The French

❧ ❧

❧

FRANÇOIS NOURISSIER

THE
FRENCH

Translated from the French by
ADRIENNE FOULKE

New York · Alfred · A · Knopf
1968

THIS IS A BORZOI BOOK
PUBLISHED BY ALFRED A. KNOPF, INC.

First American Edition
© Copyright 1968 by Alfred A. Knopf, Inc.

All rights reserved under International
and Pan-American Copyright Conventions.
Distributed by Random House, Inc.
Published simultaneously in Toronto, Canada,
by Random House of Canada Limited.

Library of Congress Catalog Card Number: 67-18626

Manufactured in the United States of America

Originally published in French as *Les Français*
by Editions Rencontre, Switzerland, 1968.

CONTENTS

The French

❧ ❧

❧

INTRODUCTION

I F AN AUTHOR were ever free to give a book its ideal title, this one would be called *The Dilemma of Being French.* Over the last twenty-odd years—since I was old enough to think independently and seriously about my country—the title would have changed in ways that can be readily imagined. In the days following our defeat, when France had fallen so low and was so vulnerable, seemingly so hopeless, young people often seriously considered exile far from Europe, and the book one would have had to write around 1946 would have been called *The Affliction of Being French.* Later, we saw France bog down in rear-guard colonial battles in Indochina and Algeria. As we witnessed the senselessness of those wars and the fumbling of the men in power, as we saw violence and blackmail become methods of government and racist brutalities go unpunished, as we watched the drift toward civil war and the cleavage of the nation into two blocs, two camps of blindly opposed opinion, our book could only have been called *The Shame of Being French.*

Of course, one could always have parodied the French

Academician on a lecture tour for the Alliance Française, or the standard political campaign oratory, in which case one would have evoked our everlasting "genius," our "mission," "eternal France," "France, eldest daughter of the Church," the "glorious principles of 1789," and so on. That book would have been called simply *The Glory of Being French.* No one who has read material still being written today, which in all seriousness pays such rhetoric the placid homage of imitating it, would dismiss such a possibility with a laugh. (Examples of this are *La France dans le monde actuel,* by Louis Dollot, 1963, and *La France d'aujourd'hui,* an anthology published in 1964.)

Let me say at once that France's situation today warrants a more serene appraisal than was possible in the fifties. Yet the moral relief that has so rapidly eased the nation's tormented conscience actually contributes to our current dilemma. Those of us who have lived as adults throughout the last ten or so years—roughly, from Dien Bien Phu to the present—still have not recovered from our surprise. France has astonished the French. The French have astonished themselves. They had no idea that as a people they could so narrowly skirt dismemberment and, after experiencing great instability, enter into a period of great stability; that, albeit after much shilly-shallying, they could rather quickly become a modern community devoted to mass consumption and mass culture. Cataclysms that the French thought they could never survive (Algerian independence, the rebellion of the army, bringing that army into line) they have taken briskly in stride. Eight hundred thousand refugee *pieds-noirs* swept back like a tide over metropolitan France without seriously threatening its ideological or economic equilibrium. The feverishly intense animosities of 1961–2 seem to have been buried. What we refer

4

to as the "Americanization" of our style of living is, for better or worse, proceeding apace. The generation reaching its forties in the mid-sixties was brought up amid lamentations over "French depopulation" and the irremediable weakening of our society because of our hereditary pusillanimity and our fear of the future. This generation now watches in amazement as twenty million young people under twenty propel the whole country toward psychological rejuvenation and a fresh historical outlook.

In short, in less than twenty years this doddering old nation, for all that it dodders still, has become young. This low-birth-rate nation has grown in population from forty to fifty million. This capricious nation has submitted to a conservative, authoritarian regime. This nation with its Marxist itch has plunged, workers included, into a vast middle-class daydream. This spent nation is experiencing a relative affluence. This nation of pieceworkers is facing up to the realities of mass production. This agricultural nation is being urbanized. This nation of miniature businesses—our beloved "small industry"—is witnessing the formation of large industrial concentrations. This stay-at-home nation travels. This nation, still exhausted from one futile war and from one lost war, talks and acts with all the snappishness of an invalid on the way to recovery. People of my age have witnessed this metamorphosis, have lived it—have undergone it rather than produced it—and when they look at their own country today it is with genuine curiosity. If other observers see a "French problem"—something irritating or a bit mystifying about us—we feel the same way ourselves. The Frenchman today is frankly dumbfounded by his country's rapid and at time unforeseeable evolution; he finds himself confronted by a rhythm and demands from which his old European's nostalgia and indolence would, he thought, protect him. This Frenchman does not know exactly who he is, much less who he is becoming. He asks—or rather, he would ask, if his recent trading in peace and prosperity left him the leisure or taste to do so—as many questions about himself as foreigners do. Of course, he does not spontaneously welcome this mixture of paradoxes and challenges, of formerly sluggish and currently feverish activity, which the novelist Roger Vailland termed as long ago as 1950 "the peculiarity of being French." However, with a vague uneasiness, he does perceive the disparity between the myth and the reality of France, between the idea that he believes has been created of her, the idea of her he has himself created, and the idea that might reasonably *be* created. The Frenchman's historic sensitivity and his intellectual comfort quite naturally posit his own country at the nerve center of the world. At the same time, his good sense, his travels, and what objectivity he has salvaged thrust on him instead a sense of her being small and overwhelmed—for example, she accounts for only 0.1 per cent of the world's surface, 1.6 per cent of its population, 0.37 per cent of its land area. All these things— vanity, humility, illusion, acerbity, pride restored and simultaneously disappointed—cohabit in him. He feels himself a survivor, but the survivor of a *grandeur* of a French, a European importance—in the liturgy of which he was brought up. He envies (with a hint of disdain) the flowering of materialistic civilizations from which he long believed he was debarred and of whose fruits he knew himself deprived. He keeps telling himself, with great satisfaction, that of the fifty-eight most widely translated authors in the world, sixteen are French. From childhood, it has been drummed into him, as a self-evident truth, that France has a universal mission. That his altogether remarkable country has been successively the embodiment of Christianity, Monarchy by Divine Right, Liberty, the Rights of Man—of this every Frenchman is inwardly if not consciously convinced. Like knowledge acquired along with his mother's milk, he drank in such notions when he was learning to talk and read. Every French schoolchild, even before he knows how to multiply, lives for several years on the peaks of History and the Universal. But at the same time, the whole myth-making machine called education —the osmosis, the multiform pressure that makes a man what he is—also imbues the French child with a respect for parochial and petty notions. He is taught pell-mell that love of country is "sacred" but that juggling one's taxes has its charms, that "money does not make happiness" but that "a sou is a sou." Outmoded images are exalted which will shackle him for life. He is taught a quasi-religious respect for bread in an age when dietetics advises him against eating it, and for the symbols of flag and bugle in a society fed up with supporting its military. He dreams of immortal principles and national grandeur and the lofty civilizing mission incumbent on his country, but his realistic self is alert to the virtues of prudent husbandry, tight purse strings, and the strict correlation between good fences and good neighbors. One day he sees himself a citizen of Brobdingnag, the next day, of Lilliput—that is, of a former empire now shrunk to the compact hexagon of metropolitan France. The Frenchman thinks of his national culture as a soaring cone poised on its tip. It is dinned into his ears that the French language must be preserved in all its "purity," but simple addition tells him that French is the mother tongue of only sixty-five million human beings, and the second "working" language of several tens of millions of black and yellow people, although no one can count on the latter figure's remaining stable. He has been imbued with a superstitious

7

respect for the "three *départements* of North Africa" and the
France "from Dunkirk to Tamanrasset"; solemn commitments
were made in his name never to abandon Vietnamese Catholics
or "our Algerian friends"—yet he has witnessed the collapse,
disappearance, or abandonment of all these notions, with
France only the better for it. The civilizing mission of France,
which was somehow made compatible with colonial wars,
has fared no worse since freedom was bestowed on people of
color. The grandeur that used to oblige us to defend our
"possessions" was equally well (and more realistically) expressed in our falling back within the frontiers of metropolitan France. These acrobatics were not only political maneuvers, blackmail, tests of patience and strength, and military
disengagements that we saw with our own eyes; they were also
robed in abstractions and crowned with slogans. Men did not
merely manipulate facts and figures; they played with
ideologies.

SINCE ABOUT 1962, the Frenchman has been venturing out
from the shadows of his legends as if he were issuing from
a long dark tunnel. To meet what? To meet a world that has
changed, accelerated, and grown younger while France was
wasting thirty years by shutting her eyes to reality or disguising
it in uniforms of another century.

When she finally opened her eyes, what landscape did
she see? Germany? The ancestral antagonism was all of a
sudden removed. The once greatly feared Nazi occupier came
back, a bit heavier around the middle, as a tourist behind
the wheel of an indestructible little Volkswagen or a reassuring Mercedes. In a flash, the German once more became the
workingman, the rich man, the strong man of Europe. The

8

collapse of 1945 seemed redeemed a hundredfold by General Marshall and the miracle of economic recovery. General de Gaulle went off to address the Ruhr workers in German. Together with Chancellor Adenauer, he scaled a historic summit to plant the dream of a Lotharingia capable of imposing on Europe the law of the old Frankish and Germanic peoples. In the space of fifteen years, the hereditary enemy had become the efficient competitor, the partner and peer, the pleasant visitor. The adolescent of 1962, born in 1945, had only the dimmest notion about all that business of persecution and Maquis and Resistance. A film released in 1962 expressed this well: its twenty-two-year-old producer called it *Hitler—Never Heard of Him!*

England? That intimidating old island, that stubborn, self-centered, prudent nation that had nonetheless symbolized hope from 1940 to 1944, seemed to have been as poorly repaid for her heroism as Germany had been well rewarded for her sins. People soon became accustomed to the image of a weary England. When you went to London, you deplored the fact that so many little Italian restaurants were replacing the traditional pubs (the French are more Anglophile than the English). The pound was the sick currency of Europe. No justice in that, either. Then, when it became apparent around 1964—from films, actors, popular singers, painters, fashions— that England was coming to life again, young Frenchmen commenced to dress like colonels in the Indian army and their parents gave up sending them to Brighton for the summer "to learn English," although this had been a well-established family ritual. People stopped being interested in a country they no longer understood. London—that is, a mysterious combination of tonsorial extravagance, casual haberdashery, and provocative skirts—London was in vogue. Details of such capers filled the papers but they did not concern public opinion in depth.

The USSR switched from its "eye of Moscow" role to that of churlish old ally just as French communism (always quite isolated in the nation as a whole) was losing members, virulence, and its bugaboo function. The image of Maurice Thorez —suffering by then not only from paralysis but also from being congratulated by De Gaulle in his *Memoirs*—was replaced by that of the irrepressible Khrushchev, who arrived to talk corn and pigs in the wine cellars of Languedoc. Having washed its dirty Stalin linen, launched satellites, and been nibbled at by the Chinese, the Soviet Union became a rather indifferent topic of conversation for the French. Building socialism loses its appeal when everyone owns a car. Simultaneously, people stopped worrying about Soviet armored-tank divisions and believing seriously in the danger of a European war. In a word, the USSR amuses no one.

Italy? Its little miracle—Vespas, Gio Ponti skyscrapers, *espresso* machines—dated from the fifties. It did not last. Election brawls and government instability quickened disagreeable memories for the French. (In the eyes of the Gaullists, Italy is a kind of Fourth Republic, only a little more clerical and a little more sunny.) That left vacations. But here again disaffection has set in: Spain is cheaper and just as warm.

In fact, since the mid-fifties Spain has been the great French toy. Eleven out of twelve months you had a Spanish maid, and the twelfth month, every summer, together with several million other Frenchmen, you vacationed somewhere between Cadaqués and Marbella and enjoyed at a very low cost the illusion of being a millionaire. Someone could have made a movie called *Franco—Never Heard of Him!* (The

sound track would not have been exclusively in French!) Who
still cares about the old days of the Spanish Civil War? What
can the French hold against a regime whose austerity enables
them to treat themselves to villas rented complete with swimming pools and palm trees in exchange for a loaf of bread?

I have kept the United States until last, in accordance with
our music-hall hierarchy that christens the performer who has
the honor of appearing last on the program the "American
star." This is as it should be. In the postwar years, the United
States—in France people say simply "America"—has been
the great mirage on the horizon of French imaginations.

Whatever the subject, whether films—thrillers, comedies,
or Westerns; literature—Faulkner, Capote, or Frank Slaugh-
ter, depending on which public; the Paris-New York art
tussle; architecture—Saarinen or Philip Johnson; whether
it is a way of life or a folklore, Audrey Hepburn or General
Motors, James Bond in the Bahamas or Jacqueline Kennedy
in Gstaad or Seville; whether it is the New Frontier or the
Bay of Pigs, beatniks or Vietniks, Sinatra or Bob Dylan, the
growing mechanization of Western man, Louis Armstrong,
race riots in Little Rock, Watts, or Detroit, one thing is certain: French heads are full of America. The passion with which
the French followed the election of John F. Kennedy, the
warmth with which they welcomed him on his visit to Paris,
their grief at his death—all these are signs of true and profound feeling. Kennedy was the only foreign statesman in a
long time whom the French had spontaneously *loved.* The emotion was widespread and irrational, and it is by no means a
negligible item to add to the dossier of Franco-American
relations. It bespeaks not only an inclination of the heart but
also the inevitability of social evolution and an increasing
similarity in way of life. The chill between the two govern-

ments is certainly not shared by French citizens or, if it is, is felt only vaguely and passingly. Whether it be in terms of our free-moving economy, the development of our social structures, fashions, or any one of other manifold forms of imitation, France more and more resembles the United States. French teen-agers do not allow their pro-American enthusiasms to be dampened by the chauvinistic alarms that upset their elders. Some recent phenomena—like the appearance of Jean Lecanuet at the front of the stage—are direct results, in form and in substance, of the American example. Even in a world in which any hypothesis is risky, one need not be a great prophet to foresee that, thus primed, the evolution will expand and become more clearly defined. Because this projection is accepted or desired by our younger people, and by middle-class groups in particular, it is definitely part of our immediate future. It remains to be seen what traditions may be overturned, what peculiarly French qualities may be bastardized, what sluggishness may be stirred to life.

Even this rapid reconnaissance flight over the French scene reveals how in the last few years the French have often turned away from comparison and competition with their traditional neighbors. They have withdrawn within their own borders. They have become uninvolved. They have been busy enjoying an affluence long unknown to them. Pushed in this direction by a heavy population increase, they accept and for the moment cherish the promises of well-being held out by a fairly healthy capitalism. Their traditional restiveness and partisan passions have yielded to a preoccupation with the techniques of consumption and vast publicity-promoted images of happiness. Standards of family and sexual morality are changing rapidly, and the churches are puffing in their race to bring them under control again. More evenly shared wealth and ideological attrition combine to "depoliticize" the nation. Leisure and pleasure rule French tastes today, even if France is ruled by a sovereign to whom such notions are basically alien. This split, this difference in levels, can help to explain some of our malaises. The man whom President Coty called "first among the French," when he placed the Republic in De Gaulle's hands in May 1958, bears a very close resemblance to the mythical "Frenchman," that offspring of monarchism and Jacobinism, of Louis XIV and Clémenceau. It did seem then that he would be the prototype of my fellow citizens for a long time to come, but he has only a few characteristics in common with the twenty-five million young people of today who will be in charge of things tomorrow. Therefore, it will be useful to talk both about Frenchmen and about the coexistence in them of the old and the new man.

It is awkward to be French because France is now divided between two periods of her history, as she has always been, and is, divided between her conservative and progressive elements. This double division, this double conflict, is found in individuals, social groups, and ideas.

Until quite recently, when one spoke of monarchy and republic, *ancien régime* and revolution, Right and Left, one was alluding to a tension in the nation's life which has proved to be fruitful at some times and paralyzing at others. Today this dual dynamic manifests itself in vacillating ideas, a profound uncertainty about the future, and a race to catch up with the twentieth century; in short, it has caused a cleavage in time.

In terms of our national mythology, the France of the fifty-year-olds lives in the past; she is still a great world power. In material and economic terms, on the other hand, the country is facing the future—with, I must say, mixed exhilaration and nervousness. Some countries advance slowly over long periods, as if they were on a more or less successful but stationary cruise. This was the case with us in the euphoric period 1875–1914 and in the agonized years 1918–39. However, the sixties are for France a time of jolts, improvisation, and acceleration.

In speaking about my country, I feel I should avoid references that would elude a non-French reader and allusions that would be obscure—indeed, everything that is implicit and inexpressible about a culture. So I have decided to talk not so much about France as about Frenchmen—the Frenchmen of today are my subject. To the extent that they as individuals feel dissimilar and divided, they will be giving an acceptable idea of their country. To the extent that they still dwell in the past and it dwells still in them, they will not be betraying the centuries of history they bear so ostentatiously on their shoulders.

I would like to make clear the tension, the painful dislocation, and the rarefied yet smothering air of the past that my fellow Frenchmen are inwardly experiencing. Here and there, no doubt, I will be considered severe. It is not always easy for a Frenchman to choose among objectivity, aggressiveness, and complacency. Aggressiveness and complacency come to him rather naturally; his tongue trips over objectivity. I am no exception to the rule. One should remember that in my country the writer's role has been to deal not in dithyrambs but in irony and anger. Since long ago, the French have had the habit of "thinking against"—Montaigne against obscurantism, Pascal against the Jesuits, Saint-Simon against royal bastards, Voltaire against oppression, Beaumarchais against the nobility, Saint-Just against bloodshed, Stendhal against the golden mean, Hugo against Napoleon III, Baudelaire against ugliness, Zola against reasons of state, Barrès against the uprooting of rural populations, Gide against virtue, Malraux against fascisms, Céline against everyone and against God. French thought has been nourished on alarums and excursions. Our language has been forged in duels. French literature and French intelligence at their best constitute a perpetually subversive activity, a permanent dispute. The writers who have been color-bearers for the established order, zealous apologists for a sovereign, or hired defenders of a class have almost all slipped into oblivion. This country and its people are so fashioned that to love them is not easy. Insolence and verve and good sense—these are the qualities that Beaumarchais chose to ascribe to his Figaro, for whom he wrote some of the sallies we are most proud to find—taut, mocking, dazzling—molded into our language and alive in our memories. Figaro: an author might well invoke him as muse for such a book as this.

CHAPTER I:

Is France in Good Health?

H OW'S FRANCE?"
      "Fair, thanks."
      The exchange is imaginary, the question is oversimple, and the reply has a slightly bantering undertone. Bantering it may be, but how delightful to be able to say it at all! For such a long time we could not, without boasting. To understand the French today, other people must remember to think of the older generations as convalescents and of the younger as impatient listeners to tales of an illness that they have not experienced.

French well-being vanished one morning in August 1914. The 1918 "victory" was a deception because it left us exhausted, and what glory it heaped on France was senseless and too costly. The madcap decade that followed bespoke nervosity, not joy. French life had lost its traditional rhythm and flavor. The twenties were a survivors' celebration and had nothing to do with health. The thirties brought a cortege of calamities—depression, joblessness, strikes, social conflict, the threatening nearness of fascisms just beyond our borders, the collapse of the Spanish Republic, inflation, government instability—and they were much closer to reality. The men who were called up in 1939 left believing in very little, to fight a war that was lost in advance. The defeat of 1940 annihilated us but hardly surprised us. Four years of occupation amassed material damage, human suffering, and distress, but, far worse, it inflicted a dreadful moral wound. To have nothing to eat, to be unable to move about or even to leave the house after curfew, to live in fear for the lives of our men who were prisoners of war—those were nothing compared with battered pride and the humiliation of finding ourselves citizens of a nation whose honor was divided. To be seated at the bottom of the table at the victory feast (rather in the way people were once privileged to sit on a stool in the presence of royalty) was no consolation. Cold, hunger, and poverty prevailed, together with the bitterness of having issued from a tunnel only to discover no true light. Governments continued to bluff, beg, bungle, and break up; everthing, it seemed, was allowed to disintegrate. Actually, a rebirth was already stirring, but to all outward appearances France was incurably sick. Yellow men, black men, Muslims—the perennial sacrificial victims of our battles, the extras in our reassuring imperial parade— had seen us too depleted for them not to heed the murmurs of contention that were spreading over three continents. They now knew that the colossus was fragile, and they jostled it. In the face of this challenge, our military men regrouped the forces they had allowed Hitler to rout. But it was to no avail, and the defeats that ensued were not among our most glorious.

And so, in the years from 1952 to 1957, when the French began to sense that the air was clearing, that the country was rousing from its torpor and in spite of its burdens was begin-

ning to walk again, when the cruel benefits of the war began
to be evident (sometimes it is easier to start again from
scratch, to borrow and build rather than to patch up), this
pleasant surprise was received with reserve: "Let's hope it
lasts!" The old peasant mistrust could not believe in fresh prosperity. It required *reductio-ad-absurdum* proof—the Geneva
Agreements in 1962 and the Evian Agreements—to demonstrate to the French nation that it could extricate itself from
the morass it was in and could also withstand the repercussions
it feared. The tumors had been removed and we had survived
the shock of the operation! Around 1963, the average Frenchman began to breathe again. He stopped glancing nervously
in the direction of the Algerian hinterland, lamenting the
fortunes amassed in North Africa, and listening to plastic
bombs explode. He took a good look around and verified the
fact that the scene was—slowly—changing. His ritual belly-
aching was no longer entirely justified, nor was his pessimism.
Real and present problems not only concerned the liquidation
of his bankruptcies; they also involved his future.

For France, the present is a moment suspended in time,
it is prolonged by the strength of one elderly man and the experiment of one administration. However, in the midst of this
adventure, which we have been living since 1958, and which,
in all truth, resembles no other in our whole history (although it feeds on examples from history and is expressed
in their terms), we are in a position to face our needs and
our lacks squarely, and also to muster a few reasons for
feeling satisfied.

We are rich in gold bullion. We are no longer so poor
in youth. Our planes circle the earth. Our engineers achieve
an occasional success. We are exploding a few bombs and,
like modern Cyranos, we can at least take pride in having

made them ourselves (modest as they are) without anyone's help. We are proud of our Alpine ski champions and the thoroughbred horses from our stud farms. We are building some beautiful dams and, after thirty years of standing in the corner, we have even won a Nobel Prize for science! The things around us that are going badly or very badly sometimes yield place to things that are going better or even very well. Schools, teachers, housing, roads, telephones—here the picture is still black. But we glimpse a few bright spots here and there. Fifteen years ago we were the sick man of Europe. Today we are its preceptor and sometimes its pest. This metamorphosis represents progress of a kind. But what has changed above all is the frame of mind with which we view all this, our psychology, our disposition. Our diplomacy is still contentious, but our businessmen have become less inflexible. Realism is In, and it does not suit us too badly. The domestic political oppositions—the fascist and the progressive—are both disarmed by maneuvers launched against their flanks. The government exhibits a more intransigent nationalism than the Right would ever dare; it risks alliances and flirtations that the Left could never permit itself. Gaullism is accused of ultra-conservatism, yet it has shaken off its detractors by several forward leaps, even if helter-skelter ones: toward Peking, toward Moscow, toward nuclear power, even toward a European resolution. Out of this comes one novelty: the French are beginning to evaluate events in terms of results and not of principles. Tomorrow, twenty-five million young citizens may venture to rally around this pragmatic approach; it suits their nature and their age better than the old ideological pronouncements. In a people who habitually take a universalist, abstract point of view, realism can be a sign of health. No matter how modern French realism may seem, however, it is not practiced in the name of realism but by reference to traditional historical concepts. Hence the disarray among the experts. The French have been brought up on the classical disciplines; they like to put things into logical and metaphysical categories. Our present empiricism should be a characteristic of youth, but it has been sparked by an old man. This confusion between two age groups and two styles of behavior disconcerts the observer and discloses one aspect of French self-interrogation. For a long time our public life, like our theater, followed fixed rules. The repertoire was balanced between two known poles. One neither hoped for nor feared any surprises. Now we have come to a moment when roles are changing. The part of one group is being played by another. The upper middle class exhibits imagination and the reforming theoreticians drag their feet. If any recovery is taking place, the convalescence is being acted out with much shifting of sets and casts.

Let us get back to earth for a moment and down into the street, close to daily life. What do we see?

Our *laisser-aller,* our negligence, assumes many forms, from individual scoffing to administrative incompetence, from filthy streets to an inexplicably sluggish legal system; the who-cares attitude, freeloading, procrastination all die hard. The evidence is everywhere; our negative capacities sometimes seem inexhaustible. (This book will come back to them often, unfortunately.)

But in this all too familiar gray monochrome, fresh lines are being sketched in; in the midst of the slackness, some firm spots, some zones of strength appear. A nation that can win a few victories may hope to win others, and tomorrow the more than twenty million children who will reach adulthood will act like a blood transfusion; the organism will be transformed.

Despite a full-fledged agricultural crisis, in less than fifteen years our farmers have made up for a half century of backwardness. Paris, which for sixty years has been a dormant city seemingly headed for asphyxiation and paralysis, gives signs of awakening from its uneasy sleep. Administrative and professional reforms long blocked by inertia and privilege are being effected. Some cities are bursting with life and are being radically transformed. Living habits are changing. People are dressing better. People are eating better. Some of our mythological values from yesteryear are passing out of fashion with our young people. Even the physical appearance of the French, our pernicious *gourmandise* notwithstanding, is improving. We who, as a nation, exhibit so much misplaced vanity forget to congratulate ourselves on the agreeable fact that we are getting rather better-looking. To come back to France from a trip during which one has dreamily admired Bavarian blondness, the sparkle of students encountered on the ski slopes of Gstaad or in the rue de Bourg in Lausanne, the elegance of the Romans, the proud independence of the children of Naples —to come home to France is no longer like crossing the threshold into purgatory. Our girls, the youngest especially, have acquired a new kind of assurance. This can be verified outside the *lycées* of Paris or on village squares, in Val d'Isère or Cannes, or at any public camping site. Taller, slimmer, polished, and bronzed, the species has taken a giant step forward.

But now to speak bluntly, these compliments having been duly tendered: What is a healthy country? What is the touchstone of health?

François Nourissier: THE FRENCH

Is it power, prosperity, military success, peace? Is it equitable distribution of wealth or conspicuous luxury for a few? Is it reclusiveness or a general outgoingness? Is it inventive vitality, artistic creativity? Is it tranquillity in all things and for all people?

Let us say, knowing quite well that the definition is being applied to contemporary France, that we should be able to recognize the good health of a country in its realistic attitudes, its capacity to arouse the concern of its citizenry, and its ability to involve the whole of the nation in a unified forward movement.

Realism is awareness of limits; it is the denial of demagoguery and illusions. When France dispatches an expeditionary force to Suez or strives to maintain her presence in areas where she has become intolerable, she gives evidence of lack of realism. When she drapes her relative weakness in rhetoric, when she surrenders to jealousy and xenophobia, it is lack of realism. It is lack of realism, again, to strive to maintain an appearance of power to the detriment of factors making for true power. And finally, it is lack of realism of the most pernicious kind to give in to the disenchantment that has tempted us all: "We have become nothing at all, a negligible quantity, a moribund civilization. Let the barbarian wave roll on and we will sleep amid the wreckage of our greatness."

Undeniably, such forms of escapism constituted our great collective sin in the years from 1945 to 1962. Crusaders or desperadoes, visionaries or aggressors, the French seemed to have renounced once and for all dealing in exact measurements and weights. Better to drown in self-contempt than to be assigned a modest rank at a time when primacy in almost all things eluded us. Ministers hurling reinforcements into

22

lost battles that they had been elected to halt; military men pushing a catastrophic strategy to its bitter end because it enabled them to retain power; desperate and betrayed *pieds-noirs* trying in an apocalypse of arson and murder to destroy the colony they had not known how to become part of—these are but a few examples of French lack of realism. It was surrounded by a halo of patriotism and high-sounding phrases and oversimple idealism. It was prideful and destructive. At one moment, it seemed to corroborate the view that as a nation we were facing a definitive collapse.

On the other hand, to liquidate our failures, to retreat to our initial positions, and restore our economy to good health —that was realism. A neostate capitalism, even if it does not always seem to be of exemplary moral purity, is less damaging to the nation than a utopian socialism that is timid and, given our nature, dedicated to demagogic compromises. What is lost on the level of ideology is won anew in stability and expansion. Even the seductive, essential dream of the European Idea called for minute and cautious examination. The United States of Europe is still a vision; the Common Market, which is the product of sharp bargaining, is a reality. The solitary, do-it-yourself accession of France to the status of a nuclear power can, for all the usual reasons, be considered an old-fashioned, dangerous, and illusory effort. To this argument one can reply that, judging by the initial results, this decision has not precipitated all the disasters its opponents predicted: French economic expansion has not been blocked and, with or without us, atomic weapons proliferate.

If he is willing not to wear the dark and distorting glasses of the doctrinaire, the severest observer detects some evidences of independence, objectivity, and seriousness in French life over the last few years. For the first time in a long while, the clouds have rolled away. It is possible to see more clearly. All our mistakes and blunderings and slowness, which will be fully reviewed in what follows, do not gainsay this.

Have we managed to stimulate interest?

Less than our propaganda and our vanity claim. More, perhaps, than our Cassandras believe.

Viewed from the outside, the French scene has somewhat improved. Our three shirts of Nessus—political instability, military adventurism, and fiscal and economic disorder— have been stripped from us. This is not a return to "normalcy" (the word is discredited by far-fetched misuse) but, in gymnastic terminology, a recovery—a motion performed with vigor, speed, and, it must be said, with all the overtones of a salvage operation.

Speaking from inside, how is one to be impartial? I may say that it has become less exasperating to be French. In the mid-sixties one has the feeling that although the country faces innumerable problems, they are at least real problems, each of which interests some segment of the nation. One no longer has the impression that, in addition to its genuine difficulties, the country is staggering under the unaccountable crosses that once paralyzed the national life and by their very absurdity tarnished all our hopes. A student can complain about the scarcity of laboratories or his professors' absenteeism, but at least he need no longer reckon with having his life interrupted by such long and dangerous military service as we required during the Algerian war, when the length of duty was extended to twenty-eight months and, contrary to custom, draftees were not merely given basic training but were sent into active combat. (The Vietnamese war, for example, had been fought by an army of professionals and mercenaries.) France has become more acceptable to the French. Some of the regal posturings, shoddy tricks, and ugly quarrels our sovereign invents may get on our nerves, but the fact remains that we identify—almost all of us, and for the first time in a long while—with the day-by-day image of France. This image is impugned by those who yearn nostalgically for fascism. It is criticized, sometimes fiercely, by the progressives—the more fiercely when they feel someone has stolen a march on them. However, no one thinks any more of deserting. It has become less uncomfortable to be a citizen of this country, a fact which has helped to restore a sense of national homogeneity.

The battles of ideas are still lively, political parties are still divided, some regions (Brittany, the Southwest) and some employment categories (farmers, small businessmen, workers in outmoded industries) still feel outside the movement that is propelling the country forward, but it would be deceptive not to underline a progressively stronger sense of unity, of belonging to the same body politic. This community, which always teeters on the brink of a schism and which has been severely shaken over the last twenty-five years, has been reknit a little. From now on, the danger of divisiveness lies in the country's being split into two rival camps—twenty-five million young people versus twenty-five million old people. This will be a grave danger if crises arise to shake the foundations, if there is a threat of serious strikes, or if housing becomes more expensive. But for the moment nothing promises such difficulties.

This chapter would have been very difficult had it been written only a few years ago in the midst of the explosive tumult of Algiers and Oran and in the atmosphere of general disbelief in our economic growth. It would have aired the poor civic health of the French, their disarray before the choices that had to be made, their anger at or lack of interest in almost everything. It would have expressed an almost unqualified pessimism. If there is optimism now, it is newborn, still fragile and uncertain. Everything threatens it, and above all else, one unknown quantity: post-Gaullism. Will we be able to preserve stability without putting men of narrow vision in power? Will we resist the temptation to relapse into our former drifting? Will we have a better choice than to be ruled by self-seeking politicians or demagogues?

The strange thing about the problem is that any day, any hour, death could bring us face to face with it, and that no one in France is sure that the country is prepared to look with composure for a solution.

In good health? Yes. Then why the constant complaining? The great doctor, the great sorcerer, the man of unpredictable rites who has been able to tame or deflect French destiny, is already, in the drowsy peace of our creature comforts, simply an old man.

IF I AS A GUIDE were asked to suggest the ideal France to visit, my answer would be: "Spend some time in the mountains." It is a fact that the region of the Alps is in better shape than any other part of the country. There you find the only attractive houses the French know how to build, good hotels, dams worthy of our famous cathedrals, a countryside that has been preserved with respect, an industrious population that is deservedly prosperous, our only Olympic champions, air that is a delight to breathe, daring ski tows, a dynamic vitality; in short, the French Alps are a dream world that has produced both chalets and character. This is not a witticism but a surprised, pleased statement of fact. Surprised because it is an exception, pleased because it allows one to hope.

Why is not all of France, in this sense, Savoyard? Because, perhaps, all climates are not so privileged, are not favorable and hospitable to the triple flourishing of a consumer society, of leisure, and of youth. There must be some virtue in altitude that is equitably distributed; notice that Switzerland, the Tyrol, and the Dolomites are equally well off. Lastly, let me enumerate some other things France can be proud of. Our excellent horses, for example, are heroes of track and show. The fields of Normandy are as successful in their way as the Alpine ski runs. Our airplanes are good. Trains run on time. Our automobiles are better than they look. Ordinary country roads are well tarred. Several dynamic corporations, both private and state-owned, are flourishing.

To combine fish with fowl in this way may sound like a joke; it is rather like stringing mismatched pearls. Yet this is a serious list. Let a visitor travel freely through France for two or three months, and these are the items he will come up with, *if* by any chance he has been seized by the whim to appreciate in France precisely what he did not come to look for—her present.

CHAPTER II:

Living in the Past?

THE GLORY OF CERTAIN NATIONS lies in what they are; I am thinking of the United States. For others, it lies in the labor and exaltation of what they are building: the Soviet Union after 1917 and China after 1945; for still others, in the fever of chaotic growth (Brazil) or of recent independence (the young Arab or Asian nations). At least one country is striving to fulfill a millenary promise and is achieving a kind of prodigious antidestiny—Israel. Some nations that seemed trapped by catastrophe, like Germany and Japan, or entombed in solitude and memories, like Spain, have found the secret of a spectacular metamorphosis through hard work and opportunism. Even those perennial victims of oppression and treaties, the nations of eastern Europe, which have been variously absorbed or dismembered or have had their frontiers redrawn, have willy-nilly, by surviving the hazards of a gradual ideological revisionism, committed themselves to a kind of future. In our world of the sixties, lovers and prisoners of the past seem to be notably few. We watch as England struggles to keep in step with a rhythm that is no longer her own, hesitating between tradition and sacrifice, between the bitterness of her old Conservatives, the pragmatism of her Labourite theoreticians, and the insolence cultivated by her young people who, though too few in number, are at least faithful to British habits of eccentricity. And then there is France. The French are still mired in their history and their more recent misadventures, though already the body may be giving the lie to the head and the country may be about to pull out of the mire and resume its march forward along new roads and in a new style.

Psychologically, we are lagging behind the chance that is offered us. Our fetishism of the past, which produces both public rancor and negligence, has contaminated the French mind for forty years. Evidences of it still abound to compromise the possibility of the country's rebirth. The French appetite for turning a profit is stronger than our impulse to build. France had scarcely stopped suffering from stagnation when she converted herself into a society of overhasty, acquisitive consumers. Once conservative and frugal, she is now wheeling and dealing and spending. She thinks more of clipping coupons than of investing fresh capital, and this is a characteristic of old age, not a proof of dynamism.

Conceivably, a country like the USSR looks back with collective satisfaction on the triumphs that its people have already achieved and those they are mutually working toward. Measuring the distance they have traveled in fifty years, the Soviets must feel repaid for the sacrifices they made—sacrifices of liberty, of human lives, and of comfort. Their road lies upward; why should they not be full of enthusiasm? Similarly, American society, respectful as it is of the minutest detail of its short history, nonetheless faces toward the future. Whether in the matter of its more recent immigrants' gratitude and their determination to be still more thoroughly Americanized, or of the feeling of world-wide responsibility that now dictates its leaders' policies, questionable as these may be, the United States is embarked on a path of expansion and affirmation of its supremacy. The American love affair with its past, which is so lively in New England, the South, and the West (where the past is celebrated even though it is scarcely a century old, an age that in Europe does not make even furniture valuable), is simply a luxury for this most modern, all-conquering world power.

The key items in the French scale of values, however, are still antiquity, tradition, and the hundreds of ties that bind us to yesterday, though it is possible that this generalization has already become doubtful, and that every passing month makes it more so. It remains true, nonetheless, that the vital springs of the French mentality flow in the past. When De Gaulle speaks of the USSR he calls it Russia, as if the tsars still reigned under the onion domes of the Kremlin; when he visits Volgograd, he takes pains to call the city Stalingrad. This is not linguistic perversity or political malice; it expresses his most profound nature, a nature in which we—all of us—recognize ourselves.

With us the past is a habit. What do people come to visit in our country if not our past? What do we sell, boast of, take care to keep in good shape and well to the fore, if not the most accessible eight centuries of our culture? What, by choice, are we taught in school? On what do our standard reference books nourish us? The past of places, buildings, families, battles, quarrels—these are our capital reserves. Today's readers are more interested in a study of dukes, real and false, than in an explanation of the objectives of the

Monnet Plan; they would rather dwell on "our forty thousand historical monuments" than analyze our educational reform.

All refinement issues from the past. To own a house that's "been in the family" a long time and is furnished with "some good old things," that has a chockful attic, walls covered with the portraits of one's forebears, and every surface loaded with bric-a-brac that is superannuated but "full of memories"—there is your unchallenged proof of respectability. If you are not fortunate enough to possess it, you manufacture it out of whole cloth. No sooner do middle-class Frenchmen become comfortably well off than they set themselves up in some "period" style; this is the expeditious, reassuring way of purchasing status. In the last fifteen years, interior-decorating magazines and antique shops have had extraordinary success—not because of a sudden passion for collecting but simply because everyone wishes to don the uniform of good breeding. Decorators have been known to advise their clients to place in the midst of the expensive perfection of a Regency or Louis XVI salon an odd chair or some other piece of furniture, provided it is a little ugly and worn, its purpose being to make the room look more "lived in" or more "familylike." People do not reconstruct, they fake, a background. Every new fortune is suspect, and to lodge it in a contemporary setting would make it more suspect still. So it must be disguised as old, inherited wealth, given an injection of archaism that will confer dignity on it. Around 1955, when we began to construct relatively modern buildings, specialists strained their ingenuity to teach the new owners how to turn into high, narrow Louis XV windows what the architects had intended to be wide bays opening onto the trees of the 16ème *Arrondissement*. By dint of antiquated frames, cleverly

31

faked furniture reproductions, new paneling patinated at great expense, one can nibble away two centuries and set people up in a reasonable facsimile of the surroundings in which the forebears they dream of having had might have lived.

This vogue has not exactly infected our taste, because in the end it teaches the French to appreciate a certain refinement and beautiful objects; rather, it is pusillanimity, an elegant way of taking refuge in what is known and safe. Are we pioneers or museum guards? The Frenchman born around 1920 seems to have made his choice. Perhaps his children will react against it by making another or an opposite choice. One may hope so. For the moment, the fanatics of the secondhand market still find that the furniture of Le Corbusier or Mies van der Rohe "belongs in airport waiting rooms."

This respect for yesterday, when focused on periods or on individuals, has worked considerable mischief for many years. It was not so long ago that in France old age conferred a mysterious prestige on public figures—I mean true old age, with all its little miseries and touching or pathetic infirmities. In a word, public opinion was indulgent toward dotards. What it cherished in them was not a long, active life or what youth they had preserved, but, on the contrary, the thousand and one failings of advanced years. People believed in the wisdom, the prudence, of the old. Such perfectly safe virtues were preferred to the venturesomeness of the young. In 1940 it seemed the sensible thing to place the destiny of the nation in the hands of an octogenarian. Until very recently, French society behaved like some primitive people worshipping their tribal ancestors.

On this score, customs are changing almost too quickly. Too quickly because the new vogue for youth—"young bosses," "young farmers," "young employees"—is still an isolated phenomenon that may have brutal repercussions in a society where all elements are not evolving at the same pace. Already we are beginning to be wary of hiring employees who are not young, to demand that forty-year-olds take "retraining" or professional "refresher" courses—above all, to burden them with the multifaceted anguish of premature old age. In this country, where once we believed only in experience slowly acquired, in wise maturing in time, we suddenly are beginning to swear only by form, dynamism, and the style of the moment—by greenness. No doubt this swing from one extreme to another is inseparable from economic pickup and expansion and our efforts to cope with competition. It is our business leaders' concern that they may not be up to date or up to the challenge which pushes them in this direction. Although for such a long time French business has been backward, apathetic, and not geared to compete for markets, with some zeal it has begun to bestir itself. Like every other recent adult discovery, of course, the cult of physical and moral health has its silly aspects; one hears talk of nothing but dietetics, output, efficiency, rest cures, phobias about heart attacks. Since societies more evolved than ours have gone through these crises and found that they have become endemic, there is a real danger that French executives may have taken up something which for them is not only very new—a religion of Youth—but likely to be nerve-racking for a long time to come.

This exception aside, we still encounter many examples of the inverse malady. Overemphasis on or overestimation of the teaching of history; the tendency to judge the present by constant reference to precedents exhumed from the past; the acceptance of historical facts and personalities as so many familiar or guardian angels—everything conspires to make the French breathe the air of a bygone day.

It is striking that we have such trouble in relating the world around us to ourselves—to our present or future. Every fresh event automatically evokes some past event we all know and have evaluated. Our mania for historic dates is a conspicuous case in point. Let any military man get slightly too strong a hold on political power, and we cast up at him the 18 Brumaire or December 2nd.[1] It is impossible to decline a Legion of Honor award or a two-bit pension without ranting about the night of August 4, when in a burst of idealistic humanitarianism, nobles and clergy in the 1798 Constitutional Assembly voted to abolish their traditional feudal privileges; it is no less impossible to unseat some trivial tyranny without invoking July 14. An ambitious antirepublican general is a Boulanger; an author who excoriates the status quo is a Hugo or a Zola; and authoritarian premier is a Richelieu. We do not congratulate a prominent official on having devised some new policy for dealing with the economy or defense; we compare him to Colbert or to Turgot. In France, to be great, to be patriotic, persuasive, or efficient always means to continue a tradition, to remain worthy of illustrious models. France thinks of herself as if she were a succession of chapters, a chain of generations and examples, and values adaptation far more than innovation. The great models from our past are virtually sacrosanct. An amusing case in point: the radio (a government monopoly) has long been forbidden to broadcast a pleasantly anarchistic song cavalierly titled "Merde à Vauban" ("Shit to Vauban"). Two hundred and fifty years after the death of this cabinet minister (who did build some superb

---

[1] The coups d'état of Napoleon I and Napoleon III.

fortifications), the state cannot countenance any disrespect to his memory.

In all honesty, one must note that this inflation of history has as its simultaneous cause and effect the fact that so many aspects of the present are so impoverished. How can one reproach the French for preferring the noble houses of yesterday to the cardboard shanties built for them today? How can one not absolve the middle-aged man who has lived through the empty victory of 1918, the country's collapse, the crises of antagonism and cowardice in the years 1933–9, the defeat of 1940, the long postwar stagnation—how not absolve him for dreaming of Louis XIV or Napoleon? The day comes when all nations take refuge in the golden legend of their heyday and tailor to order their lost paradise.

It is disheartening only because, since the French mind perpetually looks backward, the chances of a leap forward are reduced; we tend not to see vitality, beauty, inventiveness, and health where they are waiting to be discovered, because we fail to look for them. The past forces an unfair competition on the present, and the past almost always wins. Such scorn for what is current discourages even men of good will. What is the point of trying honorably to be the contemporary of your compatriots if they dismiss all your efforts and prefer the backward glance, the copy? At times it calls for heroism—at least until now it has—to try to live in France in terms of the date shown on the calendar. Ours are always "costume" balls.

In another sense, we dwell in the past because our "big problems" are actually archaic and because a kind of paralysis seems to prevent our solving them. Ideologies are antiquated, as are certain techniques and public services that lag astonishingly far behind our possibilities and apparent wealth.

First, as to ideologies:

Our quarrels and the ways in which we continue to formulate them amaze the outsider. In this area, the foreign visitor to France feels that he is far from home, not so much in space as in time. To share in French conversations in which questions of government or our political future are touched on (the age of the president of the Republic multiplies the reasons for dealing with this subject) is to dive into the heart of the nineteenth century. Historically, this long century lasted from 1789 to 1914. Prodigious technical developments, the shrinking of our planet, ambitions in outer space, and the rise of a "third world" have made outdated nonsense of a certain politico-social vocabulary and the splitting of society into conservatives and progressives, yet a discussion of ideas in France in the 1960's would not greatly surprise characters out of Stendhal or Zola. In some regards we believe we are living under the July Monarchy, in others, under Napoleon III. Only a handful of engineers, scholars, and physicians must feel (more or less comfortably!) sure that they are living in the here and now. Whether our journals of opinion are discussing the reactionary vagaries of such and such a group or the hazy, quibbling protests of some other faction, whether they are mourning the "natural" order of Old France or the "democratic" disorders of parliamentary government, it always seems, as one reads or listens to our polemics, that nothing has happened, the facts have taught us nothing, corrected nothing in our outlook. It is as if old wine goes to our head the moment we sip it. In its own way, Gaullist empiricism represents some improvement over such chimeras, but even its defenders or beneficiaries willingly don the colors of what Stendhal stigmatized around 1835 as the *"juste milieu"* ("the golden mean"). And, in truth, France has been "golden mean" ever since her great Revolution. All the intervening violence and bloodshed do not controvert this. It is simply unbelievable how with us ideas and slogans remain the same.

As to techniques:

We have totaled the sum of our backwardness, we know what things are wrong, yet we have the greatest difficulty in applying the remedies. The necessary steps are these: we should discourage the small tradesman, the nearly destitute artisan, the small farmer; we should close down small factories and eliminate railroad lines running at a deficit; we must convince all owners of tiny, parasitical businesses that their enterprises are doomed, that evolution will crush them. Convince them that it would be better to effect change than to suffer it, that in this way endless bitterness would be avoided and resentment would be disarmed; that if this evolution were organized and controlled, it would be fertile but that if it is allowed to be anarchic and full of hatred, it will impoverish and divide the country. So far, however, we have not managed to set up the necessary controls or win over those who will be eventual victims of an irreversible forward movement. From 1940 to 1944 the regime of Marshal Pétain preached a return to the land, to small crafts, to family and local organizations, and in doing so it moved in the direction of the collective will. It was quite easy to convince the French that all virtue had fled to the past for refuge, that implicit in democratic, capitalist evolution were sins that our defeat was justly forcing us to expiate. Frenchmen of that generation had found no better answer to the challenges of life than to raise dikes— tariff walls against competition, the casemates of the Maginot Line against invasion, Malthusianism against rejuvenation— and they believed the old man when he counseled them to plant wheat and make their own sabots.

True, progress in certain areas from about 1950 on was

spectacular. Industries and techniques that had been completely overhauled overcame their backwardness. Certain sectors of our business community are now in excellent health. But these successes cannot make us forget how fearfully and reluctantly we set about making the necessary changes.

The old colonialist refrain, "We've built them roads, schools, and hospitals," is one that the French will never sing again, but it might well be replaced by another and more bitter refrain that will often be heard through this book: "Why don't we build ourselves roads, schools, and hospitals?" I do not want to belabor the point. But is it not disenchanting to note that the Paris *lycées* best equipped to offer superior scientific instruction do so in buildings that date from Napoleon I, and that those best qualified for liberal-arts training provide it in the shadow of a medieval tower? The *lycée* students, those unfortunates, also live in the past. As do the patients of a certain (excellent) hospital who, as they lie in their beds, can contemplate beams that soon will be three hundred years old. As do the people who drive at ninety miles an hour along avenues of trees, between projecting walls, along sunken roads, beside wool-gathering bicyclists, gossiping housewives, kids playing ball—rushing along roads that were laid out in the days of the kings to accommodate wagon and coach traffic.

In all this there is a kind of fey charm that will appeal to optimists and sentimental travelers. There is also a surrender to implacable routine and a laziness of imagination that can drive other people mad.

When all the farms of this country have running water and electricity, when urban slums have vanished, when getting phone service installed no longer represents a triumph of patience over red tape, the French will find it easier to exist in the current century. However, if they were already really a part of it, all this business of modernization and retooling would not loom so impossibly large. Where and when did the trouble start?

For a long time, we rocked ourselves in the cradle of our superiorities, and then in the cradle of our weaknesses. We slipped from "French genius" to "poor wounded France," and the one and the other ritornello justified our letting almost everything crumble, rust, and deteriorate. To wash away our past, we must perhaps take a shower of realism. The assorted avatars of Eternal France which our idealism has fed on we shall have to put away in the prop closet. In the twentieth century the life of a nation is no longer a poem; it is a mathematical exercise. The computer must take the place of the bard. This change is already outlined for all to see, and in our very manner of responding to it we French encounter our archaic selves once more.

Enlightened and progressive minds see only fiscal injustice in the current liberal euphoria; they see an affront to the socialist dream, the rule of privilege, collusion between the State and Big Money, etc. Although they savagely deny it, they dream of a return to the ideological debauches that lasted in France for more than sixty years. Their *idea* of justice and democracy seems more important to them than the *fact* that is exploding before their own eyes—namely, that France is centrist, and that she loves authority if authority wears the colors of prosperity. It is symptomatic that when the present evolution of France is examined by the so-called forces of progress, the discussion actually expresses a whole range of nostalgias. It is striking that these nostalgic attitudes, clothed as they are in humanitarian concern, take no account of the experiences of others, the failure of reformism, and the generally wretched results obtained by Marxist preachments every-where except in the Soviet Union, where the least that can be said is that the situation in 1917 did not resemble the current situation in Western Europe. In a word, the theoreticians who supposedly represent the forward-moving wing of our political thought, being in no position to act, are thinking as unrealistic observers of history and, all in all, as prisoners of past illusions and dreams. Intellectually, our progressives are reactionaries. Let us suppose that they were to come to power —an unlikely hypothesis for the moment: either they would stand by their principles and fail; or, having become realists, they would discover that the day-by-day management of a vital, active France is neither red nor white, moral nor immoral, but consists simply in getting the French out of the rut of time and pushing them firmly down from the clouds onto solid ground. It matters very little who it will be, and in the name of what principles they will act to catapult us into the present and keep us there. The importance of the service rendered will be well worth our disregarding the theoretical trappings.

I have already said, and I come back to it, that what I am providing here is the photograph of a living, moving organism and that the focus is therefore a bit fuzzy; very likely, every day that passes will make it only more approximate. If it is easy to say that two thirds of the French are looking back over their shoulders, it is honest to say that no one knows for sure what the other third is looking toward—and they will be the voters of 1972. The presence of this mass that must be held in check and conquered obsesses the generation currently in power. Public men begin to tailor their "image" to suit what—they suppose—will be the future opinions of young Frenchmen, and also what their parents, via osmosis, may already be thinking.

A favorite hypothesis is that "responsibility" (which I call here empiricism, realism) already sells better than the rhetorical vapors of yesterday. Is this true? And if it is, is it a sign that we are in the process of banishing our old-man syndrome and daring—if I dare to put it so—to set our watches?

The sociologists of yesterday loved to compartmentalize our society and underline the permanence and stability of its categories. The "six Frances" were traditionalist, liberal, industrial, Christian, Jacobin, and socialist. "They were at last united on the roads of the 1940 exodus," Claude Quins has said. This is true. It is no less true that the nation, which has experienced the leveling effects of television and the mass media only for the last ten years, has never been so homogeneous. The trend is toward similarity: standards of living, leisure, the press all are becoming more uniform. Hence, a hypothesis—mine about realism, for instance—can speedily become reality. If people are offered pragmatic, concrete, undemagogic programs, they will come to love realism and lose their taste for flights of humanitarian eloquence. To express it differently, it is becoming more and more tempting to manipulate and impose a direction on public opinion. Attitudes that the public would never have assumed spontaneously can be made popular in the guise of fashion. This explains the doubt that assails some of us when we see our fellow citizens zestfully behaving in ways that could scarcely be more contemporary in their nonsensicality; we are not sure that they represent the truest expression of the collective mentality. At the very least, we must say that contradictory values co-exist in France today. One group exalts history, military heroism, cultural supremacy. The other's bosom puffs out with pride over efficiency; it gets drunk on efficacy, and runs a high fever over consumer goods and installment credit. As these pages are being written, the truth about France must be found in the tensions between such desperately divergent forces.

Given the inevitability of time and the death rate, no doubt France will soon teeter on into its future. But there is the real danger that because the average Frenchman has been too long coddled in the hothouse of his memories, because he has clung desperately to the icons of his traditions, he may, at least for a generation, be a much-deceived modern man, the possible dupe of new illusion hawkers, and a poor inhabitant of the last quarter of the twentieth century.

CHAPTER III:

Paris vs. The Province

WITH ALTOGETHER DISARMING NATURALNESS, the Frenchman has long held himself to be the most charming of men, and his capital the most beautiful city in the world. To his way of thinking, both judgments have gone virtually without saying. They were manifest truths, akin to other patents of perfection bestowed on our cuisine, our roads, our fashions, even on "the incomparably mild sky of the Île-de-France." The Paris agglomeration was enveloped in a cloud of soot, our gastronomy drowned in expensive, ulcer-inducing sauces, our roads had become more lethal than tuberculosis, and our women exhibited increasingly conspicuous inelegance—all true, but no matter; the taboos died hard. In particular, the charm, pre-eminence, and the sway of Paris brooked no challenge.

Then opinion seemed suddenly to hesitate, to waver, and self-approbation came very near to tumbling into ferocious disenchantment. Confronted with a housing shortage, real-estate speculation, asphyxiating traffic, a dearth of public accommodations (from curb parking to schools to hospitals to

cemeteries), and unsettling comparisons gleaned from traveling abroad, the Parisian began to crow somewhat less over
his privileged estate. He now saw that his city was grimy,
foul-smelling, exasperated and exasperating. He dreamed only
of his weekend out of town, his summer-holiday escape, sun,
and a little place in the country. This new state of mind
coincided, around 1950–5, with his government's policy of
opting in favor of the automobile and against housing, and its
endlessly adjuring the nation to decentralize, as if building
factories somewhere out in the country were the panacea for
all our ills. Paris was getting a poor press at that time. Interminable lines of cars stretched along the roads of Île-de-
France of a Saturday morning and Sunday night, two hundred
thousand "secondary residences" mushroomed, and the "little
country house, furnished" proliferated within a radius of sixty
miles around the capital. An obsession with leisure and extended vacations governed the thinking of an erstwhile home-
loving, economy-minded middle class. Paris, in French opinion,
was sick. It no longer astonished people to learn that even
foreign travelers were lingering for shorter and shorter periods
by the banks of the Seine, and then quickly fleeing the city,
blaming overinflated bills and overaged plumbing. The summer of 1953, when a general strike imprisoned impecunious
tourists for weeks, unquesionably marked one of the lowest
points on the city's popularity curve.

Let me say at once that the situation is in the process of
being corrected. After fifty years of immobility, the city has
begun to rouse itself. The end of futile overseas wars? The
population explosion? Governmental stability? All these together, probably, although one must not disregard the mysterious currents that now and then stir the unconscious of

such a very ancient social body. No miracles have occurred, but one can sense a certain dynamism prevailing over apathy. Large public works have been undertaken, administrative reforms have cleared the way for renewing and vivifying the city, and a concern for beauty has begun to improve the appearance of our streets. The regulation requiring public-building fronts to be cleaned, which Parisians welcomed initially with hearty boos, won them over in the end. Between 1959 and 1964, or over a period of five years, they sand-blasted 335 miles of building facades and discovered an almost new city—fresh in ocher, rose, and yellow. They feel, too, that the bustling, unpredictable Minister of Culture that Gaullism offered them as a prestigious literary bonus is turning some old dreams into working realities. Some town houses in the Marais are being salvaged; lively polemics have raged over the ceilings commissioned from Chagall and Masson and the latest play by Jean Genêt. The role on which Paris had stubbornly prided itself even when it was no longer worthily played is being partially restored to the city.

Of course, Parisian nerves are still racked, Paris squares are still congested, beautiful landmarks are still threatened, and some initiatives seem rather foolhardy, yet something is taking shape at last—an intention, a hope—that in all fairness cannot be disregarded. In any event, these already heartening developments are a suitable context for the observations and at time regretful comment that will follow here. At a moment when the status of Paris is contested in several areas— by New York's rivalry in painting, London's rivalry in fashion and juvenile effervescence, the tendency of foreign corporations (American especially) to locate their European headquarters elsewhere, etc.—the city is unquestionably trying not to merit such disaffections in the future. Justice does not necessarily have anything to do with this—or let us say that justice and fashion do not always go hand in hand.

NO PREDESTINATION OF SITE, no fact of geology or geography made it obvious that a city would be built here and would in the space of two thousand years become the fourth largest in the world. At most, one might note that the fairly safe route which cut through the immense forest land of Île-de-France, descending from Flanders in the north toward the ancient district of Beauce and the Loire, at this point traversed a quiet, navigable river. The presence of an island— Île-de-la-Cité—facilitated crossing the river by two relatively short bridges. The Parisian who battles his way through the crowded Faubourgs Saint-Denis and Saint-Martin or breasts the flood of students in the rue Saint-Jacques scarcely stops to think that he is following the millenary route used by travelers anxious to escape brigands and worrisome forest spirits. Add the further facts that the riverbank at the foot of the Sainte-Geneviève hill was firm, allowing boats to draw alongside, that timber for repairing bridges and boats was available nearby, and that quarries were rich in good building stone. (The same quarries tunnel today through the Paris subsoil like giant mole burrows, bedeviling city planners and architects.) Thus was born the village of Lutetia, which in the late fifth century became Paris.

At all times it has been, and is even now in the twentieth century, a corseted city, imprisoned by walls that have been quickly overflowed and pushed back despite an apparent wish to enclose, girdle, and delimit the town. We can count no fewer than four major attempts to check the giant's growth. The first wall was built under Philippe-Auguste (1180–1223),

the second under Charles V (1356–80); Louis XIII (1610–
1643) extended it and Louis XIV (1643–1715) embellished
it with gates that are still solid today. The third wall, intended to facilitate collection of tolls, was erected by Louis
XVI (1774–92); the last was enhanced by the addition of
forts that began to be demolished only after 1918. This passion for limits has left concentric traces that give historical
Paris its aspect and shape. Lutetia is the present Île-de-la-Cité.
The eight-hundred-year-old wall of Philippe-Auguste is dis-
cernible in the rue Clovis, behind the Panthéon. The emplace-
ment of the next wall was followed in laying out today's
Grands Boulevards. The third, punctuated by the handsome
tollhouses built by Nicolas Ledoux, can be seen at the Lion de
Belfort, the Rotonde de la Villette, and the Barrière du Trône.
And finally, if the outermost fortifications did not succeed in
halting the invaders of 1870, its moats and shadowy corners and grassy slopes at least offered attractive backgrounds
for Paris folklore and the antics of the city's wild young
bloods.

I emphasize the permanence and persistence of these
traces of the past because they express so well the coherence
and continuity of the city's development as well as its tendency
to let itself be immured in centuries-old habits. No great
fire, no terrible siege, no natural disaster has ever obliged
Parisians to rebuild Paris. The city is all superposition, ac-
cumulation, preservation. It has grown reluctantly, razing almost nothing, and without any preconceived plan. Paris has
experienced the charm and the curse of spontaneous growth,
of a chaotic but always contained impetus. Why no one knows
exactly, but Paris has always seemed overgrown, overpop-
ulated, and a little disturbing. "Its head is too big for its
body." Although the sum of French technical skill was devoted

47

to the creation of this huge, greedy city, the monster's excesses and violence were feared. Paris was an invention of monarchic absolutism, an inevitable result of royal centralization. Nonetheless, it was that embodiment of absolute monarchy—Louis XIV—who created the "parallel city" of Versailles so that he could assemble his nobles there, keep them under his thumb and busy, and also shelter his authority against possible eruptions in Paris. By virtue of having been conceived as "anti-Paris," Versailles implicitly paid homage to Paris.

At the very beginnings of the great French monarchical adventure, when the king of France was such a nonentity that no one remembered to invite him to join the First Crusade, Paris itself was of little account. The early Capetians dreaded even the puniest quarrelsome baron or pillaging lord. They possessed little more than their city—Paris. When they imposed themselves upon France, they also imposed their capital upon her. As they gradually unified the country around themselves, they fashioned an amazing web of customs, feudal allegiances, laws, functions, and roads all of which converged symbolically, juridically, or geographically in Paris.

France is the prodigious, minutely elaborated triumph of the Capetian monarchy, extending over a five-hundred-year period from Philippe-Auguste to Richelieu and Louis XIV. The jurists of the Revolution, of Napoleon I, and even of the later Republics lived, as indeed the Fifth Republic lives today, on the patrimony accumulated by France's kings: the conquest of natural boundaries, the subduing of the feudal lords and cities, the establishment of a remarkable administrative mechanism, absolute concentration and centralization of power in the monarch's hands—in a word, Paris. England achieved unification at one stroke, with the Norman invasion. Spain had to reconquer hers from Islam. Germany and Italy were

still parceled out in pricipalities and rival cities in the nineteenth century. France was built like an anthill, by the unre-
mitting labor of men of law, not that of soldiers. Her great
upheavals, her dark ages—the Hundred Years' War, the
Burgundian threat, the religious struggles—weighed less in
the national scales than did the meticulous task performed by
the kings, their royal ministers, and their councilors in unify-
ing the country and successfully exercising authority over it.
Paris was the Palais-Royal and the seat of parliament; here
resided both the grandeur and the efficacy of power. To lose
Paris, to leave Paris—to be "the little king of Bourges" or the
Chief of State in Vichy—was, in 1425 as in 1940, unparalleled
calamity.

Look at a map of France. Whether it is a question of
highways or canals or railroads, you see a star, a spider's web,
the center of which is Paris. The old Roman roads crisscrossed
France in response to the various laws of trade or necessities
of military occupation. Once the monarchy was installed—
that is to say, once France existed—everything was organized
like filings around a solitary magnet. The Empire and the
Republics confirmed and completed the royal choice. The railroad routes of 1850 reaffirmed the pattern of highway and
waterway. Republican France was organized as centripetally
as the monarchy, and by the same methods. The bailiffs of
the *ancien régime* became the prefects of the Empire and of
the modern Republics—meticulous executors of the central
power, permanent and authorized representatives of Paris in
each *département*. It was granted that because all power, all
sanction, all achievement issued from the capital, the capital
would attract and absorb all the vital energies of the nation.
The highway and railway symbol is sound, for it subsumes a
similar convergence of ambitions, interests, commodities, and

wealth. Even the democratic system, which periodically returns to the source of power—the electorate—was helpless to
reverse this prodigious centralizing movement. Why? Because
politics might be practiced partially in the provinces, but the
state existed in and by virtue of Paris. Politics was a matter of
words, ideologies, passing storms. The State was permanence,
continuity. Kings followed one after another, regimes changed,
ministries fell, but the State, with its great civil-service corps
ranging from clerk to the highest-ranking administrator—
the State endured. And it endured in Paris.

During the period of his London exile, General de Gaulle
welcomed a modest prefect more warmly than a political
bigwig because the prefect symbolized the rallying of a small
fragment of the State to his cause rather than one man's
ideological adherence. On that day in August 1944 when he
entered Paris, which had been liberated by the Allied advance,
General de Gaulle did not go directly to the Hôtel de Ville,
where the victorious uprising had taken place; he went to
what in his army officer's eyes symbolized institutional permanence and legitimacy—the War Ministry. This gesture must
be understood if one is to understand anything about French
life or the role of Paris.

Paris is not merely the center stage for historic events,
popular uprisings, and retributive rebellions; it is the place
where for more than eight hundred years those institutions
have been rooted that, above and beyond revolts and regicides
and defeats, have constituted the real armature of a country
which, for all its seeming anarchism, is extraordinarily well
structured. The Paris of St. Bartholomew, the Fronde, the
fall of the Bastille, the Commune, the barricades of 1830
or 1940—this Paris exists, of course, especially in popular
folklore and the patriotic films the nation loves to regale itself

with. But it counts for less than the Paris of the Council of State, auditor-general's office, Army Chief of Staff, the head-quarters of big business corporations and banks, the Sorbonne, the École Polytechnique and, more recently, the École Nationale d'Administration.

This nebula which is Paris has no clearly defined boundaries, but today it is divided into eight *départements* and is termed "District of Paris." It comprises some nine million inhabitants, or 18 per cent of our population, with 22 per cent of our automobiles, and by the year 2000 it will number sixteen million inhabitants. Its maximum density of population is 93,265 inhabitants to the square mile (against 38,860 for Moscow, 31,090 for Tokyo, 27,200 for London, 25,910 for New York, 3,887 for Rome). It constitutes, after Tokyo, New York, and London, the fourth largest agglomeration of humanity in the world. Based here are 25 per cent of French civil servants, 45 per cent of our students, 65 per cent of our corporation headquarters. When one says "Paris," it is this enormous urban, human, economic phenomenon which one evokes, as well as the centuries of time and custom that have formed the city, the history and the laws that account for it, and its little-known genesis rather than its too-familiar mythology.

And yet, let us admit it, the mythology is based on some truth. Not the mythology of the tedious night clubs and the fixed prices for the entertainments to which tourist buses nightly cart our innocent, cheated visitors. (There is a nocturnal Paris—antic, closed, shelving—which is by no means vulgar but offers scant hospitality to the average visiting stranger, who knows neither its guidebook nor its laws. It is almost exclusively for domestic consumption.) Rather it is the legend of a brilliant, lighthearted, wild Paris dispensing wealth and glory, disdainful of provincial aspirations and international competition: that legend rightfully perseveres because it is true.

Psychologically, socially, economically, and, above all, culturally, Paris absorbs and redistributes a considerable part of French activity. Not everything comes from Paris, but almost everything ends in Paris, or depends on it. Whether a Frenchman is civil servant, professor, musician, author, painter, or journalist, he dreams of rounding out his career in Paris or of seeing his work receive the stamp of approval there. The military man does not want to sit out his period of service in some remote garrison. The diplomat, whatever the charm of being posted to Teheran or London, is always eager to get back to the home office and cultivate his connections and his reputation. It is impossible to become an established musician or singer far from Paris. Is one better off as the Number 2 doctor in Paris or as the Number 1 in Lille or Lyon? It is hard to say. Local snobberies do exist—landed gentry who woo or shun the prefect's company at dinner, ancient hereditary fortunes—but only in Paris (with its Norman, Basque, or Mediterranean annexes, depending on the season) does an important social life exist. A man can learn to play tennis or ride in the provinces, but he must prove himself at Roland-Garros, the Étrier, or the Jumping at the Palais des Sports. Perhaps a man will write a great book or produce his painting or sculpture deep in rural solitude, but he will find his publisher or gallery in Paris. It is in Paris that the prizes are awarded, that the government makes its selections for official purchases, and that the big Biennale competitions are held. It is there that the writer will pick up assignments for articles and the painter, his commissions. There the author will find the drawing rooms that will inch him toward the

Academy, the bars where he can meet the film makers and get the television offers; there the painter finds a milieu—in cafés or collectors' homes—that will stimulate him, and reassure him about his future and the direction he is following in his work.

Actually, the situation of the artists is equivocal. Creative work requires solitude, and the artist must live apart. But the recognition that counts is garnered only in Paris, after which—success being more destructive for him than ever poverty was at twenty—the better part of valor will be for him to remove himself again, if he does not want to become the toy of society, a prey to the *bistros,* the salons, and the prevailing fashion. This explains why we see the more prudent artists—painters, sculptors, and writers alike—shuttling between isolation and the social whirl, between Provence and the Left Bank, Brittany and Montparnasse. They alternate between silence and bedlam, work and talk, discipline and alcohol. Whatever the current vogue offers, they accept the part that stimulates them and rejects what would enslave them. Obviously, all this applies to artists who are already, or are by way of becoming, celebrities. For the beginner, Paris is the place where he must try his luck. To be a good painter in Nantes or a fine poet in Toulouse means, nine times out of ten, that one is a nobody in Paris and risks (such are the ironic workings of prejudice) never amounting to anything there. Much as the denizens of Saint-Germain-des-Prés, the Coupole, the Institute, and the powerful salons on the Right Bank approve of the artist's possessing a "home base" and "roots"— some place of origin, in a word—they would equally hold it against him were he to bury himself there. A man can make a career as a typically Breton novelist or Provençal painter, but he makes it in Paris. It is enough if he withdraws to Ploumanach

or the Lubéron six months out of the year "to work." The
disadvantages of this state of affairs are evident. When creative
work is almost severed from its sources, it weakens and falters.
The fashionable, the imitative, the sterile—all these lie in
wait for the imprudent artist. The eternal socializing that
goes on in Paris, the enormous consumption of theories, gossip, and casual spite, the multiform usury of the studios,
dinners, newspapers, publishing houses—these are all mortal
threats to creative work. Presently reputations come to depend
on gossip, quips, connections. At best, it becomes difficult to
distinguish the fake from the real, the solid-gold from the
tinsel talent. Add to this the web of intrigues, liaisons, perver-
sions, emotional or sexual or social complicities, the vendettas,
disappointments, *gaffes,* and connivings, and one has a fairly
exact idea of what Paris can mean in terms of luck, blunders,
fascination, and vertigo.

Tout-Paris—the "Paris that matters"—is a silly expression, but it is also a sociological reality that merits description
and analysis.

Actually, several milieux coexist, variously superimposed
on, insulated from, or relatively accessible to each other. To
try to enumerate them all would be forcing matters, but
there is a "cream" that is almost purely aristocratic and still
quite close to its ancestral landed-proprietor roots. There is a
Protestant upper middle class. There is a Jewish middle class;
this group has access to many other milieux, such as the press,
medicine, law, business, and entertainment. There are the
film colony, the playboys (who are increasingly cosmopolitan),
the free-lance journalists, newspaper and book-publishing circles, and assorted groupings from trades such as couture,
interior decoration, and so forth. People move back and forth
among social and professional contacts, class reflexes, and

special-interest alignments, from a philosophy of life to style of living, and then to simple living comfort. But *Tout-Paris* is not the sum of all these little societies, rivalries, private languages, exclusions, and collusions. To put it simply, *Tout-Paris* is the four thousand individuals among whom the two thousand who always attend first-nights will be recruited, or the one thousand invited to the opening of an exhibit, the five hundred fierce partisans of a ballet, the three hundred first readers of a good new book, the one hundred names that occur to the hostess planning an important dinner party. It is not enough to be a duke in order to be one of these four thousand persons, nor is being a minister or ambassador enough, nor being rich, nor possessing talent, profundity, or beauty. Nonetheless, aristocrats and bankers brush elbows, as do politicians, prominent doctors, lawyers, publishers, actors, newspapermen, industrialists, a few scholars, theater producers, writers, well-known models, antiquarians, painters, and even an occasional hair stylist or night-club favorite. Is there a reliable safe-conduct into this world, a password that allows one to be admitted? Yes and no. Mostly no. Beauty, birth, and wealth help; they simplify but do not solve the problem. There is no question but that talent and wit are good passports, for *Tout-Paris* abhors being bored. New faces may please, yet one is not averse to being eternally among one's own kind. Allusions, first names, silences must be quickly grasped. There is no time here for explanations. A half-uttered word or a wink guarantees that one is among one's own kind. Better to be talented and amusing, albeit from a "trade" (couture, interior decorating), than to be a soporific member of the Jockey Club. To own horses, to give generously to charities, to wield a tidy bit of political influence—this is not enough, or rather it is no longer enough. Better to have written a good book. There are a thousand and one nuances: the song or play may not be picked up, but the musician or actor will be. Film people generally strike terror to the heart—almost as much as deputies do—yet such and such an actress, such and such a member of parliament who is only secondarily the people's elected choice, will belong to the coterie. Some ministers are In; others are ignored. Foreigners are easily assimilated if they know their place. Whether a man is black or yellow or a Jew scarcely counts at all in Paris, either "for" or "against." On the other hand, a military man, a solemn provincial, or a fiery militant is firmly rejected. As for morality and personal conduct, the attitude is one of total and spectacular liberalism. Affairs, adulteries, homosexuality ruffle no sensibilities. In this hothouse of eclecticism, specialization is viewed with favor. One can be a *dame à musique* or a *dame à peintres*. Some salons are dedicated primarily to the Academy, to surrealism, to horses, or to progressive opinions or nostalgic reactionaryism. Some nuclei are organized around a successful star or current enthusiasm. And finally, notwithstanding the flexible rules of gaiety, brio, or talent, some people seem to belong as if from all eternity, by virtue of being human antiques, witnesses to the past, mascots.

Is this milieu savage, superficial, snobbish, futile? Yes, all of those things. But it is also warm, generously enthusiastic, cultivated, open-minded, and rather simple. It is easily said—by people who do not belong—that "the first-night-by-invitation crowd is the roughest public in the world." But one could as fairly point out that this same public is capable of caring passionately about the theater, that it has some notion of what the play is all about, respects the actors' performances, and shows a cast more consideration than do the smug middle-class Sunday theater goers who think that because they have paid for their seats, they have the right to shrug and grouse. And so on and so on.

Tout-Paris yawned at the plays of Claudel, yet how many crazy and delightful experiments has this same audience saved? However that may be, sanction (whatever it is worth) in art, theater, music, and dance comes via the narrow gate of snobbism. This tiny society of *Tout-Paris,* heterogeneous and polymorphic as it is, picks up where the princes and royal court of days past left off. Snobbism, we must remember, is the modern form of patronage and performs the same salvaging function. Of these four thousand people, two thirds are men and women of talent and quality, informed and advantaged consumers; many, being themselves creative, are good critics. Whenever this segment of Paris life is berated, these facts bear repeating, even if personally one may wish to skirt the fashionable fetishes and avoid depending unduly on the verdicts handed down by good breeding. Dreadful *Tout-Paris* —it can be a bore, as can the exquisite Parisian elite. Both are oversimplifications and, familiar and comfortable as they are, to be eschewed.

PEOPLE HAVE SPOKEN, in contradistinction to Paris, of the "French wilderness." The phrase denoted the deserted hinterland, the sleepy provinces, and quickly assumed the form of a warning and the force of a dogma. But let us look at it a little more closely.

We find, first, that the term was coined in the 1950's, when the mania to "decentralize" was at its euphoric peak. Since then, it has come to seem a better idea to modernize our cities rather than to evacuate them, which was proving impossible in any event. It is true that during this period, France experienced a vast urban exodus, but that primarily benefited the Paris megalopolis. From the point of view of rustic charm, this exodus was regrettable, but it was inevitable and by no means confined to France, where it was actually much less accentuated than elsewhere. Twenty per cent of our population remains agricultural. For an advanced Western nation this proportion is enormous. It reveals, in part, our archaism.

Secondly, we find that without a doubt the province less and less resembles the image which novelists and Parisians have fashioned of it.

Sociologically and in terms of the national mythology, the word *province* means medium-sized and large cities of from ten thousand to a million inhabitants—not the countryside; not rural towns and villages. The *province* is a profound French reality—that is, a product of time and human experience; it is also raw material for literature and is thus a product of anger and talent. The French *province* is a reservoir of social ambitions, a culture broth of conformisms, a terrain favorable to Radical-Socialist aspirations, a refuge for suppressed passions and criminal reveries, a hothouse where the growth of family hatreds and intrigues and rivalries can be nourished. The *province* is—or was—all these things. Or you can sing the praises of the *province* and reel off a host of great names, literary and political—Balzac, Flaubert, Stendhal, Herriot, Mauriac, Jouhandeau.

And it would be equally honest to shift from dark to rose-colored glasses and point to a relaxed, leisurely, civilized way of life, which is shielded from excess, whether of speed or of concern for money, and offers family closeness, an opportunity for a balanced education, and the mysterious charm of the small city. We would then line up other cohorts—less numerous, it is true, and with more literary vinegar than honey, our novelists having had very ambiguous feelings for their places of origin—Barrès, Chardonne, Larbaud, Maurois, and even Giono or such writers as Mauriac and Jouhandeau, mentioned above.

Yes, the *province* really does exist. It is a source of fresh energy, a springboard capable of launching its man high indeed in the national sky. One literary character in particular is most often mentioned in conversation as symbolizing the provincial man—Balzac's *arriviste* adventurer, Rastignac. During the 1965 elections, the sneering way to belittle François Mitterand—General de Gaulle's opponent for the presidency, who received 46 per cent of the popular vote—was to brand him publicly as a "Rastignac." Why? Because he "came up" from Bordeaux. No one will ever say this of Giscard d'Estaing, another ambitious man in his forties who is certain to play a large role in France's political future. Why not? Because, following in his father's footsteps, he is an inspector of finance and a product of the most thoroughly Parisian bourgeoisie.

The *province* exists also in terms of speech and accent. Too often we forget that only the most cultivated families in a few regions of the country have been able to keep their speech free of local idiosyncrasies. The Parisian ear pitilessly detects the man from Nice, Marseille, Nîmes, Toulouse, Bordeaux, the native of the Massif Central or Alsace or Savoie. (This obsession with uniform speech is typically urban and middle class. The château dweller or the country squire will pride himself on affecting local inflections and will even risk a little patois.) Only the northern Frenchman—from Normandy and Brittany—escapes a regional accent almost entirely. The Parisian himself has one, which is speedily detected sixty miles from the capital. If he has none, that means his speech would be classified by Parisians from a milieu more modest than his as "upper class." So, depending on latitude, longitude, and social origin, there are several dozen ways of speaking French. Topping the pyramid is the accent that might correspond to the Queen's English (or the English of Oxford and the BBC). This is the French spoken between the Faubourg Saint-Honoré, Porte Dauphine, the Quai d'Orsay, and the rue Saint-Guillaume (where the École des Sciences Politiques has its headquarters). This speech is rapid, a bit shrill, clipped, and there is a tendency to swallow one's words. It is rather monotonous, but affects sudden emphases and exclamations usually more characteristic of feminine (or effeminate) voices. The *province* indeed exists: it is where no one *ever* speaks like this.

Between 1954 and 1962—that is to say, in the transitional period when Paris and France together were awaking from their various lethargies, the big provincial cities expanded at rates much higher than that of the capital. Grenoble ranked first (44.5 per cent), followed by Besançon (35.3 per cent), Caen (33.2 per cent), and so on. Paris ranked only twenty-third (15 per cent). Cities that had been partially destroyed during the war (Caen, Tours, Orléans) turned their misfortune to good account and, taking a long view, rebuilt entirely. Others, like Grenoble, simply resolved that, on the strength of new blood in their populations, modernized businesses, and long-range planning goals, they would escape the curse that weighed elsewhere upon the provincial scene.

These rebuilt or expanded cities are already vigorous and lively. They offer dynamic and solid business opportunities to Frenchmen in search of them. But will they also be able to satisfy cultural and social needs, and ambition on a national scale? This is still far from certain.

When a city the size of Marseille (900,000 inhabitants), which is certainly old but suffers from no perceptible hardening of the arteries, and which has a sound local administration, is virtually the only city in all France to decide that it wishes to support a decent opera house and—what heroism!—put on original productions (a Sagan ballet, a *Carmen* with sets by Bernard Buffet, an opera based on a Julien Green novel, etc.), what does it do? In addition to *Tout-Marseille* and *Tout-Provence,* it invites a trainful of Paris notables and pays for their travel and lodging at great expense to the city. And what happens? The quizzical, incredulous Parisians discover faces, manners, and mannerisms of small-town elegance which they supposed had vanished from French repertoire and folklore at least twenty years earlier. Their faith in the capital is correspondingly fortified, even as they must applaud this attempt to break away from it; they are amused and titillated, their Parisian patriotism blooms, and in the space of three hours their prejudices are once again, in the classic pattern, centralized.

Anyone traveling through France in these years of mutation is constantly leaping from one hypothesis to another, from a conclusion to a fresh doubt. He may pass through a village that clusters intact around its church and school, and is still uncluttered by pseudo-modern constructions, a village that he feels nonetheless to be still alive and he is filled with wonder at such stability and with apprehension over the dangers of stagnation. Sooner or later he will pass through a market town disfigured by architectural excrescences and ringed by new and hideous hovels; here he will inveigh against anarchy. Later, when he comes upon an almost deserted hamlet inhabited only by elderly people, he will say to himself that the exodus from the cities is necessary and inevitable.[1]

---

[1] In 1964, out of 38,000 French communes (the smallest administrative unit in France), 22,000 numbered less than 500 inhabitants; 10,000 less than 200.

What is he to think? When he reaches the outskirts of a city—any one of the cities of 50,000 to 150,000 people that constitute the typical French *province*—he will be assailed by a dozen conflicting emotions: pleasure at seeing things on the move, fear that they may be moving toward chaos; hope that an earlier psychology and its attitudes have been toppled forever; hope that a new order will replace them. It is a statistical fact that as late as 1964, 40 per cent of the people living in the *provinces* had not been to Paris for twenty years; but this is a sign of giving up, of growing old, not of proud self-sufficiency. On the other hand, whereas in 1939 the provincial press as a whole was printing four million copies as against the Paris papers' seven million, today this proportion has been exactly reversed. The third largest French daily, with a circulation of more than 600,000 is a Catholic Breton paper, *Ouest-France. Le Progrès* (Lyon) and *La Voix du Nord* (Lille), with 400,000 copies each, are comparable to the big "national" morning dailies, *Le Figaro* and *L'Aurore*. Only the evening papers, *France-Soir* (1,300,000) and *Le Monde* (325,000) have no provincial equivalents or competition in their particular specializations, which are, in the first instance, popular, apolitical news, and in the second, substantial information and a liberal point of view. During the last twenty years of relative stagnation of the French press in general, the provincial press has carried on rather better than the Paris papers.

It is true that provincial college faculties do not enjoy as good a reputation as those of Paris. It is true that the big names in medicine, the most famous lawyers, the authors of the prestigious textbooks usually teach—or are waiting impatiently to teach—in Paris, despite often deplorable working and living conditions. It is true that for a long time large business concerns have traditionally owned or have built factories far from Paris (Peugeot in the *département* of Doubs, IBM near Nice, Citroën near Rennes, Michelin in Clermont-Ferrand, etc.), only to have middle-echelon personnel not recruited on the spot chafe at their "exile" and top-ranking employees end their careers in Paris.

However, a former president of the Council of State, later to be a minister—Edgar Faure—traveled twice weekly to Dijon to teach law. It is a fact that among the regions in full economic expansion, the North, the Rhône Valley, and the area around Grenoble are trail blazers. It is worth noting that the Compagnie d'Aviation Air-Inter, which specializes in domestic air travel in a country where the longest flights are five hundred miles, was given a very slim chance of success ten years ago, but today finds its carriers besieged by the businessmen of the new generation.

In brief—although it is rash to be brief in this shifting, uncertain world, which is still subject to all the currents of a slow-moving history—it does seem that the *province* of Balzac or Mauriac, the *province* of simmering ambitions, of devout middle-class women yearning for social precedence, of small factories and narrow horizons, subject as it still is to the tyranny and fascination of Paris, may be in the process of metamorphosis. There are Frenchmen living today—often in positions of responsibility—who are over fifty and in whom the Paris-*province* syndrome looses a torrent of fears, jealousies, superstitions, and symbols. But their attitudes and their roles are already tottering. Tomorow they will disappear. Their sons, who outnumber them, are less pessimistically Malthusian in their thinking, free of the lost-wars complex; pressures from the European community spur them, force them to experiment. This generation will quickly relegate the old *province* concept to the dustbin. These younger men will pose a healthy, high-spirited threat to Paris. One may even now wonder whether Paris will be able to meet it.

FOR THE MOMENT, however, what a strange city it is! Yesterday we were the victims of its charm; today we are the victims of its aggressions. Only yesterday we strolled about the city, happy, gawking pedestrians; today we rush, jostle, and, rather than risk asphyxiation while walking, try desperately to get about by car. Yesterday, so the legend runs, we cultivated good manners and good humor; today we snap at each other for no reason and come to blows over a parking space. Yesterday we rhapsodized about the celebrated soft mist that today is transformed into a sulfur-anhydrite cloud. The city has become weary and shrewish, at once jittery and paralyzed. It is, beyond question, the most exhausting capital in the world, the most difficult city to work in and the least comfortable to live in. Parisians are trapped on every side. It is hard to find a place to live, hard to move about, hard to telephone—even hard to arrive or leave. There is less air to breathe here than anywhere else: 85,000 trees, or 43 square feet of foliage per inhabitant, as against 97 in London, 269 in Vienna, and 1,688 in Los Angeles. Paris boasts 32 bridges, 75 museums, 250 movie theaters, and, in the big stores on the Right Bank, 113,000 microbes to the cubic foot. Paris drinks a billion liters of wine a year and teaches more than 100,000 students. The Eiffel Tower receives 1.8 million visitors in twelve months, but in thirty years Paris has built only one new hotel, and that was an American enterprise. Every evening around six o'clock 70,000 cars are brought to a halt by 800 red lights as they attempt to carry home those individualistic Parisians who refuse to use public transportation.

To shelter one car in the center of Paris requires an area that can be worth as much as six times the value of the car.[2] People complain about the lack of space, but an edict of Colbert—a three-hundred-year-old edict—forbids the construction of buildings higher than 101.7 feet. People complain about lack of space, but in Paris 3,460 acres are occupied by stations, railways, cemeteries, barracks, bus depots, slaughterhouses, public markets, wine warehouses, and prisons. The cemeteries alone occupy 1,140 acres. By count, there are twenty of them, more than the number of swimming pools (nineteen) or sports stadiums (seventeen). Whereas Mont Blanc has been tunneled under, an automobile has yet to be driven under the Seine. The Métro, built with pick and shovel by our grandfathers around 1900, has not been significantly improved since then. If Parisians did not abandon Paris *en masse* each August, they would face a water shortage. If one fine morning all the students enrolled in the Sorbonne were to decide to attend their classes, only the police could disperse the mob. If decent precollege education were to be provided, it would be necessary to have not 80 lycées, as at present, but 130 of them. Were there to be a nuclear explosion, the *département* of the Seine would be able to provide shelter for 120,000 of the city's 5,650,-000 inhabitants. At the Saint-Louis and La Salpétrière hospitals, some buildings date from 1607, some wards from 1635.

Le Corbusier wrote in 1933: "Paris has become a monster sprawled over an entire region, a monster of the most primi-

---

[2] About a dozen underground garages are either in construction or now completed; among the more spectacular of them are those under the Champs-Élysées and in front of Notre Dame. However, they will accommodate a maximum of 10,000 cars, whereas the automobile population of Paris and the *faubourgs* is nearly 500,000.

tive biological type—a protoplasm. It is a swamp. People talk endlessly, complain twenty-four hours a day, the years pass, and the city atrophies."

A monster, a protoplasm, a swamp—how did it come to this? It is fair to say that in almost two thousand years of accretion and spontaneous disorder, the city has known only four kinds of real planning: (1) the construction of the walls; (2) some miracles of beautification; (3) partial redesign in response to police and military interests that were disguised as a concern for public hygiene and city planning; and (4) the provision of suitable residences of the bourgeoisie of the *belle époque.* These actions and only these have variously stemmed or channeled the urban torrent, and they account for Paris's appearance today.

We can quickly skip over the walls, which were mentioned before. Only their general outline remains, kidney- or bean-shaped, plus traces of a few curves, avenues, squares, names, and some tidbits of folklore.

The embellishments are of another order of importance. We are their solicitous guardians and their prisoners. Little by little, they began to make up our capital of beauty and gild our legend. Individual pride and religious faith were the great dispensers of display in the past. Although churches and chapels cannot be said to have figured importantly in the will to build Paris, proud rulers did transform the city. Louis XIV loved only Versailles; out of a spirit of opposition and austerity, his minister, Colbert, wrought miracles in Paris. It is to his influence that we owe the enlargement of the Louvre, the Place Vendôme and Place des Victoires, the Observatoire, the Val-de-Grâce, the Gobelins, the Hôtel des Invalides, the Saint-Denis and Saint-Martin gates—and the first sewers.

Paris vs. The Province

The completion of the Louvre dates back to Napoleon I, as do the rue de Rivoli, four bridges, two canals, the Bourse, the Banque de France, the Carrousel, the Colonne Vendôme, the wine market—and running water.

But, beyond question, it is to Napoleon III and his prefect, Baron Haussmann, that Paris is indebted for the fact that it is still a half-habitable city. This is, perhaps, the biggest debt of all. Haussmann's motives were mixed, but he gave the city the appearance that it still preserves, and for a hundred years, 1860–1960, Paris remained his creation. Haussmann discovered that vast public works eliminated unemployment and that wide avenues allowed air to circulate—and cavalry to charge. Ergo, public order, public health, and full employment could be achieved by a single policy: town planning. With one stroke, epidemics, idleness, and barricades would be done away with. This many-sided and optimistic discovery transformed the city into a prodigious workshop for almost twenty years.

A north-south axis was cleared. The big avenues that still serve as the addresses of the well-to-do were laid out: the boulevards Malesherbes, Saint-Germain, and Raspail, and the avenues George V, Marceau, and Bosquet. The Opéra, Les Halles, and the railway stations were built. The Bois de Boulogne and the Bois de Vincennes were converted into great parks. Paralleling these official, centrally planned upheavals, private wealth, elegance, fine manners, and snobbism were establishing their own quarters at costs that ran into millions. The Plaine Monceau was overgrown with ostentatious mansions. In this fussy Napoleon III style, which was opulent and showy but remarkably sturdy, rose the ornate town houses that we, sneering perhaps a little rashly, have been tearing down over the last decade. This Paris of bankers and cocottes,

67

of wealth and gaiety—Offenbach's Paris—may elicit a smile, but one must concede that since those orgies of bad taste nothing has been done that equals Haussmann's city planning. Gingerbread ceilings and Regency fake gilt must not make us forget that the city was laid out, simplified, and made viable for traffic with such talent that we can still fumble along today. Without Haussmann's great axes and the Métropolitain of the *belle époque,* the Paris of the sixties would quite simply suffocate.

Paris underwent its fourth and last civic operation around the turn of the century in response to *fin-de-siècle* aspirations toward more gracious living. This yielded the city 112.5 miles of subway lines, those two examples of architectural delirium which face each other at the end of the Champs-Élysées, the Petit-Palais and the Grand-Palais, some fine Rodin statues, that squawk of modern metallic vanity known as the Eiffel Tower; and the countless private residences, somnolently overfed in the true 1900 period style—potbellied, convoluted, festooned, carved with caryatids, thistle, and heliotrope, crowned with pinnacles and belvederes. For more than half a century these dwellings have sheltered families who, for all their smiles, have been well satisfied to live amid the reassuring décors conceived in an era both wiser and more adventurous than we have conceded it to be. To live here is to hew oneself an easy conscience out of building stone.

Anyone who walks about Paris with his eyes open, seeking the key to the city, will see that basically it is superimposition: five hundred monuments designated as historical; slum areas that have been four hundred years abuilding; a working-class and lower-income city-within-a-city that is about a hundred years old and utterly lacking in character; the powerful imprint of Napoleon III; countless relics of the 1900 era, ranging from folly (Eiffel Tower) to banality (the streets in the "better neighborhoods"). Around these five elements we could embroider a thousand and one arabesques, but they would not alter this structural pattern and succession. Such a simplification highlights the nature of the separation between tourists and Parisians. The first group visits one and perhaps two Parises; the second group inhabits the other three. Virtually none of our city-planning problems is related to the monuments—the palaces, churches, public buildings, squares, fountains; everyone agrees they should be preserved, restored, cherished, and revered. Our problems revolve around all the rest—slums to be torn down, low-income sections of town to be remodeled, business districts to be rescued from asphyxiation. These problems are rooted in a lie, a lie which we have lived with for several decades. It is that we must mortgage the future and paralyze the present on the pretext of safeguarding historical beauty. Absurdity reigns when people refuse to build upwards on the pretext that skyscrapers would overwhelm Notre Dame and obscure the Sainte-Chapelle. Can they not see that verticals are precisely what is needed if we are to break out of that swamp that Le Corbusier spoke of. Twentieth-century Paris needs towers—that is to say, skyscrapers—just as medieval cities needed belfries and spires. Verticals are the dream and the saving grace of cities. Without towers, without steeples and belfries and minarets and campaniles and domes, cities would look like cookies or omelets. However, if—Colbert notwithstanding!—one manages to wrench the authorization from the appropriate authorities to build a 590-foot-high structure on the site of the former Gare Montparnasse (a hideous section whose folkloristic interest is zero), what happens? Immediately one runs up against horrified outcries, petitions, and assorted campaigns mounted by the "associations for the defense of Old Paris" and other self-appointed trustees of the past who sadly misconstrue its real value. When one seems about to snatch victory away from these diehards and to build—finally—upwards, one discovers that a hodgepodge of professional and bureaucratic absurdities (cost of land, artificial scarcity of sites and permits, taxes, a plethora of administrative requirements, lost time, speculation, etc.) will bring the square-foot price of office space in our first skyscraper to such a figure that no corporation will ever locate there and no promoter dare risk construction.

What is it that threatens, distorts, and perverts beauty? Modernity? The buildings of Chandigarh, Brasilia, Chicago, New York? No. What threatens beauty is, quite simply, ugliness. What disfigures Notre Dame is the abominable Prefecture of Police. What ruins the Sainte-Chapelle is the gray boil that serves as dome for the Chamber of Commerce. What offends the eye in the vicinity of Saint-Germain-l'Auxerrois and the Pont-Neuf is the huge department stores, the Samaritaine and the Belle Jardinière. Since the eye does get used to almost anything, in Paris one is no longer shocked by the grievous promiscuities, the stone pimples and warts that deface our streets, but injured taste moans at the mere idea of putting up clean steel and glass in place of some piece of 1900 gingerbread. People raged when Zehrfuss and Nervi erected (only two steps from the École Militaire!) a building for UNESCO which was elegant in its economy and subtly integrated with the surroundings. But ten years earlier they had tolerated the gigantic pat of butter that accommodates the Faculté de Médecine, and ten years hence would tolerate a parallelepiped rectangle that we owe to the imagination of not one, but seven, architects, and that crushes four *arrondis-*

sements of the city under its mass at Maine-Montparnasse. The capitulations of Paris opinion to *laisser-aller* are as unforeseeable and aberrant as its spasms of nervousness and intolerance. This city which prates so much of beauty lacks all sense of it, and lacks as well the legislation to foster it. It is miraculous that in the course of four centuries a few sovereigns and numerous great nobles, churchmen, and wealthy personages have, on their own, invested Paris with an architectural ensemble which, though less prestigious than that of some other cities, is harmonious, coherent, and wisely adapted to the light and the climate. Paris spoils much but destroys little, so a good part of this heritage we will preserve. Now we must see to it that the city is not condemned to the distinguished lethargy of a museum on the pretext of protecting it from any blemish. No need to worry over that; the blemishes are there already. Some of them, mellowed and well integrated, are by now pretty much part of the sacrosanct "historical" Paris. Contemporary Paris must be curetted, sorted out, rearranged—made livable once again. It will also be necessary to invent around her, beside her, even inside her, a new city unshackled by taboos and the curse of antiquarianism. The more contemporary such a city will be, the less it will shock any sensibilities. When Parisians come to understand that what they love in the Place des Vosges is a once-modern Louis XIII, in the Place Vendôme a once-modern Louis XIV, and in the rue de Rivoli a once-modern Empire, and that even their beloved old Opéra, slightly touching and ridiculous today, was avant-garde a hundred years ago, then, perhaps, they will concede that a modern Gaullist style would not compare too badly with the long-cherished urban art that they peer at through gas and oil fumes. Perhaps they will discover that while it has been a good thing to scrub the old stone faces of their buildings, to dare design and build new structures would be even better. Adding Chagall to Garnier, installing a Maillol before a seventeenth-century palace is all very well. But to install the works of modern artists in modern buildings in a modern city would be better still.

Paris risks dying of simultaneous ailments of the lungs, head, and heart: death by asphyxiation, exasperation, and discouragement. How could visitors who are here for one week —and generally a week in midsummer when the city drowses in the heat—notice this? How could they sense that the passion with which Parisians love their capital and cling to it sometimes risks becoming a hopeless passion? How could they understand that the city is in fact suffering from capital ailments; that is, the kind that affect the head, the ability to invent, the imagination of genius?

Yet some solution must be found. It may lie under the Seine or be buried three hundred feet beneath the city, or may even be suspended from rails, bridges, and towers between sky and street. Perhaps we shall have to hack out expressways or bypasses or radials or tunnels[3]—or look ahead to the time when the absurd tyranny of the automobile will end. It may become a matter of extending the city in the shape of a star or blob, chopping it into sections or dispersing it like a nebula, converting lakes into reservoirs, replanting woods, opening up to the sky. In the end it will amount to one and the same task: to restore to ten, fifteen, or twenty million

---

[3] The expressway from Auteuil to Bercy, which will run under the Place de la Concorde, the length of the Louvre, etc., is a gigantic undertaking that is utilizing the most advanced techniques and crews which work around the clock. It is an efficient and striking project—and hopefully one harbinger of a larger Paris awakening.

people the pleasure and honor of living rationally in this ancient, history-saturated city. Tomorrow, let us hope, cities will not be classified by population statistics or relative wealth in historical beauty, but by the capacity of each city to preserve and foster human happiness. May Paris—where once Saint-Just thundered his noble vision from a revolutionary tribunal: "Happiness is a new idea in Europe!"—may Paris win a place of honor in such a competition!

CHAPTER IV:

Affluence?

THE QUESTION CAN BE PUT SIMPLY: Are we living in a period of true prosperity from which the whole nation benefits, or are we witnessing merely a surging consumer's economy that conceals under a flattering exterior active social injustices and backwardness that we have yet to rectify?

For some twenty years, we French coddled our nostalgias and woes; now we seem to have come to, and the national mood today is even euphoric. Evidence of our poverty long obsessed us; now it is the evidence of our wealth which blinds us. One hears talk only of prosperity and growth. "Growth" has become a magical word. Government and opposition bombard each other with production statistics and indices that prove or challenge them. Especially since 1962, a satisfactory annual rate of increase in the gross national product has become our prime election slogan. Even President de Gaulle, who loftily scorned the "economic factor," no longer disdains to quote, in his heavy, mocking voice, optimistic figures—"loaded figures," his adversaries hasten to claim. It does seem that the average Frenchman, for whom the three pillars of security are the gold reserves of the Bank of France, the ownership of a car, and vacations in Spain, is finally beginning to trust in a prosperity that he had been feeding on without daring entirely to believe in it. He hears his ministers promise simultaneous change and conservation, expansion within stability, greater wealth for all and the preservation of old privileges. He does not ask himself whether these aspirations may be contradictory; because they are compatible with two traits of his own character, he happily accepts them at face value.

It is true that many minor facts and many impressions corroborate them. They also serve as reminders. The president in uniform who came to power on the wings of a plot, but who was later endorsed by staggering majorities; the intimacy between government and big banking; the fact that Paris has become once again a vast workshop; speculation in new construction; twenty-year-old singers who are great celebrities, and are perhaps the Offenbachs we deserve—France has known all this before. The same was true of the Second Empire, the almost two decades from 1852 to 1870 which witnessed the triumph of money and the middle class, a tardy industrial revolution, and a nation-wide spree that screened the rise of some and the poverty of others. Historically, will Gaullism be a kind of tailpiece to the reign of Napoleon III? Affluence, formalism, and bourgeoisie: just one hundred years ago, these were the guiding ideas of a fairly prosperous period. What equivalents characterize the controversial era we live in?

In 1965 a well-informed, objective journalist, Paul-Marie de la Gorce, published a study defiantly titled *Pauper France*. It might be compared to Michael Harrington's investigation, in 1962, of poverty in the United States. Although La Gorce's book came out in the midst of full expansionist euphoria and did not deny the progress that had been made, it was dedicated to "the other France," to the clouds which are sometimes so black that they allow one to doubt what we rather comfortably term "the French miracle" (which happens to be the title of a book by M. J. Guyard, also published in 1965). The privations of our old people, the painful situation of those "over forty" and of small businessmen and farmers, the distress of those who are badly housed or live in the poor regions of the nation, the neglect of immigrant labor—those were the main chapters of this harsh and much needed reexamination.

Before delving deeper into these issues, let us consider this question: What initial *impression* does France make?

A traveler, for example, who had first come to France in 1945, then again in 1955, and who is now putting together impressions received in the course of a third visit would certainly be struck by semblances of wealth today. He would notice squalid old houses still, but now crowned by TV antennas and adorned with fairly shiny cars parked in front. He would notice many new buildings also, since today we are putting up almost 400,000 housing units annually, as compared with a total of 500,000 units from 1944 to 1954. He would note that one out of every two families owns a refrigerator; that eight million cars crowd our small roads; that on the farms, tractors have increased from 56,500 in 1946 to almost a million today. He would observe that people are less poorly dressed and notice how many young people there are and how readily money circulates. As he traveled about the country, he would sense that some cities are experiencing a fever of growth whereas others remain dormant and unchanged; that big farms are finally functioning well, but that small ones are run down; that supermarkets and Prisunics are multiplying, but that millions of small shops are dying behind their dusty windows. He would sense, would share, a certain relief and euphoria, but at the same time he would detect a malaise. What malaise?

Our traveler would ask himself some questions.

He would ascertain that although the expansion has been real, its benefits have not, perhaps, been equitably distributed. By virtue of these economic developments, on one hand, and by political choice on the other, prosperity has created its own advantaged and its own disadvantaged groups. The spread of income ranges from one to one thousand. (These figures are quoted by J. F. Revel in *En France,* and were used in a survey published by *Le Monde* on September 13, 1962.) Our financial system has always been antidemocratic, and now, instead of establishing a better balance between extremes, it is accentuating the imbalances. It is pitiless toward wages and salaries—i.e., earnings of workers, white-collar employees, civil servants, and the military—but actually tolerates tax evasion on industrial and commercial profits and on the earnings of the liberal professions. As a result, a class of people has come to exist which is not rich but at least earns a comfortable living that is not too seriously diminished by the income tax. This class is fairly large, perhaps one tenth of the population. These people are not the timid *petits bourgeois* of once upon a time, but neither are they the holders of real wealth and its attendant power. They are simply those French people who, in a restaurant or on the road, in stores or on vacations, spend a lot of money. They are the people who create the impression of affluence and ease. They are the people to whom advertising and fashions and the thousand and one consumer appeals, the magazines, the films, and—in politics—a brawny, rejuvenated liberalism are directed. This

77

advantaged group is large enough, J. F. Revel observes, to make one forget that it is only a minority; its members "serve as a screen rather than as a target;" they spread "the myth of general prosperity because one sees them often and everywhere."

Our traveler might ask himself, like Revel: Are we in the presence of true wealth or of a gilded mask placed over the real face of the French economy? Have we for the last ten years been appeasing appetites or satisfying needs? Selling records and T-shirts to teen-agers is not building them schools; selling sunshine and bathing and vacations is not building houses, and so on. A society that produces, buys, and sells luxuries is not necessarily an economically sound society. Is there not a bit of fraud here? Have we not satisfied secondary wishes instead of fulfilling primary and urgent needs? Have we not bought social peace, and demobilized our old political watchdogs too cheaply? If the French feel vaguely uneasy in the midst of their recent well-being, is it not that they have struck—and guess that they have struck—a poor bargain?

This calls for a straight answer and, first of all, a tally of what progress has been achieved. I have already rattled off a few figures for tractors, household appliances, construction, and automobiles. I could cite others. They indicate that from 1930 to 1965 the French standard of living has risen by about 200 per cent; this takes into account that between World Wars I and II, 1929–30 was our brightest year, and that the 1939–45 years piled up heavy losses, setbacks, and material destruction. (By 1945, 66 per cent of our rolling stock, 66 per cent of our cargo ships, 75 per cent of our oil tankers, 80 per cent of our barges, 115 large railway stations, 9,000 bridges, and 80 per cent of our dock facilities had been destroyed.) In 1946 our industrial production fell below what it had been at the close of the nineteenth century. The year 1949 equaled 1939, but was 20 per cent below 1929; the production level of 1929 was only regained in 1953, which was, however, a bad year on the political and social fronts.

What can be measured in statistics is no less apparent in daily living. A Frenchman would hardly believe in a prosperity celebrated only in graphs and speeches. The rich Frenchman believes in wealth because he eats, drinks, displays, and burns it. He never wearies of this manna, and he talks about it with equal parts of relish and false modesty.

He forgets only one thing—that this expansion is normal. He forgets that it is implicit in the rationale of our society's evolution; that it affects all industrialized western Europe; that growth is expectable and that nongrowth would be the surprising phenomenon. The Fifth Republic would be very wrong to act and talk as if it had invented French affluence. The prototype of the (intelligent) man of the Fourth Republic, Edgar Faure, presided over the most spectacular advance our national economy ever knew. Recalled to the government and presently assigned to revitalizing our agriculture, he must feel not that he is a renegade from one system or a hostage of another, but that he is a versatile technician in an evolution that makes sport of political changes. Let me just mention in passing that governmental stability, which is a Gaullist achievement, certainly facilitates economic growth. That the French, who had a long and hard postwar road to travel, now register pleased surprise, well and good. But it would be absurd for them to call their advance a miracle. Again, one must weigh one's words when speaking of that long hard road. A ravaged Germany and her millions of victims, the torn and humiliated Italy of 1943–4, the Franco ghetto, famine in Holland—in any competition to decide which nation had suffered most, other countries would have been ranked before France. Actually, the root of our surprise goes still farther back. For thirty years we had stopped believing that our economy would ever take an upward swing. We were defeated in advance, and we remained defeated long after a victory in which we figured only *pro forma.*

This no doubt accounts for the numb disbelief with which the French calculated their chances around 1945. Almost two years went by without the situation's seeming to be notably improved. The idealistic fervor that characterized the summer of 1944 and the optimism sparked by the official end of the war on May 8, 1945, were followed by political vendettas, international humiliations, and the personal joys and tragedies arising from the return of war prisoners and deportees; above all our obsessing poverty persisted.

Today we realize that among the various incitements that were spurring our economy on even then—consumer demand, hope for social renewal, the Monnet Plan, foreign aid— the most disappointing was the impetus toward a revolutionary social overhauling and the most effective was American economic aid. From 1946 to 1958, in various forms—the Marshall Plan, military aid to the member nations of NATO, the off-shore contracts, and sale of surplus goods—American assistance reached a figure of 4.6 billion dollars, or 43 per cent of our balance of payments for those years. In particular, for ten years (1947–56), when taxes fell dangerously short of covering government expenditures in France (in 1945 they supplied only 42 per cent of needed revenue, in 1949 only 70 per cent), the aid that came from the United States was essential. It financed, alas, some futile adventures, like the "first" war in Vietnam, but for our economy it was a genuine blood transfusion. It enabled Jean Monnet as early as 1946 to set up his General Committee and, in 1947, to launch his first four-year plan for the modernization and equipment of industry. For a twelve-year period our economy was planned as follows: priority to six basic sectors (electricity, coal, steel, cement, railways, and agricultural equipment); a buildup in exports; recourse to inflation and to foreign financial aid. These options worked out well. Economic recovery was achieved by 1950, though a bit skimped and deceptive because our economic structures had not been essentially improved. Also, it mortgaged the future by neglecting housing and road construction and in countenancing financial decrepitude. As to the hopes for social justice so dear to the men of the Resistance, one can only say that not much remained of them. As early as 1947 economic uncertainties were translated into political tensions; Communist ministers were dropped from the government, whereupon strikes and social conflict resumed. General de Gaulle created an opposition party, the Rassemblement du Peuple Français (Rally of the French People), whose elected deputies or sympathizers, rancorous and rambunctious, made life in parliament hard for the successive governments up to 1958.

This foray into the jungle of statistics and political quarrels has been necessary if one is to understand the origins of our economic contradictions: the liberality, safeguards, and prudent policies of 1946 are bearing their fruit today, but so are things we overlooked or neglected. The striking disparities between our successes and our failures were conceived in the haste and bickering of the years 1945–9, when there was everything and too much to be done. Surely some things had to be sacrificed? Today, if we are pessimists, we see only the bad consequences and not the battles won then by the "Monnet team."

What are these bad consequences?

I have mentioned them already, and we shall keep meeting them again and again. They are groups in our society who are forgotten or discriminated against or doomed: the old; the relatively nonspecialized workers of forty-five and over; workers confined to the purgatory of the "minimum living wage" (about five hundred francs—say one hundred dollars—a month); and the immigrant workers (about two million), who are treated with indifference and often disgracefully housed. Standing before the shopwindows on the rue de Faubourg Saint-Honoré or at a big reception at the Élysée or by the port of Saint-Tropez around seven of a summer evening, who would think about the France of the Little Sisters of the Poor, the suicides of desperate old people, the gas-can shanty towns, the hovels where Arabs and Negroes are herded together, or even the France of the ashamed, hidden poverty of people who live on crumbling incomes, the artisans out of work, the workers languishing in long unemployment? In capitalist countries there is a fundamental poverty and a residual poverty, the latter inseparable from the exigencies of the machine. To what category do the poor of rich France belong? How does one classify the Portuguese worker, the lawyer's widow left penniless, the village or city grocer who survives solely on the charity of a few old customers who still drop by for a few canned goods?

These people are the victims of an indispensable and fierce forward movement. They are caught in the pincers of progress and they will be pulverized. The demographic torrent pushes the older man out; the economic torrent sweeps the little fellow away; the technical torrent drowns the untrained worker; the well-to-do consumer devours his poor neighbors; prosperity in the north aggravates poverty in the south. Per-

haps these ills were avoidable; surely they were not necessary. At least, by being the exceptions that prove the rule
they show that fruitful progress is being made.

Having thus bestowed our blessing on poverty, let us not
be taken in by wealth. It, too, is real, but its fine outward
appearance also feeds on injustice and bluff—on injustice
because wealth is very unevenly distributed; on bluff because at
times affluence has been granted priority over primary needs.
Depending on the degree of realism and intelligence which
her technocrats display, and depending on the proportions of
egoism and realism in her upper classes, in the years ahead
France will either complete her metamorphosis or slip into
the inflation of short-term economic gimmicks. To talk unqualifiedly of France as affluent would be like believing that
the moon is made of green cheese. To speak of France as poor
without defining the areas and the causes of this poverty
would be to misunderstand the current context of wealth
in all western Europe. We at the westernmost edge of the Continent are a slightly feverish, astonished, pleasure-seeking
nation, but one that is perhaps beginning to take its new opportunity seriously. May our Prince-President and his Ducs
de Morny preserve us from any repetitions of Crimea, Mexico,
and Prussian cannon!

CHAPTER V:

The French Are Growing Younger

OF THE VARIOUS POSSIBLE EXPLANATIONS of the French upswing over the last ten years, the most satisfactory seems to be the fact that our population is growing younger. A demographic awakening precedes, demands, and stimulates a psychological and economic awakening. Certain rather hazy aspects of the national scene come into meaningful focus the moment one realizes that this dynamism is like a flood: far from letting itself be dammed back, it requires room for expansion. France is moving precipitately—yet at the same time much too slowly—from lethargy to activism, from Malthusianism to a faith in large numbers, from a cult of the small to dreams of vast concentrations. We are justified, I believe, in explaining this by a single but all-embracing factor—the demographic *volte-face*.

Here, in one sentence and four statistics, is our situation: France has a population of about fifty million; one fourth of the people are under fifteen years of age; one third under twenty; two fifths under twenty-five. In 1938 we had the oldest population profile of the old European nations; today we have the youngest. Statistically, this rejuvenation is still relative, but it is of immense importance in terms of psychology and perspective. For the first time in a century and a half France is looking toward the future rather than turning away from it.

As a nation, we had begun to grow old in the late eighteenth century, the result being the slow depletion of our society. Furthermore, between 1914 and 1945 two wars and two invasions snatched two million men from the best and most vital section of the population. Take the France of 1938: she was overwhelmed by the exuberant birth rate of her two totalitarian neighbors; her own annual death rate exceeded her birth rate; her sixty-year-olds (15 per cent of the population) were weighing her down at the very moment those born between 1914 and 1918 (the low points on the birth-rate graph) were reaching employment, university, or military service age. France in 1938 was unquestionably at the lowest point on the curve of her decline. Why then? Why not a little later—at the time of the 1940 defeat, or during the Nazi Occupation, or in the chaotic days of the Liberation? Because, as we are in a position to realize today, it was as of 1939 that our demographic upsurge was primed and its legal and psychological framework was established. In a country that was the prisoner of its own comforts, Malthusian inertia, and historic fatigue; in a country of cabaret singers, apéritifs, pettiness in private life and resignation in the nation at large; in a country beguiled by its graybeards and annoyed by its children—in such a country, two politicians, Paul Reynaud and Édouard Daladier, concieved of family-subsidy legislation, which perhaps began it all.

This legislation was disconcerting, even revolutionary, and seemingly ill-timed; yet the Code of 1939 elicited no opposition. People saw that henceforth children were going to yield certain "benefits" to their parents (what grist that was for the mills of Montmartre cafés!), but what did not register with them, luckily, was the size of the bill. Was it bad conscience or unawareness on their part, a spurt of energy or indifference? One cannot say for sure. As Alfred Sauvy wrote, "It all happened as if the nation had acted deliberately yet without anyone's realizing what was coming about." The "baby bonus" was hailed gaily, and one had to be very clever to see in it the instinct of self-preservation of a community teetering on the edge of the abyss.

In the heart of timorous, provincial, *petit-bourgeois,* penny-pinching, calculating France, a current began to stir and soon to swell which was to improve the betting odds on our national future. It is amusing to note that from 1939 to today, from Daladier and Reynaud to Debré, and including Marshal Pétain, General de Gaulle, Communist ministers and reactionary ministers—everyone has been agreed on at least one score: the national birth rate must be encouraged. The French of 1940–4, who gave themselves into an old man's keeping and, through him, to the illusions of the past, as well as the post-Liberation French, who with delight recovered their sacred dotards and their septuagenarian star public performers, whose National Assembly president had to be hoisted bodily into his chair, whose actresses had been born under the Second Empire, and who evinced a positive passion for senility—these same Frenchmen imperturbably went on making babies under the generous protection of the law. Our maternity legislation was the most advanced and most effective in the world, comparable to laws the fascist states had fabricated for more questionable ends.

The result? More than eight hundred thousand births

86

annually (as against six hundred thousand before 1939), the highest rate of population growth in Europe, and 2.5 children per family as against 2.0 previously. These figures are still modest. With 226 inhabitants per square mile (compared to Holland's 910), we are not threatened with overpopulation tomorrow. But here again, while not so striking statistically, the development seems both unsettling and heartening to the collective French mind.

What does French society look like today? It includes both many old and many young persons. What with the augmented birth rate and successful efforts to prolong life, France is caught between two duties, two responsibilities. The duty imposed by the old people is a passing burden; the other looks to the future. As of now, and for at least ten years to come, a few productive Frenchmen must maintain many who are either no longer producers or not yet producers. This situation gives rise to a certain anxiety and to conflict between consumer dreams and the obligations of a collective morality. Unquestionably, there exists in the psychology of the French, as in the economy of their country and the decisions of their government, a competition between cars and housing, births and vacations, refrigerators and education, washing machines and professional training, pleasure and reason, social lethargy and a progressive orientation.

For families it is tempting to prefer a summer on the Costa Brava to another child. Similarly, for the Fourth Republic it was tempting to opt for a pro-automobile policy rather than one of basic investments (housing, schools). The small car for everybody guaranteed that the working class would become nonpolitical in its thinking and that social stability of sorts would be assured. Relax credit and encourage impulse buying; from there on, strikes are less to be feared.

A kind of public tranquility is bought on short-term credit by sacrificing long-term prosperity. It is common knowledge that in France the proletariat has often poured into the streets to defend its wages, but no one will go on strike or raise his fist to claim the right to a roof over his head. For that matter, strike against what? Raise one's fist against whom?

Accordingly, the vogue for youth, which is rampant in France, is not unwelcome because, combined with the approbation and assistance of the law in the form of various bonuses, it helps keep the demographic flame burning brightly, whereas the appetite for material comforts would threaten to let it die out.

On the other hand, the short-view policy that successive governments pursued blindly for fifteen years has led to today's catastrophic situation.

A simple perusal of the figures showed exactly what the needs of the young would be, year by year, in terms of secondary education, professional schools, teachers, sports stadiums, new jobs, and housing. Three factors probably explain our refusal to consider these figures and the consequences of that refusal: (1) a deliberate policy—make France the European country best provided with roads and cars and the worst supplied with dwellings, colleges, telephones, etc., because that is the surest way to comfortable social stability; (2) the unrest and expense created by the wars in Indochina and Algeria, by changes of government and the political anarchy that lasted until 1962; (3) a kind of traditional sluggishness, a difficulty in shaking off the fears and passivity of yesterday in order to face the problems of our young people. After all, it is easier—in any event, faster—to rejuvenate a society than to reform it. The shock of the awakening has not been overcome yet; some of the old stiffness persists. A horde of undaunted youngsters, the results of twenty years of booming birth rates, is now pressing hard against decrepit institutions and worn-out administrative personnel, but the national mood, confronted by this wholesome onslaught, remains backward-looking, overwhelmed.

True, we are building schools—it appears that in 1966 ten million francs a day were so spent—but not enough of them. Teachers are being hastily trained, swimming pools are being dug, school curriculums are being feverishly revamped to produce more technicians and fewer unusable fine-arts graduates, but these measures are still poorly organized and inadequate. The magnitude of the problem, which could easily have been foreseen fifteen years ago, is still greater than the scope of the solutions. The slowness, the disproportion, the failure to adapt to reality, the signs of panic, the statistical or budgetary lies, the bluff that is called every year in October at the terrifying moment when the school year starts—all this is the penalty we continue to pay for a century of stubborn sleep.

No doubt these are passing difficulties; we are in a period of transition. The efforts put forth so far will bear fruit in time. Of the three great challenges that the new France hurls at the old—education, jobs, housing—doubtless only education will continue to be the victim of our recent dark ages. We will have culturally underprivileged generations trained in haste by emergency teachers in overcrowded classes. Intellectually and technically, this will represent a total loss. Housing? In time, housing will be put up, for whatever it will be worth —ugly and unplanned, of course, but everyone will probably have a roof over his head in the next ten years. As to employment, it does not seem that young people are seriously threatened with a dearth of jobs. On the contrary. Thanks to the economy's expansion, and assuming that it continues, all of them will find work. It remains to be seen whether they will have been sufficiently trained, adequately specialized. It remains to be seen also what will be done with the "forty and over" citizens, whom the demographic explosion is driving from offices and factories and transforming into premature oldsters on the job market. In the years ahead full employment will be for Frenchmen from twenty to forty; the rest face hardship. Promotion from within, retraining, and understanding will not avail much. In this sense, the problem of our young people is actually a problem of our no-longer-young-enough citizens. One can imagine the disenchanted fate that awaits the average fifty-year-old Frenchman in a few years. If he loses his job, he will not find an equivalent, for the twenty-five-year-old applicants will be systematically preferred over him. His ridiculously modest rent, which he has come to consider his due, will have multiplied ten or twenty times, for one can build houses for the younger generations only by charging rents comparable to the interest rate on the capital invested. (For forty years, this fact was merrily denied in France. The "low-rent tenant" was "protected" even if it ruined the landlord and discouraged anybody from putting up a new building. To house your fellow citizen in return for rent became pure philanthropy. Hence the massive sales of apartments. Around 1950, to find housing meant inevitably to buy it, and the owner sold it rather than lease it for some paltry amount. Here again, from 1920 to 1960 or so, we encountered protectionism, holding back, pusillanimity.) Let us add the fact that our fifty-year-old will feel excluded from the new way of life; because of changes in things such as the use of leisure time, communications, and morality, he will be out of his element. Let there be no mistake about it: the rapid rejuvenation of French society will have as one effect that of prematurely aging a percentage of the population which, by atavism and education, is poorly prepared to withstand the assault of youth.

One can already sense the uneasiness setting in. One feels it among the young themselves, and in the efforts of the older generation to make adolescence fashionable, to flatter and exploit it, either by apathetic astonishment and resignation in the face of its onslaught, or, conversely, by a hasty, awkward acceptance of it. Our entire social life is affected by the vogue for youth. From the Radicals, a party once symbolized by the white beards of its soothsayers, to the Communists, from Lecanuet to Mitterand, our political leaders talk youth and nothing but youth. The rise of Robert Kennedy, which would have been inconceivable in France twenty years ago, fascinates the ambitious politician of the sixties. To be popular with today's adolescents is to sweep the election of tomorrow. In the slump in which our magazines find themselves, the only successes in the last five years have been periodicals aimed at teen-agers, whether the very Americanophile papers of Daniel Filipacchi or the Communist equivalents (the only Communist party publications that are not financial losses). Astutely, all the designers, manufacturers, publicists, and sellers of radios, records, books, motorbikes, etc., now have their eyes fixed on this vast purchasing power, both real and potential. In the choice of a car or holiday or vacation spot, it is the teen-agers who, by their advice or ridicule, make the decisions via their parents. In only a few years, they have become superb money-making machines. With blatant cynicism, the business world has strained its ingenuity to manufacture made-to-order tastes for them and the wherewithal to satisfy those tastes. Every serious sociologist will agree that the idols of our young people

—the singers or musicians—are the fabrications, pure and simple, of specialists. Rarely has one witnessed so systematic and unscrupulous an exploitation of a whole age group; if one had to choose whether to blame the organizers of this market or its victims, there is no doubt that the victims, silly and conformist as they are, would deserve our forbearance. Everywhere one hears it proclaimed that "youth is a market." Sure it is: a sucker's market. It is hard at sixteen not to be duped when a prodigious mobilization of press, radio, television, films, publicity, advertising, etc. conspires to make you the center of the world and supplies you with fads masquerading as values. The slogans, the publicity pitches, and hidden persuaders are all aimed in the same obsessive direction. Step by step, the obsession takes over. Young men in industry organize themselves into a Young Executives Association; farmers form a Young Farmers Union. The fever is raging in vast sectors of our daily life; it favors both wheeler-dealer and demagogue; it claims the attention of newspaper editor and cabinet minister, priest and policeman, the market researcher, the film producer looking for a scenario, the decorator of a new shop.

Is this perhaps a normal stage in the expansion of a liberal capitalist society? If we had studied American society fifteen years ago, for instance, we could have easily foreseen how ours would evolve. Allowing for a certain time lag, which is shrinking, all the typical attributes of American society are being, or soon will be, acquired by our own. It now takes scarcely more than two years for young people's fads in clothing, speech, reputations, and behavior to cross the Atlantic. "The era of the completed world is beginning," Valéry wrote, without having exactly these things in mind; that is to say, we are entering a period of osmosis, of almost instantaneous imitation, and tomorrow we will enter the period of absolute simultaneity. From Warsaw to Mexico City, from Paris to Tokyo, it is only differences in the standard of living which still delay or retard this irrational adherence of adolescents to the gilded, nonchalant, brimming, marvelous adventure of American adolescence.

Is *Papa* mildly nationalistic, perhaps, and *Maman* vaguely xenophobic? That will not suffice to deflect their children from the American example, which fascinates them. Folklore, music, films, clothing, vocabulary, customs—everything that comes from over there is destined to triumph over here. The young people sense this and press toward it.

Those among their elders who hoped that this identification would feed exclusively on Louis Armstrong and Sarah Vaughan, Jerome Robbins and Gershwin, Hemingway and F. Scott Fitzgerald, Humphrey Bogart and James Dean are the worse off for their all too eclectic illusions. They will have to endure Paul Anka, Elvis Presley, and their innumerable progeny—the beatnik by-products and the carbonated drinks, the cowboy-style jeans and the flowered shirts, saccharine imitations of Bob Dylan (and Bob Dylan himself). Happy are they with children whose *fureur de vivre* is confined to blaring records and broken-down seats at the Olympia without progressing to marijuana and switchblades!

Actually, these young people, who are so numerous, who are treated at once badly and too well, who are crowded into cramped *lycées* but courted by merchants, who not very long ago were packed off to fight for nothing while being wooed by every electioneering orator—these young French people are exceptionally *nice*. From the New World they are borrowing its romantic fancies, its lacquered and hygienic pleasures, but not its violences. Our young people are not brutal or rebellious or vicious or despairing or drugged or headed for assorted extremist adventures. Indifferent? Yes. Nihilistic? No. In France, the hooligans are Polish; the rival gangs that terrorize family beaches are British; the attractive *West Side Story* toughs are New Yorkers. In 1960, the only year when there was rather a lot of talk in France about black-leather jackets, juvenile delinquency, teen-age gangs, and so on, the oncoming demographic wave had not quite reached the age for such excesses. Of course, in the streets of small French cities and especially on the street corners of big dehumanized housing developments you come across leather-jacketed boys mounting motorbikes they have caparisoned in Mexican style. They are simply today's version of the eternal small-town show-off. They pursue the marginal dreams of the confusion of their age and are acting out their crisis of juvenile originality. Paris is said to be becoming an increasingly violent city. Pigalle and Saint-Germain-des-Prés seem less disturbing, however, than Soho or Times Square or MacDougal Street in Greenwich Village. Alcohol and drugs do not play important parts. Sexuality seems perfunctory, dedramatized, almost meager. No one appears to give much thought to revolt—revolt against whom? Against "old people"? One little nudge will be enough; they will soon be quietly walking offstage, thanks to the force of figures and of events.

If it is plausible that popular songs say something about the mentality of a generation, we may be variously dismayed or reassured. French teen-agers today sing only about nice feelings, nice pals, and a syrupy, stereotyped good will. Their idols do make an awful racket. After which, the boys take off for their peacetime military service and become excellent soldiers—widely photographed with the complicity of colonels hipped on the "psychological approach"—and very soon thereafter, they become good husbands who settle down in Neuilly or in small country houses. The meteorlike career of an idol —the cherished dream, apparently, of some 90 per cent of French sixteen-year-olds—is simply the dazzling acceleration with which bourgeois ambitions of yesteryear now come true. One acquires a Citroën "D.S.," a Ferrari, fifty suits, a huge house, and a chain of laundromats, all in the space of three years instead of putting in thirty years of hard work to accumulate these treasures. The irritations and hesitations and political passions, the "lyric illusion" of the preceding generation—my own, and I know it well—have given birth to little brothers who are realistic, casual, and not in the least prone to impulsive excess.

Obviously, one would be very ungracious to loose any thunderbolts over such charming, conspicuously blond heads, or to appeal for a trifle more aggressiveness, more ferment. And yet let me put it in other words: Can we hope for vigor, depth, distrust, and passion in young people? Vigor to demand worthier treatment; depth to decide what to believe and what not to believe, on earth as in heaven; distrust of sycophants, passion for pleasure and love. If youth is no longer insurrection, disgust, bumptious defiance, then what has happened to youth?

THE GENERATION NOW REACHING TWENTY has inherited from its parents and grandparents their big—and empty—words, their parsimony, their nostalgias and defeats. Young people know or feel as much. They themselves have been brought up with relative liberality. Or at least in a realistic atmosphere, in which a taste for pleasure has flourished, religious faith has weakened, and political conflict has subsided. Can it be held against them that they settle for what is simplest

and most immediate, and repudiate castles in the sky? They
have not known enough of the harshness of life that tempers
a heroic soul or enough of the sweet things in life for their
gorge to rise. They have not really been tested yet either by
adversity or by an excess of ease. They stand exactly halfway
between two possible self-images—fervor and exasperation.
They have experienced nothing in life which might warrant
these two extremes. The senior members of this young generation arrived on the scene two years after the Liberation and one
year after the end of the war. They were eight years old when
the expansion began to make rapid strides and when France
jettisoned Indochina. They were ten years old on All Hallows'
Day, 1956, when the Algerian revolt erupted; eleven at the
time of the battle of Algiers; sixteen at the time of the Evian
Agreements. Had they been of age to vote in December 1965,
they would surely not have opted for de Gaulle. This not out
of any spirit of opposition, for they rather fancy that venerable
character, but as a natural reaction—to them he seems too
remote in time, blurred, imprisoned by an archaic, overardu-
ous concept of life and of France. What on earth *is* that "battle
of Teruel" about which political opponents are forever up-
braiding that minister . . . what's-his-name—Malraux. We
really ought to see that film of his, *Espoir,* next time it's shown
by a film society. What a crazy title for a movie about a defeat!

I venture these thoughts the way one fumbles to focus
binoculars or a camera. I am looking for the right distance,
the clear image. But time has passed quickly, brought many
new things, and swept away a goodly number of illusions. Accordingly, the image remains a little fuzzy, and I am filled
with admiration for the specialists and official administrators
who are so expert in drawing up the list of youth's "problems"
and its "questions" and its "insecurities." I readily confess

that what I am afraid of is, rather, that these fifteen or twenty million new arrivals may suffer from the lack of classic trials that used to constitute the standard by which men in the making were put to the test. Traditional education recognized that human beings are not shaped without tensions and restraints. Our big Catholic schools (which, together with the elementary schools, were the one coherent form that education of the young ever took in France and which for years molded our childhood), were not afraid of a little turmoil. (As Henri de Montherlant put it: "O priests, stir things up—systematically!") Today it is as if one had polished the form and allowed the content to deteriorate. We offer adolescents an abundance of comfort, money, and consideration, and permit their own inclinations to dictate their behavior—but do we respect them? Educating them in haste in ramshackle old buildings and at the same time insolently throwing their study programs into utter confusion; tossing them into the labor market without genuine professional training; allowing them to believe in a life of ease in a country where things have not yet sufficiently changed for life to be truly livable—is all this not deceiving them?

Perhaps I tend to distort the argument, to weight it too heavily with facile illustrations from folklore and today's picturesque behavior. To present a more balanced picture, I could evoke the famous Olympia cabaret less and the earnest concerts of the Jeunesses Musicales de France more; the insipid sweetness of the currently fashionable young girls less and the success of the old die-hards of song—indomitable champions of antimilitarism and anarchy—more; the seed of violence less and the seed of diplomacy more; the leather-jacketed hoods less and the militant unionists more; the knuckleheads less, the serious students more.

I would reply that statistically the knuckleheaded, saccharine, conformist image is truer than the edifying image. If our political parties, Left and Right alike, are experiencing a severe crisis in recruiting new members, it is because there is a crisis of civic involvement, a lack of zest for ideas. As to the students, how many are there, and where do they come from? In 1966 there were a hundred thousand in Paris and four hundred thousand in all of France; the enormous majority of them came from the middle class. Are young bourgeois more interesting, then, than others? They are, of course, because their background already represents a certain selectivity, even if merely on the basis of money. The young bourgeois are more cultivated and more ironic; they have numerous bases for making comparisons, efficient weapons for judging and being on their guard. If they play at following the style of the moment, if they play at being a little silly, they do so for pleasure and provocation without being deeply involved. They are wrong only in that their laughter underwrites buffoonery. As for the others—the grinds, the eager beavers, the young people nobody could accuse of having compromised in the slightest with the inanities of some current fad—their defense (or their indictment) would have to be placed on another level. In what are, if you like, nobler terms, one would have to posit the question of their faith, disinterestedness, civic sense, the yardstick by which they intend to measure their values. One would wish them not to be too realistic or technocratic; to be capable of uncalculated passions and immoderate impulses; to be slightly infected with our well-known concern for the national "grandeur," and eager to fashion a society free from the inertia of which they see themselves the victims. Are they like this? Why not? It would be as absurd to imprison the best of a generation in the behavior patterns of the average as it would be not to dare denounce the mediocrity of the average because of the quality of the best.

Here we have the important word—quality. The only questions one may ask about a generation to which one does not belong have to do with its quality. However, youth is not a milieu in itself, not an entity born of chance. It is the result of a given upbringing, it reflects particular circumstances. Its worth derives from what has surrounded it and been given it. Its quality goes hand in hand with a hundred hard facts, none of which it is responsible for. Youth will be sturdy if it is exposed to trials, healthy if its health is cared for, foolish if it is compromised by foolishness, deceived if it is fed on lies. The quality of youth will be high if it has been reared by intelligent rules.

However, since the Liberation there has existed in France a vogue for youth but not a policy for youth. We have cooked up slogans rather than fired imaginations. Free enterprise rushed to meet the new opportunity faster than the state responded with suitable legislation. The record companies and the comic-book publishers have often evinced more dynamism than the Ministries of National Education, or of Youth and Sports. Is all this changing? It is, none too soon, after a long period of neglect. Oversupplied with gadgets and undersupplied with certainties, French youth is an enormous capital poorly invested. Schools and stadiums are not everything, but they symbolize the nation's concern for one of its vital sectors. They fit more readily into statistics and polemics than do the aspiration and dissent, the indifference and zest, the collective mystery that make the life of a generation.

Today's opposition is composed of the same men who were the inept administrators of the Fourth Republic; let us not forget it. Furthermore, it is not really true that the Bomb is depriving us of schools. Or if it is depriving us of schools, perhaps it is supplying us with laboratories. What is a fact, on the other hand, is that one consequence of our population's aging has been, and still is, a certain indifference toward youth. It is yesterday's citizen who is not managing to organize a France where today's child can be tomorrow's citizen. One would like to believe that the malady is on the way to being cured, but it has not been so much political as psychological. One cannot hope to erase in a few years all traces of an anemia that has dragged on for decades. Commercial speculation has been quicker to seize on and exploit the phenomenon of our rejuvenation than the public at large to see it for what it is worth. People were weary, snared in a nationwide pessimism. And in masochism. Let us not indulge in a futile competition between the skiing champion (good) and the pop singer (bad), between the estimable science student and the inveterate loafer. They are all members of the family. It is much more worthwhile to understand why the family was "badly brought up," why for such a long time parents reneged on their jobs. In this particular court hearing, there are enough guilty parties—indeed, witnesses who refuse to testify—for us not, this time, to damn the innocent.

CHAPTER VI:

The French and the General

I T IS AMUSING to watch the pundits of the opposition in France wax indignant over the flabby inertia that, to their way of thinking, is the only explanation for the doting fatalism with which the French give themselves into de Gaulle's keeping. It is just as amusing to hear the irritated protests from abroad that greet this strange, long honeymoon. Most of France is Gaullist out of laziness, perhaps, but not so by chance. The laziness is part of her nature or her good sense or her weariness. If France is Gaullist, that is because she must be. She loves what Gaullism offers her and the image of herself that it holds up to her. This is no reason to be scandalized or irritated. Or it is not the General who is to be criticized, but the French people. In 1965 J. F. Revel wrote in *En France*: "General de Gaulle is right in thinking he is the living embodiment of France. He is wrong in thinking this a compliment." The judgment may be sharp, but it has the merit of being sound. The marriage between France and the General, nourished, like every long association, on quarrels, disappointments, and misunderstandings, is essentially legitimate and easy to explain. "All Frenchmen have been, are, or will be Gaullists," the General is quoted as having said— one more disdainful but firm and well-justified opinion from that realist. Calm analysis produces many more reasons for the French to be Gaullist than not. Perhaps the reasons are not often good, but to study them will let us penetrate further into the psychology not of the General but of the fifty million Frenchmen who, in their daily lives, their recollections, their cares—and tomorrow in their textbooks—find and will find everywhere this huge, embarrassing figure.

PERHAPS THE MYSTERIOUS ASPECT of the Gaullist bland-ishments has to do with the unconscious horror the French feel for oversimple statesmen. To say that they dote on military men or old men or literary men would be too super-ficial an explanation. From Pétain to Clémenceau, from Gen-eral Boulanger to our own General, each of these claims could be proved as to detail, but what counts is the ensemble, the conjunction of several of these fascinating qualities in one man —age, uniform, eloquent voice or eloquent pen. Apparently the French detest one-sided personalities. Public opinion offers popularity, confidence, forebearance, caricatures, satiric verse, and supporting votes—every shift of ephemeral political devotion—to great men who are endowed with a gift for multiple, ambiguous roles. The French love enlightened des-potism, brutality embellished by style, literary intelligence as much as political. Unquestionably, what one cherished in Léon Blum, beneath the Socialist leader, was the aesthete of the *Revue Blanche.* And in Édouard Herriot, what the people perceived behind a vast amount of political baggage and cam-paign oratory was the nostalgic, fervently admiring biographer of Mme. Récamier.

The French and the General

On the other hand, the intelligent, energetic, lucid, austere statesmen—the pessimists, that is—from Mandel to Mendès-France are only reluctantly followed by the sentimental demagogues that we French continue to be. As to the "born politicians," the virtuosos of the republican tremolo and of parliamentary arithmetic—from Mollet to Mitterand, say, to keep to the present—the public accepts them, but with no relish whatever, as tools, as characters in the political comedy to which the French vouchsafe an unfathomable, smiling scorn.

In General de Gaulle, however, the French gradually discovered a personality full of ambiguities, complexities, and stratagems. Far from reproaching him for his contradictions, the French accept them *in toto,* insofar as his contradictions endorse their own political uncertainties, their civic irresolutions, and the mental confusion in which they have existed for so long. Do they perhaps unconsciously recognize their own vagaries in this haughty, chameleonic president? Subject as they are to their own hesitations, why should they not subject themselves to a monarch who clothes his every hesitation in luxuriant phrases, in bullying or majestic reaffirmations of national stability? Then, too, the General's contradictions, albeit magnified and expressed with his by now familiar bravura, are rather those of an old people worn out by countless quarrels, fed on too many and varied ideologies, wounded by profound internal conflicts. How could the French fail to recognize their own best and worst traits in this teacher's son, born ten years before the turn of the century, who emerged from dreams of bringing back the king to win the esteem of Communist ministers, who was wounded and imprisoned in France's real war, the Great War of 1914–18, who was a scornful yet grieving observer of his nation's aimlessness between the two wars, his head full of visions, his mouth full of words from the past, a man of uncommon stature and unshakable obstinacy—all this, too, belongs to the General's contradictions and is very familiar to us.

Although from a modest and traditionalist middle-class background, de Gaulle has come to be—at first with distaste (1940-4), then realistically (1944-6), and finally, lucidly (from 1958 on)—if not a fellow traveler of the Leftists, at least the only effective instrument of their programs.

This uncompromising admirer of the Empire found himself announcing the decolonization of France in Brazzaville in 1941, and in 1960 actually carrying it out.

Brought to power in 1958 by fanatic partisans of the French presence in Algeria, he led that country, through four years of maneuverings, half-lies, and half-truths, to independence.

Born of provincial middle-class conservatism, and married to the daughter of the owner of a small biscuit factory, he presided over the great nationalizations of 1944-5.

A soldier—and a soldier persuaded of the almost sacred importance of his caste and of the military's pre-eminent place in the nation, yet at the same time convinced that the military must be subordinate to law—he was brought to power with the complicity of officers who were flirting with a seditious movement that he later crushed mercilessly.

A rhapsodizing and intransigent nationalist, he probably feels only disdain for the far-flung, many-sided millions of individual Frenchmen.

An idealist when celebrating some abstract notion of the state or of "grandeur," in practical matters he demonstrates the most brutal realism, the most empirical belief in force.

Meticulous to the highest degree about formal perfection,

a coiner of elegant phrases, an attentive listener to Malraux, a scrupulous editor of his own *Memoirs,* which he hoped would not be unworthy of Saint-Simon or Chateaubriand, he also excels in sarcasm and tough language that would do credit to an army sergeant.

Possessor of a striking name and a striking appearance, he has known how to exploit the noble handle of his "de" and the symbolic value of his surname, as well as that great awkward silhouette which, with the passing of the years, is no longer caricatured as a semaphore, but as a pachyderm.

Long an admirer of Edmond Rostand, he early learned that Cyrano's nose appeals to the French more than Christian's fine mustache and, accordingly, he converted his homeliness into an asset, made his odd elocution attractive, and turned the quaver in his voice into a weapon of irony.

A man of aristocratic aloofness, a great manipulator of silence and mystery in politics, he became the apostle of the appeal to the people in its most striking but most ambiguous form—the plebiscite.

A man of the all-embracing view, of the long-range perspective, of geopolitics and of history, he has not hesitated at times to base his actions, whether they involved America or the *pieds-noirs* of Algeria, on private grudges or the memory of personal slights that through him were raised to the dignity of national calamities.

After some seventy years of life, a half century of meditation, and more than twenty years in the political arena, he seemed at once fragile and indestructible, a jingoist and a dreamer of vast dreams, an old Colonel Blimp who detested army men because he so loved the army, a patriot wary—in the name of France—of the French, a man of public order and of the *coup de force,* of the Republic muzzled and the Republic rescued, a man who had successively excommunicated, exploited, and charmed the Communists, a bourgeois with the manners of an aristocrat who loved nothing so much as to mix with the crowd, a literary man, the artist of his own destiny, a Louis XIV with the manners of a bandit chieftain, brutal, good-natured, mocking, a hundred times more cynical or artful than his best opponents, harmed more by the unqualified adulation of some than by the hatred of others—this is how, around 1960, he looked to the French in the long empty mirror in which they were accustomed to see themselves, and as such he offered them an inexplicable, flattering image of themselves, which they accepted with the gratitude of well-trained pet dogs.

The heroic nation of Verdun, which was crushed in 1940, the nation of ancient and proud unity which was tragically shattered by four years of Occupation, the nation torn between yearnings for past glory and the wish to forget everything so as to move firmly into the future—such a nation could form no coherent idea of itself except by reference to some vast, multiform, and moving contradiction. This living, breathing contradiction who spoke successively to the nation in all the languages it hoped to hear, who embodied successively all its will-o'-the-wisps—how could it have failed to invest him with almost absolute power? When Pinay kept saying: "Relax! Relax! Everything is going to be all right!" and Mendès-France played Cassandra, the former's unruffled good nature was possibly reassuring, just as the other's nervous clear-sightedness was variously a cause for interest or alarm. But both men were monotonous. Their repertory consisted of a single role. One man suited the shrewd provincial middle class, the other appealed to high officials bitten by the bug of progress and Anglomania. Neither penetrated the shifting subsoil of the national unconscious. The French may be sober, but they are not rational. Whether the nation's finances are sound or whether intelligence stands at the helm of government, such trifles do not greatly move anyone. On the other hand, let this big son of a gun seize the tiller, and things begin to happen! (Or they seem to.) De Gaulle has the knack of simultaneously lulling his fellow citizens to sleep and quickening embers that are always smoldering inside them. For the French, politics is a theater, a show at which they are satisfied to be spectators. No one is less of a militant than a Frenchman. His business is to appreciate, applaud, and whistle. De Gaulle may be this or that, but in any event he is the greatest actor to occupy the French stage since Napoleon and—thinking now in terms of distinguished troupes rather than stars—since the cast of the Revolution.

Passing from the realm of dreams and great compelling images to daily governmental reality, one must agree that the General satisfies other French hopes, whether fearful, crafty, or honorable.

The majority of the French endured the shame of 1940 and the more insidious shame of never really resisting Hitlerian oppression, of having (95 per cent of them) accepted Vichy, racism, and national subjugation. By dint of an amazing exercise of will, bluff, testiness, and visionary genius, de Gaulle has washed them clean of their humiliation—and cheaply, at that. Free France was what you will, a ripple or a tidal wave—no matter; objectively, it saved the "national honor."

The majority of the French wanted the Algerian war ended. They knew that not a single man from among the ordinary political ranks had the power either to enforce common sense or to perform the necessary surgery. De Gaulle took on the job and, whatever the style, the pace, the means, he finished it. There is no question about it: this man excels in ridding the French of the skeletons in their national closet.

Deep down, the French view the politician as a finagler, a wheeler-dealer, a man who is clever at manipulating ideas and money. In contrast, the General is disinterested and also possesses the art of balancing official splendor against the edifying simplicity of his personal life. Both things make Gaullists feel comfortable about admiring him and force the opposition to stay clear of the terrain where political scores are, by preference, usually settled.

In other areas, the General satisfies needs that are somewhat less exalted. For some time, the French have rather relished striking poses, indulging in trickery and dabbling in make-believe. Something in them shivers with pleasure every time the old Gallic and Gaullist cock puffs out his feathers, raises his hackles, crows a captious sermon for the benefit of the world at large, and hoists France up onto the peaks of prestige. We have all been brought up in an extraordinary, exhilarating chauvinism; we may be excused for preferring *bel canto* to realism, the opera based on the "Marseillaise" motif to cold figures. The French are cantankerous, mocking, grumbling people; the General is the same. They are so in little things; he, in big things. The alchemy whereby bad temper is converted to national myth is one of the sources of Gaullist strength. The General plays constantly on the little faults he knows so well (he shares them) and transforms them into great qualities. With a pinch of peevishness, a dash of xenophobia, old jingoist memories, and the miserable awareness of France's having shrunk in size, he brews pride, independence, and *grandeur*. True? False? In any event, the trick is performed with skill, and the French have the impression that they are losing nothing by it. Finally, these prodigious powers are in the hands of the kind of person whom, deep down, public opinion prefers above all others— an old man. For a nation that believes with all its heart that wine improves eternally by aging and that no architecture can be beautiful that is not historic and centuries old, age is a virtue in itself. It would seem that even our teen-agers, if they ever ask themselves the question, give the same answer. Traditionally, France is a gerontocracy sparked by tantrums and historic pronouncements. For so long now the "saviors" of France have been old men—there was Clémenceau in 1917, Doumergue in 1934, and Pétain in 1940. People keep saying that France has never been so young. That is true. Or it will be tomorrow. One must not forget, however, that what with the longer life expectancy the 1967 electorate was both the oldest and the largest we have ever known. By the time of the next presidential election, in 1972, the electorate will be the youngest that France has ever had. Those new voters, all born since World War II, represent a still-unknown political quantity, which is why it is so hard to foresee what the political life of the country will be. By 1972 we may well have witnessed radical changes. And already, to be sure, Gaullism seems a thing of the past.

THE WORD "GAULLISM" has cropped up several times here. Is that fair? Can one pass casually from the proper name to the abstract word, from the General to his troops? Of course not. Gaullism includes several strong personalities (who will survive de Gaulle), some likable people, and a larger number of opportunists. Will this heterogeneous team hang onto the reins or not? And if so, how? That is the only question, and not a very absorbing one at that. The General scorns men too much to tolerate many lieutenants around him, and he has too much contempt for political parties to have fashioned one of his own. A majority, certainly—who would refuse a sure thing?—but not a party. For that matter, the French by nature surrender readily to a man, but never to an ideology or to an association. Gaullism has been acted out between M. Dupont ("John Doe") and the baroque, sensational General whom all our Duponts have chosen to be their master. It is not charisma. It does not function via the magic exercised by a chief over the masses, but via the mystery of innumerable imaginary tête-à-têtes. To each his own general. There is no mystique involved in this: simply a "yes" vote cast in the secrecy of the polling booth after the endless "no's" of ordinary conversation. To judge from the most recent presidential election, there must be about thirteen million different species of Gaullism; to be precise, on the basis of the December 19, 1965, balloting—13,-183,699.

CHAPTER VII:

Great Principles

H E'S A MAN OF PRINCIPLE," people used to say, and for a long time it was a compliment. Men of principle were the *rentiers,* the mediocre career soldiers, the strait-laced teachers, the zealous civil servants. They constituted the highly edifying image that middle-class France had of herself.

Principles were enhanced by being couched in slogans. The more striking the slogan, the more readily the person who had invented it joined the repertory of our great French roles. At school all history teaching was (and is) founded on the equation: a man+a principle=an outstanding action. So many luminaries dominate our national legends thanks to a happily turned slogan—Cardinal Richelieu, who invented the expression "*pre-carré*"[1] in addition to his better-known political battle cries, "Down with dueling" and "Down with the power of the great lords"; Louis XIV: "I am the State!"; Danton: "Dar-

---

[1] The Cardinal is credited with originating this term to denote the national territory as defined by natural frontiers: the Atlantic and the Straits of Dover, the Rhine, the Alps, the Mediterranean, and the Pyrenees.

ing, more daring, and ever more daring"; Mirabeau: "Go tell your master that we are here by the will of the people and we shall leave only at bayonet point." The principle may be libertarian, witty, arrogant, egalitarian. Sometimes it is so dazzlingly ambitious that it need not be sloganized at all. This netted us Napoleon I and the Civil Code, Jules Ferry and his colonial empire plus compulsory education. The slogan can also be laconic, bald, or biting. Thus Guizot, the minister of Louis-Philippe, flashed a green light to the bourgeoisie: "Get rich!" Clémenceau leaped from the Left ("The revolution is indestructible!") to become the crusty Old Tiger ("I am declaring war!").

We should also note that there are disobliging slogans, whether authentic or apocryphal, that undo their man's reputation. "After me, the deluge," Louis XV is supposed to have said. And: "France, your coffee is leaking like hell!" Du Barry is supposed to have said to him. (These alleged remarks, relating to the last moments of the old monarchy, are obviously intended to convey the idea that revolution, exile, and the guillotine were no more than just punishments for those who trampled principles underfoot and allowed the sacred trust given them as rulers by God Himself to go to the devil, to the point of preferring a good time to wielding power and of letting the nation be familiarly apostrophized in the person of her king—and this on account of a leaky coffee pot.)

All these catch-phrases are refrains we learn in childhood. They are found in all our schoolbooks and they echo in everyone's memory. They provide a summary but picturesque portrait of the nation. Thanks to them, Pascal is no longer a burning mystic or an astute adversary of the Jesuits; he is the author of a metaphysical avowal so sensible and so banal ("The grandeur of infinite space frightens me") that all French fathers murmur it at least once of a summer evening in the country as they peer heavenward and try to teach their children how to tell Cassiopeia from Ursa Minor.

The most prestigious form of these principles expresses the destiny of our privileged nation, the nation invested with a universal, civilizing mission—"France, mother of the arts, arms and laws"; "France, eldest daughter of the Church"—these were not pompous or hollow formulas; they just stated the obvious. The Republic had deemed it essential, in the beginning, to adorn the brow of every public building seized from the Church, the nobility, or simply from the past, with the tripartite slogan "Liberty, Equality, Fraternity." In 1940 the Pétain government judged it indispensable to substitute another trinity: "Work, Family, Fatherland." Every ideological quarrel, every change of government, every restoration is accompanied by the ritual replacement of one slogan by another. At one point, for example, we saw the official emblems of royal lily and imperial bee switched back and forth four times in fifty years.

The private but no less exalted form of the principle is the maxim. Those of La Rochefoucauld have done more to spare Frenchmen the chore of thinking and making up their own minds than ten tyrants manipulating ten systems of censorship would have done.

The regional, household pain-killer form of the principle is the proverb. Its vaguely peasant character is reassuring. The French are armed with an inexhaustible arsenal of such sayings, which are adjudged expressions of "folk wisdom." Any event that can be reduced to the dimensions of a proverb, any attitude that can be summed up in one of these commonplaces is, *ipso facto,* justified. The fitting of fact to formula is an end in itself. To deliver oneself of a proverb suited to a given circumstance is to bind this circumstance to eternal principles—to project what is merely contingent into the realm of the transcendent.

Too bad if proverbs contradict each other, as they often do. Such disorder in the realm of common sense just goes to prove the basic ambiguity of all things. "Like father, like son. A rolling stone gathers no moss. A penny saved is a penny earned. Money isn't everything. You can't have everything. Where there's smoke, there's fire. Sing before breakfast, cry before night. Good fences make good neighbors. The bird builds his nest a twig at a time." Every Frenchman has at his disposal dozens of such magical formulas, enriched by folklore, history, the army, and so on, and at any given moment they save him the trouble of having to think for himself. The whole kit and caboodle forms a vast anthology of foolishness such as a society made up of petty *rentiers,* small businessmen, and small farmers is capable of putting together. What strikes us about most of these expressions is the fact that they belittle everything—whether appetite, folly, or anger. The world defined by such laws, circumspection, and good behavior is the miniature world of the little old retired clerk, puttering about and doing his gardening. From the pride of a Louis XIV to the modesty of the lowliest citizen, from "I am the State" to "He who lives happily lives unnoticed"—here you find the gamut of French principles, which somehow always diminish the world. And, like the river losing itself in the sea, they always lead back into the same old timorous inertia.

In contrast to this traditional arsenal of clichés, another is now in the making. Newly coined slogans are enriching earlier ones that have proved their worth: "One must keep up with the times. Better to be envied than pitied. You can't make an omelet without breaking eggs. You only live once. He who pays his debts grows rich." These battle cries express a new morality—that of the borrower, the installment buyer, the high-liver. The strange thing is that even the youngest Frenchmen feels that before he takes the plunge he must recite the justifying, sanctifying litanies. The risk must be related to a principle of risk, the anarchy to an anarchistic principle. French revolutionaries (they above all, perhaps) are indefatigable sloganeers. The anarchists at the turn of the century were terrifyingly prolific scribblers and remorseless debaters: in one hand Ravachol's bomb, in the other, the inkpot. One of the few men who sang the praises of realism, the royalist theoretician Charles Maurras, was a sedentary all his life, a man given to polemics, never to action. Great empiricists shock our French hankering for a system of rules and formulas. One acts only according to some guiding rule. We forgive Richelieu for his implacable brutality in imposing royal power because he took care to dress specific actions in the generalized slogans mentioned earlier. One of de Gaulle's traits that most shocks the French is his empiricism. People think they can dodge the issue of principles by invoking Machiavelli, but this simply means that they reassure themselves by invoking Machiavellian principles. Let a French politician talk of balance of power or conflict of interests, and he will be taxed for his cynicism and immorality. Any government enterprise, however opportunistic, must be clothed in some high-sounding phrase, must plead some eternal verity. The butchery at Verdun was the war of Right against Barbarism. Colonial expeditions were crowned with the halo of missionary spirtuality. One could go as far back as the Crusades, those adventures in profitable pillage and warrior sport, which claimed as their excuse—sincere at first but quickly forgotten—the rescue of Christ's tomb from the Infidel.

This illness of universalism has visibly afflicted the French through the centuries. Its manifestations have at times brought us glory—when the world believed in our principles or when they were genuinely beneficial—and at other times they have imprisoned us in verbalism and abstraction. The crucial periods of our history were those in which two systems of thought, of belief, of world view, confronted each other: the wars of religion, the battle between Jacobin ideology and the old monarchic ideas, the struggle between secular and Catholic influence at the turn of the century, and so on. No one in France would understand commitments that had not been preceded by rhetorical exposés. All this is resumed in two words that have nourished, since the 1750's, all our bursts of political eloquence: "eternal principles." When the Republic refers to its own rules, it quite naturally invests them with maximum authority by the use of the word "principle"; it confers on them a sacred character, invulnerable to time and human opposition, with the word "eternity." This way of speaking is not a stylistic locution. It is part of our daily pattern of thought and speech. It seems normal to us to liken political choices, which are by nature contingent, to the timeless laws of humanism. Try to explain to the average Frenchman that British law is based on custom, that there is no constitution, but simply a respect for tradition, and he will think you are talking gibberish. On the one hand, the law is sacred; on the other, it is made to be circumvented. Constitutional law and finagling, these are the twin breasts that give suck to French civic life. Also, try to explain that, under present-day circumstances, Americans or Russians act against commonly accepted precepts because might makes right, and you will gravely wound a certain French susceptibility that is not moral but simply insists that, whether one acts out of brutality or cynicism, one should first present a rhetorical justification.

IF WE TRIED to define more precisely the seminal ideas that determine our group responses, what sort of list would we make?

In the conditioning that forms the French child, the early experiences that open the way to what will be his education, from family conversations to his first lessons in school, a few great principles are already set forth. Some are contradictory, as it happens, and so they often go in pairs.

Morality remains, on the whole, Christian and, more particularly, Catholic.

Good citizenship teaches respect for the state (as an apparatus) and scorn for government (as a product of "politics").

Respect for law is tempered by a predisposition toward anarchy.

Individualism (with its offspring: suspicion of one's neighbor, distaste for group endeavors, a partiality both for making it on one's own and for free-loading) is honored as a cardinal virtue.

An appreciation of order is almost as deep-rooted as the mania for stirring things up. The complex of tensions, tolerances, customs, and usages by which we live as a nation is not termed "established disorder" merely for the sake of argument; the many shades of opinion require that the state, although apparently solid, should also appear full of cracks.

Chauvinistic passion and a warrior tradition demand, for purposes of survival, a strong dose of verbal antimilitarism.

And finally, from the chivalric romance to the triumphs of our "bred to win" race horses, all of French psychology is tainted and gilded by what J. R. Pitts (*In Search of France,* 1963) calls the "sense of prowess." Don Juanism, setting a new record, heroism in battle—it can take many forms. Primacy in some sport, military feats, exceptional longevity, conversational brilliance—for French pride it is all grist to the mill. A teacher's son getting the highest entrance grades at the École Polytechnique; General de Gaulle going about during the bitterest cold spells without a coat, hat, or scarf; the loves and triumphs of Brigitte Bardot; the mechanical refinements of our Citroën—all these are manifestations of French "prowess." The famous Gallic cock with his crest, spurs, and multicolored plumage is the perfect symbol of this passion to bring it off big. Mr. Pitts is right to see in this, together with what he calls "the delinquent community" (and what I call here anarchy, individualism, pointless agitation), the dominant traits of the French character. But these are something more than psychologically dominant characteristics; they are rules of behavior that are unanimously accepted and that every Frenchman can justify to his own satisfaction.

Let us take a characteristically French type as an example —the rowdy, the hero of his *lycée* class, and the live wire of the student snake dances which flow down the Boul' Mich' every year in June, when examinations are over, and which always turn into riots.

The rowdy (not to be confused with the dunce, because the rowdy is not necessarily a poor student) is the spontaneous and glorious emanation of that little society which lives in permanent rebellion, a French class. A class—thirty to fifty students, as the case may be—is *in principle* against the establishment—that is, professors and administration. The professor is not an enemy but an implicit partner of the students in a tug of war. Aside from his duties as a teacher, he is expected to demonstrate his authoritative character and his intellectual superiority. If he carries the day, if he brings his class to heel, he will be respected, feared, and admired. He will have played his part in the game and he will have won. If he is the weaker, he will be cried down by the scornful pack. Pitiless nicknames and sarcasm will be heaped on him. The rowdy is the leader in this skirmish, the soul of the revolt, the one whose impudence astounds the others, whose sallies delight them. He is a hero. He does deeds of derring-do. If he gets punished, even expelled, he will be respected—all other considerations aside—as if he were a vanquished soldier. It pleases a Frenchman to read in an important man's biography that he was "expelled from six schools," or was "a hopeless dunce." The connection between a poor record in school and a glorious adult career delights the French; it flatters both their taste for disorder and their admiration for brilliant careers. Lack of respect paving the way for respect, rowdiness as a revelation of exceptional character—all this they like.

It is remarkable, furthermore, that, nine times out of ten, parents are more or less consciously the accomplices of the student against his teachers. They generously write false notes asking that Johnny "be excused." They are always ready to reproach the teacher for his strictness and to defend their unlucky offspring. Organized in a kind of powerful trade union—the Association of Students' Parents—every year they protest against the severity of the examiners more energetically than against rundown and inadequate buildings. The scholastic standards of young Frenchmen are steadily dropping, yet their parents, who are so timid when it comes to requesting new buildings, loose a barrage of aggressive criticism against the teachers. To give a zero to a student who deserves a zero is held to be an antisocial act. Thus two permanent and parallel factions nibble away at the base of academic authority: the students and their families. However great our superstitious belief in the value of baccalaureate and diploma, our taste for anarchy is stronger still, and this taste is shared by all members of the family—father, mother, and the young scamps themselves. The idea of parent-teacher collaboration does not occur spontaneously to the French mind. The teacher, though of slightly higher status, is deemed infinitely less formidable than the policeman or the tax collector. Therefore, everyone thinks the teacher more or less deserves to be ridiculed, underpaid, and aggressively criticized. The idea is not readily admitted that teaching, like the exercise of authority or the administration of public funds, might be a *service* necessary to us all. The child with his report card inveighs against the "clunks" (teachers) the way he hears his father, assessment in hand, inveigh against the "bureaucrats" (tax collectors). Fraudulent tax returns and academic baiting are manifestations of one and the same emotion: the permanent animus of the Frenchman against all the institutions which he nonetheless maintains and from which he expects culture, order, and personal comfort. The average Frenchman tends to behave like a potential delinquent. The policeman, the woman postal clerk, the bus starter, the municipal employee, all seem to the man in the street—as does the teacher to his students—like so many public watchdogs or overseers who embody the limits placed on his individuality.

The same Frenchman who complains that his highways have become death traps will try to make deals with the police and boast of violating traffic regulations.

The same Frenchman who accuses the "bosses" of every

malpractice in the book will approve calling out the army against strikers.

The same Frenchman who is amused by off-color jokes, and considers himself something of a specialist in adultery and illicit sex, will react with offended virtue if any irregularities touch him too closely.

The same Frenchman who inveighs against "bureaucrats" will know no peace until his children pass the civil-service examinations and go to work for the state, that tight-fisted, constantly abused boss, but a boss who is stable and not too particular about performance.

The same Frenchman who speaks ill of our deputies will demand favors from his own; he is sarcastic about cabinet ministers but will commit any base trick to get to meet one; he belabors the government throughout the legislative session but will vote to keep the majority in power; he despises "politics" but will dream of someday wangling the most modest municipal post for himself.

The same France, or very nearly, that voted for the Popular Front in 1936 voted five years later to accept the authoritarian rule of Vichy.

The same Frenchmen, or their sons, who, with indescribable courage, let themselves be killed in 1914–18, broke ranks before the enemy in 1940. The same Frenchmen who curse the military adore uniforms. They needle the state all their lives long but they take part in innumerable official commemorations of "those who died on the field of honor" before innumerable public monuments.

The same French, or very nearly, who stood on the sidewalks of Paris to applaud Pétain in April 1944 stood there to acclaim de Gaulle in August of the same year.

The important thing is that these switches from one opinion to another, these contradictions and juggling acts, must always be based on some general idea. A principle and a slogan must always furnish some sort of noble sentiment, and good judgment be damned. One must always be able, with due honor to rhetoric, to glide from the *"liberté chérie"* of the "Marseillaise" to the necessary authority, from "eldest daughter of the Church" to secularism, from Balzac's ragamuffin Gavroche to chatelain. The important thing is not to live by chance; that is to say, not to live without being able at a moment's notice to adduce some ephemeral truth in the name of some eternal verity.

Family, upbringing, education, and culture must, amid anarchy tempered by conservatism and adaptability qualified by reverence for the past, allow the young Frenchman to feel equally at home in his own immediate present and the collective past. It isn't easy. It calls for acrobatic skill and a flair for paradox. To analyze the successes and shortcomings of our educational system is like trying to photograph a moving train. However, since twenty million young Frenchmen are on that train, it is worthy trying to find out where they are going and how they expect to get there.

CHAPTER VIII:

The Heart of the Matter

ONE POSSIBLE AREA to explore in any discussion of France is the past. Another is the family. Perhaps more than any other people, the French are conditioned by their roots in time and in their place of origin. Why more than other people? Because history—an infinitely varied, ramified, lived history— is ever-present in contemporary French life, and because family and social milieux have long been unusually homogeneous in France. Neither migrations nor catastrophes nor foreign occupations have ever destroyed the continuity or the stability of the nation.

The roots hold the secret of the impoverishment or richness of the sap; in the case of France they are easily found. Trying to describe an American, for example, often means plunging into contradictions and the upheavals of immigration, exile, and assimilation to a new way of life. Family customs and social adjustments vary rapidly from one generation to another, sometimes within a single lifetime. On the contrary, no Frenchman is ever far removed from his origins; understanding them, he has intuitive knowledge of who he is and who he will become. Rapid changes will probably soon take the place of this long-standing immobility, but they have not yet swept us away. The married couple, the family, the village, the French social classes: all can still be examined as phenomena that make for stability. We can return to the source; it is not yet out of reach and it rarely dries up. For some time to come a Frenchman will bear a strong resemblance to his family circle and his social background.

EVERYTHING BEGINS with the married couple, but how do they begin?

Nothing is more futile than descriptions of people's love life; they seek to be objective and prove to be dull, or they seek the "truth" and are vaguely scandalous. How can we reduce the behavior of millions of young men and women to a few set patterns? The simple, almost animal promiscuity of the countryside may seem quite different from the freedom which our well-to-do city youths know so well how to exploit. Yet the kisses exchanged in far corners of attics in huge old family houses are the same as those behind the wall of the orchard where one steals apples. Does the early freedom that working girls find in the shop differ so much from the freedom conferred by luxury flats on young girls who enjoy playing the party seductress? What are we to think of the sorry statements and confusing percentages regularly released by the psychologists? "I no longer know a single girl of eighteen who is a virgin," one doctor declares. "Nothing has really changed in half a century," says another. What are we supposed to think?

At best, we can say that many factors make for greater freedom. Religious morality has fallen into desuetude; opportunities for meeting (coed schools, beaches, skiing, dances) have multiplied; everything considered "American" is imitated; a generation brought up in postwar freedom has reached the age of parenthood—all these things conspire to loosen the bonds of the adolescent. Tomorrow, after interminable discussion, contraceptives, whether used legally or by tacit consent, will eliminate the drama attached to sexual freedom.

Along with all this, however, we must note that marriage remains *the* big event for all Frenchwomen, that people marry young and that the contracting parties bring to the conjugal adventure an impressive seriousness of purpose and will to succeed.

It almost seems as if sexual freedom has enhanced the meaning of marriage. One rarely finds young French people marrying with the reassuring consolation at the back of their minds that divorce can always provide an escape hatch. People love each other and get married "for life." Fidelity and children are in fashion. The wind of morality blowing on young French adults is more symptomatic than the passing storm which shakes up the adolescents. The swinging sixteen-year-olds (relatively untouched by passion and more worried about the latest fad in hair or clothes than about sex) will be transformed tomorrow into classic *petits bourgeois*. The young father now dares to boast of his paternity. The age-old and very Latin dichotomy of the hearth—housekeeping and children for the wife, the outside world for the husband—is rejected by the new generation. Yesterday, depending on the region and the season, the male's lordly superiority would admit of no pastimes other than his café, his bowling, or his hand of cards. The wife, meanwhile, scrubbed, cooked, and changed diapers. She enjoyed a letup in her labors only in the hour of socializing when she went shopping. Today, men's pride in being fathers is gradually making the mother's chores less implacable. You see young men walking their children, taking them for rides in the car, playing with them, and so on—a sight that only yesterday was most uncommon. Young actors and singers know the publicity value of being photographed with their arms full of babies. Who could have imagined Rudolph Valentino, or even Jean Marais in 1942, beaming on some plump-cheeked baby girl?

In short, girls may make love earlier than before, and perhaps without feeling a swooning grand passion as they do so, but they never lose sight of their main goal, marriage, or of the goals of marriage, permanence and children. Because young men now enjoy freer access to the opposite sex and greater equality in age and economic and social status, they have given up the time-hallowed partitioning of their lives into a "before" and "after" marriage, "sowing one's wild oats" and then "settling down," the brothel and the wife. Without feelings of guilt, love is first practiced between comrades, not to excess, then in the family; extramarital drinking and amorous adventures are becoming a thing of the past. The France of the alcove is dead; gone are the rooms draped in red velvet, the bottles of cheap champagne, and the cocottes. Even the world of the five-to-seven date with easy women is dying. Parisian night life is now limited to about two thousand persons; in the provinces, to a few score of their imitators. To judge all Frenchmen by these few would be ridiculous. If one wished to choose the least foolish among a horde of foolish and false generalizations, it would be that France has loosed her stays and grown more flexible but also rather more moral. It seems that peasant sensuality is less bestial than in Zola's day, middle-class license less vapid and hypocritical than during *la belle époque,* and worldly depravity less heady than in Baron de Charlus's circle. Other sources of information will, obviously, yield contrary views with examples to support them. I believe they would be less fair than mine.

ONE STATISTIC bears me out: the average distance that separates the homes of French fiancés is seven miles. The least one can deduce from this is that people seek their mates on familiar ground. This little fact, this negligible distance, is very significant. It explains, in some measure, the stability of our society. Adventure is never farther away than the street corner or the far side of the neighboring town.

In the country, childhood friends often marry. If a man has gone to the city to work, he comes back home to find a bride. In Paris on Sundays, in the public rooms of the town halls, there are dances for people from Brittany, Auvergne, Charente, and so forth. The purpose is not so much to cultivate folklore as to try to prevent people from the same region from becoming lost in the big city. Like village dances, these play a great role in the love life and matrimonial plans of young people. Even persons from Africa and the West Indies may meet every Saturday night at the Blomet dance hall, in a street in the Vaugirard district, exactly like people from Toulouse and Normandy. Many little cafés in the vicinity of the railway stations serve as rallying points for Parisians who come originally from the regions linked to the city via those stations. You are most likely to find Flemings around the Gare du Nord, Alsatians near the Gare de l'Est, and Bretons at the Montparnasse station.

The parlor of the suburbanites is the train that transports hundreds of thousands of them twice a day between their jobs in Paris and their homes. In the evening between six and seven o'clock the Salle des Pas Perdus ("Hall of Lost Steps") of the Saint-Lazare station is a scene of prodigious sentimental effervescence. Before the monument to the fallen soldiers that adorns this hall—a legendary trysting place—innumerable idylls have been born between salesgirls from the big stores near the Opéra and employees of the insurance companies in the Lafayette and Châteaudun districts. If you really want to understand French life, this is where you must come to feel its heart beat. Beneath the apparent incoherence of the big city, you sense the permanence of local characteristics, the almost villagelike solidarity of people loyal to the charm of their own little corner of the metropolis: Chatou, the sidewalks of the rue Tronchet.

The middle class, which travels more and is more cosmopolitan, will not disapprove the exotic notion of marrying someone from another town. Yet a single statistic lets us see the force of local custom under this appearance of freedom. In Lyon, people marry people from Lyon; in Lille, people from Lille; in Bordeaux, people from Bordeaux. These simple statements hide a whole web of prejudices and certainties. In Paris, each "good" *arrondissement* has its own flavor. The sixth is more academic, more intellectual and bohemian. The seventh is more reserved, haughty, provincial. The eighth is more affluent, more "big business." The sixteenth is the village of vanities gratified, the first rung up the ladder of ambitions coming true. There is a kind of religion of the sixteenth. The smart shops (clothing or antiques), the beautiful young girls, the contentedly dignified matrons, the flashily elegant teen-agers, the rich displays of florists and luxury grocers—everything bespeaks a special style that all Parisians recognize at once. It isn't so much what is best, but rather what best conforms to the canons of an upper-middle class that is very sure of itself. Needless to say, people from the sixteenth like to marry people from the sixteenth. Tennis-playing members of the *Racing Club* pair off with girls who go to Mass at Saint-Honoré-d'Eylau; alumnae of the Cours Lamartine marry alumni of the Lycée Janson-de-Sailly; members of the Trap-shooters Club choose mates who live on the avenue Georges-Mandel and frequent the Bois. The solidity of middle-class social structures and the subtlety of their methods of exclusion or assimilation owe a great deal to these fetishes of place, school, club, and so on.

THUS MARRIAGE REMAINS a far from negligible factor in social stability. We enter into it impulsively but carry it through with serious intentions. Although the old Catholic repugnance for divorce is on the wane, only one marriage in ten ends in a separation.[1] Divorce is not taken lightly, but it is no longer—or almost never—surrounded by suspicion. The equation divorce = chaos was axiomatic at the turn of the century; tomorrow it will be completely forgotten.

Until the sweeping reforms of 1965, marriage laws in France were based on the ascendancy of the husband and the dependence of the wife. Our laws were misogynic, almost oriental. As late as 1938 the marriage ceremony solemnly specified that the wife owed her husband obedience. Until 1965, she could not open a bank account or dispose of her own paycheck without the consent of her husband. Couples who took the precaution prior to marriage of appearing before a notary to draw up a contract by which their worldly goods remained separate have been considered in recent years a bit

---

[1] Divorce was introduced in France by the Revolution. It was very much in style under the Empire (Napoleon himself divorced); it was suppressed in 1818 and reintroduced at the close of the nineteenth century. It is still condemned by the Church. There are today 35,000 divorces a year in France.

crude. In earlier times, such precautions had been the object
of detailed dispositions and heated discussion between the
two families. Without a marriage contract, a rich girl marrying a poor man could be ruined in the most legal way in the
world, and she had no recourse. The combination of a law
which favored the man and contractual negligence parading as
delicacy of feeling tended to keep the married woman in a state
of subjection.

This is the impression conveyed by the history books, at
least, but the real state of affairs was quite different. The legal
weakness of the wife's position was often compensated for
by her psychological strength. Pressure for divorce was rarely
exerted, social pressures and the personal desires of those
concerned tending to bolster a limping marriage rather than
break it. Male gallantry and matriarchal tendencies still dictate
the general attitude, so that for the past century and a half the
Frenchwoman has actually ruled over her family. Organizing
the house, bringing up the children, determining the household budget, planning and arranging marriages—of these
powers she made efficient use, wielding an authority that was
hardly ever seriously questioned. The disparity between her
status in terms of the Civil Code and her status in terms of
the common practice has long been a peculiarly French characteristic among all classes. Hard-working, devout, circum-
spectly authoritarian, the married woman was the pivot of
social balance. Today she is still an element of stability and
prudence in the life of the nation. When General de Gaulle
gave women the right to vote in 1946, could he have foreseen
that twelve years later this "progressive" gesture would have
apparently reactionary consequences, and that he, an aging
military man surrounded by prominent men, would reap the
harvest of women's suffrage? It is a fact that the moderating

influence women exercise is felt as much at the political level (they constitute more than fifty per cent of the electorate) as in the home.

From now on the Frenchwoman, legally emancipated, her physiological well-being treated with greater solicitude— at last—by doctors and priests, her admission to careers and executive positions at least grudgingly conceded, will probably continue to exercise her stabilizing power in still other directions. She will defend morality less, security and wealth more. Her prudence will be a check on inflation. She will throw her weight against adventures that would jeopardize the comfort and security of her family and of the nation. She has always been for free public schools, the Church, proper sentiments, and piles of clean sheets in the cupboard. She is becoming the organizer of installment buying and the Mediterranean vacation. She was the soul of frugality; now she wants her own car. If you stop and think about it, she is still playing her old role; her power, which has many forms, is applied so as to ensure a calm and happy life for her family. The Frenchwoman of our present expanding economy resembles her grandmother more than one would suppose. Her blue jeans, her Austin-Cooper car, her robustly healthy children, her house in the country translate into today's terms dreams which must already have been full-blown in 1880. Analyze the four-color advertisements in the magazines and compare them to the paintings of simple pleasures bequeathed us by the Impressionists: you find the same vision of the ideal life to which all families aspire, the same comfortable, familiar world, the background of lawn or lake, the summer picnic in the sun-flecked shade, the romping children and dogs. The barbecue and—over there—the bright-red convertible would not be out of place among the straw hats of Monet or the beautiful, languid women of Renoir. With its revived economy, France is emerging from a quarter-century of military misfortunes to invent afresh a concept of happiness which it has preserved intact in its subconscious from the days before 1914.

A YOUNG COUPLE of today could serve as guide and witness to anyone wishing to examine contemporary French problems. Their worries and their behavior could illustrate an economist's article or a government report.

Two specific national difficulties, which actually combine into one, greet newlyweds on the threshold of their great adventure: lack of housing, and the obligation to help maintain a large community of elderly fellow citizens. A young couple of limited means has the greatest difficulty in finding a place to live. They cannot afford to buy. To rent is impossible or very expensive. Often one or another aging parent cannot be left alone. And so the two generations share a house or an apartment. They also figure that if the young wife works the grandmother can help bring up the children. This is how the couple's life together begins, ostensibly made easier by this sharing of space and duties, but in reality mortgaged from the very start in several ways.

The customs of the two generations conflict, the inevitable slights of daily life are aggravated. Instead of serving as a bond, children soon become a cause for quarrels. The great drama of the in-laws—mothers, sons, and daughters—opens. They judge each other, spy on each other. Everyone pokes his nose into squabbles that are none of his business. The merest scratch becomes a wound. Soon the very future of the couple is threatened. Suppose that, thanks to concessions and compromises, things get straightened out: it is still a shame that children should receive from their grandparents an upbringing that is out of step with their own time. Since 1945—that is, for an entire generation—the mass of conflicts resulting from old and young sharing quarters has caused serious psychological and social damage.

It is true that money can now begin to resolve these problems; with the number of housing units increasing, their prices will be lowered, and so on. It is nonetheless also true that this quite new social experience—old and young remaining chained together by necessity, young women finding their emotional adolescence prolonged into marriage and maternity, young men not managing to assume total responsibility for their families—will have left its mark on the institution of marriage and weighed it down with senseless difficulties. The reaction now taking place to the extent that circumstances permit will no doubt lead to a separation between the generations all the more brutal because their mutual ordeal has been long and unpleasant. In any case, that altogether successful and exemplary social institution, the middle-class family, which long served as a point of reference, an example, and a model for all Frenchmen old enough to get married, that ultimate product of a development begun at the end of the *ancien régime* (see Molière) and brought to a high polish in the nineteenth century (see Musset, Balzac, Bourget, etc.) when it was a rich quarry for romantic literature, that scaffolding which was so admirably suited to social ambition and conservatism, for good or ill will never be the same. Marriage is changing—has changed—and all the sociological patterns it has crystallized will be transformed. Behavior today may seem like that of the past, but the results will be different. Setting and psychology have changed too much for the basic structure of the family not to have changed too.

Yesterday, the complex ties among members of the same

family were the result of a drive toward power and security. Middle-class status was the more solid because in its broadest sense the mechanism of the family was functioning well. Each member expected from the others complicity, support, and incitement to do his best.

Everything has helped to break this earlier family mold. Property acquired fifty or a hundred years ago has been fragmented and parceled out among successive heirs. The long crisis that afflicted French society between approximately 1930 and 1955 was corrosive for the family. A new middle class is appearing; it is growing rich and acquiring power, but it no longer practices the family solidarity it needed to accomplish its aims two or three generations earlier. Ambition, business success, and making money are now more individual pursuits. The mythology of the bourgeois family was bound up with an unconscious desire to maintain a *status quo,* and later with nostalgia. Today social plasticity and personal success call for mobility and a "risk" mentality. After a long plateau period that coincided with the country's progressive deterioration, social dynamism has reappeared, but the actors are new. Mr. Pitts is perhaps right when he places the French bourgeois family in the pantheon of institutions—along with the Catholic Church, the Roman army, the American corporation, the German general staff, and the British Commonwealth—as one of the great creations of the human spirit, but this accolade is also a prestigious death certificate.

The society now taking shape in France is beginning anew the adventure that earlier led to the formation of the bourgeoisie, but it is not yet clearly defined. For the moment, in its nascent and fluid state, it seems to combine elements of nostalgia, snobbishness, and a striving after some style which will link it to the past, yet it is also manifesting the will to adapt to practical realities that tomorrow may determine its "new look." In any case, the privileged system of the bourgeoisie is no longer endorsed unqualifiedly. The old pattern called for a Catholic school, reading law at the university, long years of apprenticeship in the family business, a marriage of convenience, submission to the will of the head of the family, prudent investment; then, everything coming full circle, the whole process started over, with children brought up according to indefinable principles, sent in turn to the traditional Catholic school, and so on. This chain of rules respected and customs repeated—after all, they had "withstood the test of time"—is no longer necessarily binding in the view of the younger generation. Certainly, in some more conservative families people still strive to live according to this pattern; solid and honorable men are still formed by this code. Yesterday, these men were the archetypes accepted not only by the bourgeoisie but also by the majority of people, who dreamed of acceding to their style and to their privileges. They were heroes of liberal management, skeptical intelligence, and circumspect vanity. Today they are perhaps ministers or the presidents and board chairmen of great corporations, but for the first time in over a century they are no longer quite sure that their sons will be like them—or even that they would wish them to be.

As far as upbringing is concerned, Freud and the spectacle of undisciplined, blooming American babies have suggested to French minds something that was inconceivable yesterday. It is a vague, a very vague sense of guilt. That a child needed discipline, strict rules, inflexible traditions, even at the price of some conflict—this was an article of faith. The much-heralded beatings distributed in some English schools bolstered the French educator's taste for education thought of rather

in terms of dressage; in practice, the great Church schools
brought that concept to a peak of perfection. Then this scruple
about harming the child intruded. Was one perhaps giving the
child complexes? Was some delicate impulse being blocked
at the source? Soon the fashion of the child-king took over,
and parents felt confusedly guilty. Guilty of what? Of having
been unable, as yet, to reform or replace authoritarian training. A little anarchy has insinuated itself into the very coherent
network of yesterday's rules. Which is to say, order has been
succeeded by drift. The development has not gone so far as
liberalism, not so far as a genuine and intelligent understanding of the child. Things have stopped midway. Slaps are still
distributed and great principles are still invoked—but now
with a bad conscience. People have begun to talk about "confused mothers" and "problem children." These psychological
and family problems have been added to the already existing
crises in teaching, urbanization, housing, population explosion,
and teen-age styles. It has become as hard to be a child in
France as to be a parent.

For the time being, education in France is incoherent. It
takes some of its standards from a mistakenly interpreted
past and others from an uncertain future. It is clumsily per-
missive about the "rights" of the child and too pliant in cater-
ing to parental scruples. The fact is that no one in France
since Montaigne and Rousseau has given serious thought to
how you make a man. Now this neglect is beginning to be
noticeable. A few "good Jesuit fathers" and a few "pilot
schools"—the symbols of yesterday and tomorrow—do not
pay the debt France owes her children. These children are
obliged to maneuver on very shifting terrain and are subject to
too many contradictory influences. Whether their grandparents
are the old-fashioned kind (increasingly rare), with white

hair, armchair, and endless patience, or the active and dynamic breed, children can no longer play with them the subtle game of flattery and seduction which used to demark their own zone of freedom and ease within the family. Today the family pyramid is too dislocated to allow for that kind of almost unconscious social apprenticeship. The grandfather is likely to be tyrannical still, and to hold opinions even more vindictive and bitter than those of his children. The grandmother is a sort of supergoverness, playing a more active and efficient role with regard to the children than her daughter. The hasty couples of the postwar period, when it was in style to marry early, now have adolescent children. These youngsters do not find their parents sufficiently mature, and they find their grandparents somewhat too full of vitality. Between this lack and this excess, their margin of uncertainty is great. They tend to withdraw from the family circle, because it no longer offers them the harmony and assistance they had hoped for, and to aim at building an independent life, which strikes their parents as absurd and superficial. Adolescents would not go in so wholeheartedly for the fashions, provocations, and posturings which grownups find so unacceptable if adult society offered them a homogeneous framework in which to learn to live. It is not enough to blame the "inhumanity" of the vast, impersonal housing projects, the confusion that plagues farm communities, the incoherence of the school curriculums, the lack of sports stadiums and swimming pools, or the manifold tensions of urban life. We must go to the source, that is, to the partial destruction of the family fortress—or rather, to a persistent vacillation between rigidity and laxity, between the excessively authoritarian attitude that reigned yesterday and the embarrassed negligence of today.

The more spectacular problems of youth—the black-leather jackets, juvenile delinquency, and so on—have not taken hold in France in their more virulent forms. It is nevertheless true that the signs of a semirebellious autonomy, an almost total lack of moral or spiritual referents, and a disturbing taste for ease and softness, are on the increase. So we dream that by distributing free education according to a sacred principle of the Constitution, the state will succeed where family discipline is wavering. Unfortunately, the dream has not yet come true.

CHAPTER IX:

The Making of a Young Frenchman

THE TASK OF SUMMING UP in a single chapter the traditions, incoherencies, successes, shortcomings, and present
evolution of the French educational system calls for something like prestidigitation. How is one to describe an academic
system which is being reformed so rapidly that the students
themselves do not know in December what examinations they
will be expected to take in June, or if they will take any,
while their parents have, little by little, given up any hope of
understanding just what subjects their children are taking and
to what end? Am I exaggerating? Scarcely, and I write from
experience.

The best approach is probably to try to catch the intent
of the different "cycles" of our national education, to see
how it is in the process of changing, to list a few of its more
monumental absurdities, and, lastly, to attempt to describe the
behavior of a young Frenchman in terms of the things he
studies. This last may strike the non-French reader as particularly exotic.

There is much truth in the statement that there have been

and still are three distinct types of France: a "primary" France, a "baccalaureate" France, and a "university" France. The three definitions point to two social realities of unequal size, and to one vast illusion, "baccalaureate" France, which pretends that the diploma automatically confers distinction and opens the way to a higher social level.

The France of the primary school is on its last legs. It may rightly be called small and old-fashioned from now on, yet we must not forget that the establishment of nation-wide free elementary schooling was one of the great achievements in our history, a real step forward for democracy. Its hour is past but it was a glorious and colorful hour, and in retrospect its achievements are becoming more apparent.

It was toward the end of the nineteenth century (in 1882, to be exact) that the great republican leaders in our government—bearded, doctrinaire men, but less unrealistic than they have been pictured—turned their attention to the problem of public schooling. This was after the threats of monarchic restoration (real enough until 1876) had been laid to rest. Their principles were simple: schooling for everyone, free schooling, compulsory schooling. Not only must the schools assure literacy for one hundred per cent of the French population but, in the process of distributing homogeneous instruction in all parts of the country, they must also consolidate national unity. Regional differences, accents, and dialects were to be attenuated by the primary schools, so the centralizing, egalitarian dogma of the Republic specified. For the duration of the Third Republic, 1875–1940, and especially until the 1914–18 war, the two great forces fostering national unity were the communal—i.e., public lay—school and military service, for in the latter, too, officialdom took care systematically to break down social and regional differences.

But one should not underestimate the political intentions of Jules Ferry, the "father of the secular school." His aim was not only to homogenize all young Frenchmen but also to turn them out republicans. It was time to put a stop to clerical control over education. The Church had big secondary schools for the children of the bourgeoisie and confessional schools in the villages for the children of the peasants. When, in 1907, the government turned to the radical measure of expelling the religious orders from France, the teaching orders were its chief target. The State wanted to attack its enemies at the root, where they threatened to form a new antirepublican generation.

In order to understand this, one must try to imagine the political atmosphere of the time. The Church was almost totally compromised because of its dealings with the conservatives, many of whom yearned for the return of the king. The ever-present threat that the nation might be divided into two antagonistic blocs had just been underscored by the revisionist plot of General Boulanger and by the Dreyfus affair. The republican regime felt that it could not risk any mistakes, any show of weakness. It was essential for the government to win the hearts of the new generation, which was tantamount to saying that the State must have a monopoly in its upbringing. The Republic would be a pedagogue or it would not be at all.

In the crusade for secular education, the supporting troops were the teachers. No words can overstate the importance of their role during a half-century of French life. They were the saints in this struggle against God, the soldiers in an ideological and bloodless battle. They were the bulwark of the Republic even in the remotest countryside. Everywhere, in the space of a few years, rose the *mairie-école* (the town hall plus public school) whose silhouette even today is an inevitable feature of ninety per cent of our villages. In the center is the commune headquarters, never without the Liberty, Equality, Fraternity inscription and bust of Marianne, symbol of republican France; in one wing, the boys' school; in the other, the girls'. Back then, the teachers were generally man and wife, the man often filling the post of secretary at the town hall as well. They voted, depending on the period, Radical, Radical-Socialist, or Socialist. They were not revolutionaries, but Jacobins—that is, liberals or Whigs. The Establishment was only too ready to label them "reds," but they were simply very *petit-bourgeois* persons, non-churchgoers, strict, devoted to their work, equipped with a fine, sloping script and a few magic formulas. In the end, their uprightness and their extraordinary pedagogical faith won them the respect of nearly everyone.[1]

However, for a long time rivalry and strife raged in every French village. On one side were the teachers, backed by a few fiercely anticlerical, democratic souls—often free-thinking doctors and pharmacists. On the other were the priests, the teaching nuns (later defrocked), the local noblemen and reactionary gentry. All of rural France, so important because of its numbers and its stability, lived for a half-century amid this tension (which, in the end, proved useful enough) between

[1] The powerful S. N. I. (Syndicat National des Instituteurs) had a membership of 275,000 in 1966. Seventy-five years after Jules Ferry, its style and vocabulary have not greatly changed. During a debate at the 1966 S. N. I. convention concerning possible reforms in the *écoles normales d'instituteurs* (teachers colleges), a representative from the south shouted: "Let them not expect from us the blow that would decapitate the tender shoots of secular thought and democracy which our *écoles normales* have always represented!"

"old" principles and "eternal" principles. The tiniest hamlet gave itself up passionately to the ideological battle. While colonial empires were being built and great industries were emerging, while Germany was arming and England and the United States were growing rich, all France was fighting for or against "the priests," for or against Captain Dreyfus, for or against the Jesuits or the Brothers of the Christian Schools, for or against eating meat on Good Friday, for or against the inventory of ecclesiastical holdings and the separation of church and state. Never was modern France more herself, which is to say, never did she so narrow her own horizon. In the name of universal principles, she got all worked up over small-time politics. In the name of the Freedom of Man and the Declaration of Human Rights, she turned Radical-Socialist. In the name of the Nation, she cooped herself up in village quarrels.

And yet it was the teachers in their little village strong-holds—with the blackboard on one side and the multiplication table on the other, and the map of France on the wall (the France from which Alsace-Lorraine had been amputated, the sight of which fired the young to dreams of revenge)—it was the teachers who assured the country a solidity that not even the butchery of 1914–18 could seriously threaten. It was the teachers—versatile guides, professors of life as well as of sums—who gave to each little French child dressed in his black smock a historic folklore, rules of civic behavior, clear handwriting, respect for bread, a few simple dreams, and the certainty of belonging to a generous nation. This idyllic yet modest picture may seem anachronistic today, heavy with jingo-istic promises and phraseology. It is, it was. Yet it was also the picture of a well-balanced France, even with all its familiar defects, which at that time were egocentricity, a disproportionate concern with keeping things in the right proportions (often the smallest proportions), and nationalism.

What has replaced this picture?

We have organized student bussing and closed all schools with fewer than sixteen pupils. This hastens and guarantees the abandonment of the countryside. The closing of the schools in numerous communes symbolizes a necessary social evolution. Yet we may well ask if new methods, rules, and civic morality have been invented which are as coherent as those of the old primary school. It is not enough to stop dispensing one form of teaching; we must know how to replace "old-fashioned" nourishment with fare suited to the new intellectual dietary laws.

"Primary," in French, is both a beautiful word (that which is first, at the origin and base of everything) and a derogatory adjective. We call a man *primaire* if he has narrow views, if his mind does not rise readily to the level of our beloved abstractions. Let us say, then, that the evolution of French society has passed from the noble sense of the word, through attrition of the educational establishment, toward its pejorative meaning.

But who accused the teachers—whom one also called simply and proudly "masters"—of being *primaires?*

This leads us to the next question, the France of the *bacheliers.*

The baccalaureate, or *bachot,* is the examination which was formerly taken at sixteen or seventeen (now at eighteen, its academic level falling as the average age of the candidates rises) and which terminates the cycle of secondary studies. It is the *bachot* that opens the way to the university and the *Grandes Écoles.* Without this examination successfully behind one, no college study is possible. One can see why this threshold exam, this diploma key which seems to open all the doors of culture and success, has had a magic hold on the imagination.

But we have long confused the *bachot* as something which enables you to go somewhere with the *bachot* as something which says you are already there. From being a threshold, it became a goal in itself, at the same time that a more generous awarding of the diploma was lowering its relative value. All French *petits-bourgeois* dreamed of having a son—and more recently, a daughter—who would be a *bachelier*. People no longer wished to become *bacheliers* in order to pursue their studies (for which, in many cases, they were ill-suited), but simply in order to possess the title that supposedly symbolized a first step up the social ladder. After which, too often they would do mediocre college work (thereby lowering the general level), which they soon abandoned to swell the ranks of the poorly trained who, having no skill, no proven ability, no profession, still could consider themselves as above the common herd because they "had their baccalaureate."

This virus of a cut-rate diploma wrought havoc. It helped to establish a rootless class of petty employees who were an easy prey to their own discontents. Disappointed by a society that had not treated him according to his merits (that is to say, according to what he expected from his little two-bit diploma), the embittered *bachelier* felt free to become a bad husband, a harsh father, and a disaffected citizen. The whole problem arose from the fact that the trusted logic of social advancement was too often frustrated. The equation of the old French dream can be put thus: a great-grandfather who was a peasant; a grandfather who became a teacher at the primary level; a father who taught in the *lycée* (a rise, through the secondary schools, into the bourgeoisie); a son who is a graduate of the École Polytechnique or who becomes an Inspector of Finance (the possibility now being present, with an assist from marriage, of entering the *grande bourgeoisie*). This was the rational progression by which a society that was both flexible and sensible, democratic but hierarchical, might hope to evolve; the steps seemed "natural"; that is to say, they were in agreement with principles. And, in fact, many families advanced along these lines in the course of a century, sometimes even faster, going from the farm to the civil service, to the prefectures, to industry, to the university. The son of grade-school teachers would go to the École Normale, teach in a *lycée*, go up to Paris and there slide into politics or literature. Radical France has never preferred any other image of herself to this one. She was not so far wrong.

So this is not the France I am thinking of when I denounce the hocus-pocus that surrounds the *bachot* and that just barely permits the possessor to hold down a white-collar job rather than work with his hands or in a store. This obsession, with its puny ambitions and wrong attitude, has aggravated the intellectual poverty and pretensions of the fussy, stay-at-home French "center," and closed it to all the great winds of history that are now blowing.

The new-style *bachot* of 1966 was passed by less than a third of the candidates, despite the tremendous liberality and "comprehension" required of the correctors.[2]

This *bachot,* what with its chaotic curricula, its recondite specializations, and the laxness it is heading toward, is more discouraging than ever. More than ever it seems symbolic of

---

[2] In 1965 41 per cent passed; in the June 1966 session, of a total of 219,000 candidates, 31 per cent passed—the lowest figure ever achieved. The figure rose to 51 per cent at the end of the fall session of 1966.

aging institutions and of a confused effort to renew them, both spectacles being equally pathetic. Moreover, the situation is alarming because it involves the quality of our future standards and the caliber of our future leaders. Every year it throws on the work market tens of thousands of young people whom it has prepared for—nothing.

Must this drift toward mediocrity, which has been going on far too long, be attributed entirely to the adolescents, or are they victims of an inescapable web of negligence and inadequacies?

To put the question thus is to invite a disenchanted but widely shared answer. How easy it would be to rail against witless ministers or lazy good-for-nothings! But no doubt young people have the teachers they deserve, and nations have the young people they create. This equivocal statement does not, however, diminish the distress one feels in preparing a case against youth or against those who are responsible for the trouble it is in.

Four problems beset secondary teaching: a lower caliber of teachers and difficulty in recruitment; overloaded curricula, inadequate classrooms and classes that are too large; and a constant lowering of the average academic level. The four problems are obviously inseparable; one scarcely knows which to attack first.

Restoring the prestige of the *lycée* teacher would be an initial remedy from which other benefits would derive. Fifty years ago a teacher was someone to be respected in the middle-class world. He combined the prestige of culture with that of service to the state. He was not badly paid. He had earned solid diplomas, more often than not had the French equivalent of a Master's degree, and was sometimes a graduate of the École Normale Supérieure. He was somebody.

As government concern for education declined, the status of teachers deteriorated. They were, relatively, more and more poorly paid. Teaching became a vocation in the true sense of the word, especially in the sciences, where industry could offer a young competition winner in physics or mathematics a salary two or three times his teacher's stipend. The result has been growing disaffection for the profession and a crisis in recruitment, so that increasingly large and restless classes have had to be turned over to less and less well-prepared teachers. Within the profession itself several different types of exodus have occurred: there has been the flight of the competition winners from the provinces to Paris, from teaching to research, and from secondary-school teaching to college teaching. The status of teacher having lost much of its luster, it became more flattering to teach in Paris than in Périgue, at the university rather than the *lycée,* at the Sorbonne rather than at Poitiers or Montpellier. A sort of cultural aristocracy developed in the better universities (or at least those nearer the capital), in Paris, and at the C.N.R.S.,[3] which was attracted by literature, lecturing, journalism, and politics, and which progressively lost contact with the vocation of teaching. It soon seemed quite normal to spare outstanding personalities the burden of a teaching schedule. This attitude would be understandable if we had a plethora of university-caliber personnel; it is dangerous when the number of students is rising and that of teachers is tending to drop. The secondary school in France has been deserted in favor of personal careers or university professorships.

This depletion has been aggravated by the lack of class-

---

[3] Centre National de la Recherche Scientifique, an organization that attracts researchers in different disciplines, most frequently professors on leave of absence.

rooms, with, as a result, swamped classes (from forty to fifty students per class in the Paris *lycées*) and, of course, lower standards of teaching and therefore weakened performances by the students themselves. Many *bacheliers* of the sixties would never have passed the examinations thirty or forty years ago. It is ironic that these phenomena should occur at the same time as flaws develop in the study programs. The latter remain too encyclopedic, too broadly humanistic and rhetorical. No reform is made; something is simply added. French children of fifteen struggle with schedules and school requirements that would floor an adult. No serious sports activity is offered (or required) to make up for this intellectual inflation. Perhaps if playing fields and stadiums were available to our secondary-school students we would be less struck by the unreal, archaic nature of their academic pursuits. Spending hours each week on dead languages and endlessly annotating and commenting on the tragedies of Racine and Corneille or the letters of Mme. de Sévigné may impart some mysterious essence of "classical culture," but for future doctors, electronic engineers, and chemists it may also be a waste of time.

Sacrifices for the sake of tradition are so deep-rooted with us that when an objection such as this is raised from time to time it always unleashes a storm of protest in the name of Humanism and Eternal France. However, the most cursory inquiry among students reveals that they do not care a rap about the cultural nonsense that is being rammed down their throats, they do not digest it, and their natural bent will lead them in quite different directions the moment the diploma is in hand. What has happened to common sense in all this?

Is it right to require *all* secondary-school students to participate in this cult of the classics, this intangible worship of the "humanities" which has been going on for some three hun-

dred years, exactly as one once sought to have *all* children in
the communal schools acquire secular republican ideals?
Would it not be better to departmentalize instruction and
adapt it as soon as possible to the individual capacities of the
student? Surely this desire to weigh everyone down with the
same cultural baggage merely reflects our old universalist illusion.

Today, these problems have all been pin-pointed. Amid
maximum confusion, we are seeking solutions and we hope
to find them. We are counting on the population explosion to
furnish not only new students but also new teachers; on the
labor market to draw students toward technical subjects; on
the spirit of the times to turn them from Socrates, Montaigne,
and Robespierre toward mathematics; on the rise in standards of living to convince them that, on Sundays, it's fun
to have the whole family take a little exercise; on some legislative and financial miracle of the Plan to find the land, the
concrete, and the funds that will be transformed into schools.
Finally, we are counting on the civic responsibility of those
who already have their diplomas and on the generosity of the
Ministry of Finance to refurbish a little the image of the
teaching profession. They have thought up a new catch-phrase
to characterize this problem. "Youth," they say (in the opposition as well as in the government), "is 'the most prior
priority.'" Better the truth late—and redundant—than never.

French students form a community mysteriously and
perpetually on the brink of delinquency or revolt. By tradition,
hell-raising, hazing, and demonstrating in the streets are
enormously important to them. These are the three pillars of
an initiation ritual stemming from adult domination and
youthful rebellion. The relationship between the students
and the rest of society is strange; no one ever expects any-

thing good of them. Ribald, stupid, or seditious songs apparently express best what they have to say. It seems natural that the Latin Quater in Paris should be under constant police surveillance. No sooner do the students creep out of their lairs and gather in groups than the patrol cars and paddy-wagons appear. In the lecture halls, the professors must always be steeled for an outburst of catcalls or tendentious questions. The small, closed world of the student is always in a state of subsurface boil which his working and living conditions only exacerbate.

Let us draw a clear distinction, at the college level, between the *Grandes Écoles* and the faculties of the various universities. The *Grandes Écoles*—they include the Polytechnique, the Centrale, the Normale, Sèvres, the Institut d'Études Politiques, the École Nationale d'Administration, and the École des Hautes Études Commerciales—are well differentiated as to curriculums, well organized, and well staffed. Admission (and often premature departure) is on a competitive basis, the period of study is limited, and there is a strict correlation between one's academic standing and one's eventual professional opportunities. All these factors tend to make *Grandes Écoles* students rather like deferred adults; i.e., they are studying but are already involved in real-life problems. A *polytechnicien* is already a kind of officer, the pupil at the École Nationale d'Administration is a high-ranking civil servant in embryo.

On the other hand, the students in the universities are often poorly housed, poorly nourished, and uncomfortable in their vast lecture halls and libraries. They are taught in a solemn, distant, desultory fashion, as they wait for the mimeographed copies of their courses which will permit them to catch up with material their teachers have not covered. They float in a half-world, inchoate and closed in on itself, and they are ripe for any anarchy. Because they do not have any space that is really their own, their quarrels, meetings, and demonstrations are perforce held in the street. Hence they "disturb the peace" and are treated accordingly. The hatred that reigns between the students and the Paris police is really stupefying. To believe it, you would have to witness the refined brutality of the police charges, in which social jealousies and political hostilities are all jumbled together. The moment French students start shouting anything, they start to shout political slogans as well. Whatever the slogans and of whatever color the party in power, the police reply is to lay about them with their night sticks. Their response is non-political and automatic, and it is highly instructive. Order, like money, has no smell, and the guardians of order operate on the theory of a blow for a blow; they knock you out on general principles.

The constant suspicion that hangs over the university —symbolized in Paris by the little groups of policemen stationed at street corners in the vicinity of the boulevard Saint-Michel—contributes to the mounting tension between the students' world and the real world. Saturday-afternoon scuffles between militants of the Left and Right, triggered by the news vendors, have become routine. Unfortunately, when the same or other students turn out to demonstrate in the street for increased government appropriations for education, new laboratories, or decent university cafeterias (in the last instance they are often accompanied by their professors), the two types of demonstration resemble each other so closely that they get the same response from the same whirling clubs.

While this picture is true today, undoubtedly it will become less so in five or ten years' time. We are building and will continue gradually to build new classrooms, laboratories, and living quarters. Certain cities that have been redesigned since the war (Caen) or that are particularly alive (Grenoble, Dijon, Mulhouse) already offer their students normal working conditions. Near Paris, several university departments are being physically decentralized, with the double advantage of dispersing an overturbulent community and giving it a little fresh air to breathe. Two "university cities" now exist, one of them—wonder of wonders!—actually surrounded by trees! These signs of progress are touchingly modest when compared with accomplishments elsewhere, but nonetheless leave their beneficiaries mildly stunned.

The behavior and the psychology of the student population will also change.[4] Already one can say for a fact that healthy and more attractive living conditions are alleviating the futile tension in which the students have been caught. Hopefully, the annual crop of springtime jitters and nervous breakdowns will decrease. The Algerian war, to which students reacted more vehemently than did the average Frenchman (they faced the threat of having to take part in it), sparked the last great blaze of political enthusiasm. The peace that came in the summer of 1962 "demobilized" them. Also, those who had sided militantly with the F.L.N. and the diehards of the O.A.S. returned to their exams (both sides leaving some companions in jail). From now on efficiency and the

---

[4] Some 400,000 are enrolled in twenty-three academic districts, 220,000 of them boys. Forecast: within fifteen years, one Frenchman out of five will have attended the courses leading to the *bachot*. Note also the presence of 30,000 foreign students in France, as against only 40,000 in the U.S.A. and 17,000 in the USSR. This figure, in proportion to our population of only a little over fifty million and in comparison with the number of French-speaking people (scarcely more than a hundred million), is considerable.

practical point of view apparently will replace the "lyric illusions" (as their ex-idol, André Malraux, would put it) on which our young people had been nourished. They themselves use the word "folklore"—slightingly—to denote the whole traditional student mess. "For the students of 1965," Michel Friedman wrote in *L'Express* (October 18, 1965), " *'folklo'* embraces political parties, dilapidated classrooms, student unions, French education, the Resistance, battling with the police, Dreyfus, Zola, Blum, novels, the Army, poverty, and guards who stop you from going up to girls' bedrooms. To which list one can add, pell-mell: the Boul' Mich', street demonstrations, and hazings."

So the French students of tomorrow are already beginning to take shape today, although the quote above seems to me a little precipitate in stripping all their legends from them. They will become obsessed by "concrete" considerations. Exiled at long last to American-style campuses, far from the local color of the old university neighborhoods, they will travel by car and go home for weekends, like workers with jobs out of town. They will be less and less picturesque and more and more serious. They will be determined to sell themselves to the highest bidders. They will constitute a transition generation. At present, their world is far from being adequately organized, but it has broken away from a more than thirty-year-long immobility. Already students are frequenting cafés less; if they do go, they drink innocent fruit juices; they spend their leisure time skiing, skin-diving, or traveling. Their physical appearance has changed. They are blonder and taller. The new middle-class generation gives the lie to the old caricature of the dark-skinned, gesticulating little Frenchman. Better nutrition and a bit of sport have begun to improve their looks.

The Making of a Young Frenchman

Students realize how numerous they are, but take no comfort in numbers. Jobs will be few; they will have to be competed for and earned. The airy way in which the young are getting ready to elbow the older generation aside shows they are learning that elbowing and being elbowed are part of the current behavior pattern and that they might as well acquire the knack. Hard work is becoming popular. In student slang, one prides oneself on being *polar*—that is, a grind. If a student is still politically involved (militant Catholics and partisans of the two extremes are the only active minorities), he no longer acts in a spirit of ideological euphoria but supports the students' "social" demands: more scholarships, more lodgings, more classrooms, more professors, and—their most radical demand—a goverment-guaranteed stipend for university students, which would enable them to house and dress themselves, and even to marry. They defend this last demand on the ground that as college students they are already effectively participating in the national life; the idea is still rather utopian, but in the spring 1967 elections parties of the Left gave it some attention in their campaign promises.

Whereas a gust of dandyism, song, and changing styles is sweeping over the *lycée* crowd and the very young working people, with college students the wind is veering toward empiricism and hard work. The students' quasi-delinquent impulse to revolt still survives and sets the tone in some academic areas (fine arts, law) and in some university towns, but it is on the way out. The realistic outlook of science students and of future technicians is gaining ground. The change threatens, furthermore, to deepen the gulf between past and future. Because student "folklore" used to remind parents of their own youth, and because it prolonged adolescent dependence, it was tolerated willingly enough by adults, who were after all in the saddle; it made them feel secure. But now the "old folks" must expect to be confronted by a mass of increasingly tough, and less and less recognizable, youth.

Already adults are surprised at times by the tone their children have assumed. In the spring of 1966 a TV series presented a career survey that included interviews and discussions with students at the École Nationale d'Administration. The E.N.A., which is hard to get into, is a training center for top civil servants, the nursery of future Inspectors of Finance, Councilors of State, prefects, diplomats, etc. TV viewers were astonished by the rather pompous seriousness of the boys who were questioned. Words like "power" and "efficiency" and "élite" came up constantly—and always in reference to themselves! The technocratic ideal, the eagerness to run the economy and the state on a tight rein and on the basis of rational principles, was implicit in everything they said. There is no doubt that at the Polytechnique (which sends its top cadres into big business, the army, and various executive levels in the ministries), and also—to a lesser degree—at the École Normale Supérieure and among those working for degrees in history and science (the more intellectual and inquiring), the mood is the same. A serious France, a France resolved to manage its capital vigorously rather than live on it, is in the process of formation. All these young men are interested less in getting rich than in capturing key positions. One senses that the real, the attainable power has switched from ownership to administration. The big technician now wields the power of a big magnate. Liberalism is definitely moribund. Twenty-year-olds are inclined to dream of playing a role in our state-organized society rather than of amassing a great fortune. The romance of industry and finance is getting to be beyond the scope of individual ambitions and liberal principles. State capitalism (in both its bourgeois and socialistic forms), planning, management of resources, and so on henceforth offer more and surer possibilities than the spirit of adventure of the nineteenth-century capitalist pioneers.

In the tradition of her great stewards, whether monarchical, Napoleonic, or republican, France has been particularly well-endowed to train upper-echelon civil servants. Today these men are energetic, imbued with a sense of their importance, yet in their way disinterested and passionately concerned for the destiny of the state; despite an occasional excess of red tape and scorn for day-by-day problems, they are an effective group. The future of organized liberalism —capitalism curbed and supervised by the state—belongs to them. It is not distasteful to realize that abilities are even now maturing in our midst that in fifteen or twenty years will be guiding the nation. Amid the dangerous confusion characteristic of the regular universities, these minorities from the *Grandes Écoles* form so many little islands of resistance and stability. Any general survey that failed to take account of this would be misleading. Unrealistic, out of date, and chaotic as our educational system may be, our future technocrats have not been unduly affected. General de Gaulle has systematically chosen his ministers and collaborators from among top-ranking civil servants; in doing so, he has not only pursued a policy of ridding the government apparatus of partisan politics, he has mined a rich vein. Among his achievements, this one irritates the old-line political parties; yet it is admirable, and all the more so for going against a stubborn tradition.

WITHOUT my having expressly planned it, all the principal problems of our educational system have now been stated.

The most serious are lack of classroom space, understaffed faculties, devaluation of the teacher's status, almost total neglect of sports, an archaic curriculum, chaotic and hasty efforts to reform it, social injustice in the recruitment of university students,[5] and too great an isolation of the student community from the nation at large.

The students themselves, the French generally, and their government are quite aware of the crisis. Essentially, it has arisen from long-accumulated delays; ten slow years cannot be allowed to mask a century of inaction. It would be too convenient to claim that the *force de frappe* is depriving the French of everything they presently lack. It is true that when one confronts the scope of what must be done and the chaos in what is being done, the temptation to lapse into black pessimism is great. Yet in the space of fifteen years, pitch-black has lightened to gray. True, there is a disparity between the urgency of our needs (especially scholastic) and the solemn, unhurried performance at the Elysée palace. True, there is a striking difference between the dynamism in construction (left in the hands of private speculators and too often marred by scandals) and the sluggishness of ad-

---

[5] Social background of students in the *Grandes Écoles* (1962):

CHILDREN OF:	PERCENTAGE OF TOTAL STUDENT BODY	PERCENTAGE OF GROUP IN TOTAL POPULATION
Farmers	6	20.8
Farmhands	0	6.0
Businessmen	18	12.0
Professional men, top echelons	29	2.9
Professional men, middle echelons	26	16.8
Workers, foremen	6	33.8
No occupation	6	4.5
Miscellaneous	9	3.2

ministrative reform. However, it is fair to say that the end is now in sight. There is no cause to run up the flags yet, but neither should we guiltily put them at half-mast. Gaullist France is also the France of M. Giscard d'Estaing and of the twenty-year-old emulators of M. Giscard d'Estaing. Let us not be obsessed by the France of Antoine.[6] For that matter, wasn't Antoine a good student at the École Centrale? The elaborate hoax, another student tradition on the way out, acquired a whole new dimension with him. But that's no reason for forgetting to laugh.

---

[6] A singer afflicted with the long hair fashionable in the mid-sixties. Why not mention him here? After all, Dranem, Mayol, Josephine Baker, and Maurice Chevalier are also, alas, part of the history of France.

CHAPTER X:

The Real Frenchman

T HIS CHAPTER is meant to atone for all the others. May it fully confess to the presumption and naïveté of trying to portray the French as a unique species—colorful, consistent, generous, and logical in their behavior.

Every time a Frenchman tried to replace the traditional caricature of the "typical Frenchman"—chubby, dark-complexioned, wearing a hat, decorations, and a mustache, and dressed too warmly—with an image he felt to be nearer the truth, he drew another, rather bittersweet, caricature that satisfied only himself. The typical Frenchman does not exist, any more than what I will presume to call here the "real Frenchman." Or at any rate, he is only an archetype, fated to be placed by the humorist and the anthropologist with the eccentric English traveler and the romantic German devouring Wagnerian sauerkraut. There has been a certain utility in these stereotypes: they were reassuring; they exempted us from traveling and permitted us to make war without too many subtle misgivings. Perhaps the current habit of taking international vacations and—in Europe, at any rate—disenchantment with militarism have made such oversimplifications old-fashioned. The diversity, within themselves, of other societies, and their similarities to us, strike us nowadays more than their homogeneity and strangeness. The same holds true for each individual in relation to his own country. What Frenchman would still dare generalize about his country without making the usual reservations that I have been mentioning?

As opposed to nonexistent stereotypes, one may mean by "real Frenchmen" those individuals who seem to be on the verge of realizing who they really are, what they want, and what they can achieve. One may also mean those who have only recently become relatively well off and who, rather like pioneers, are seeking to establish themselves in still virgin social territory. Tomorrow they will comprise a France that no one could have imagined twenty years ago.

The doctrinaire royalists of l'Action Française, followers of Charles Maurras, at least had a gift for creating slogans. In contradistinction to what they termed the "legal country," they christened the solid, permanent, wholesome foundations on which, according to them, the nation had been built, the "real country." Obviously, those foundations were connected by thousands of subterranean paths to the traditions of ancient, royal France. On the other hand, the "legal country" lacked profundity or reality. It was a mishmash of parliamentarianism, prefectural dictatorships, foreign, Jewish, and Protestant adulterations. It was the cracked façade of the republican state, destined to be soon overthrown by a purifying leap forward.

Although permeated with bad faith down to its smallest detail, the distinction between "real" and "legal" had the merit of pointing to the very French opposition between groundswell and surface ripples, between our roots and our burgeons.

By now it may be the roots that have become illusory, although we still revere them, and what is new, what is amenable to influence and change, is preparing the *real* face of the country, which soon will be. One must not overlook the interplay of these two constants in our national make-up when assessing the hypotheses that follow.

For a long time, France has claimed to be the "eldest daughter of the Church," although perhaps Italy and Spain would have had more right to the title. She remains largely submissive to the moral doctrines of Catholicism and feels at home with the more spectacular aspects of its ritual. But the genuine importance and vitality of religious faith have diminished enormously. Eight out of ten Frenchmen are baptized, but not more than one or two out of ten are practicing Catholics. If this figure rises to sixty or even eighty per cent in certain provinces (Vendée and Alsace), it falls below five per cent in the so-called de-Christianized regions (Brie, Creuse, Haut-Var). Religion is less important to men than to women, to the young than to the old, to the workingman than to the bourgeois. How many churches on Sunday mornings seem to be populated only with local gentry and old ladies!

Yet the French Catholic tradition was once belligerent (religious wars, persecutions) as well as adventurous (Crusades, missions in the New World and the colonies). Thus, it would be useless to speculate on a definitive weakening of the Catholic Church in France. It has suffered from unfortunate alliances and complicity with the reactionary factions of the nation. "The Army and the Church," "the Throne and the Altar" were popular—and effective—slogans, based on truth. Having disassociated itself from the source of wealth and power, and having been constrained (for its own good) to break with the state, the Church hierarchy in France has on occasion aligned itself with the working classes and shared in social leadership; it has given more attention to young people than to old maids and retired generals; as a result, it has staged a real comeback in the last thirty years. The faith is growing stronger by appealing to the young, to an active, practicing minority, not by remaining just a reassuring habit for the sedentary well-to-do.

Thus the program for agricultural reform is led in part by young elements of the Jeunesse Agricole Chrétienne, an independent and particularly dynamic labor-union offshoot of the prewar Jeunesse Ouvrière Chrétienne. The Catholic press is organized, powerful, and rich. It often takes courageous stands on public issues. The free Catholic universities of Paris and Lille are active, as is the Centre Catholique des Intellectuels Français. Important writers, from Bernanos to Mauriac, from Paul Claudel to Julian Green, have spoken out for their faith. This gives easier consciences to people of good taste. The help given to the persecuted during the war and today's ecumenical efforts reassure the liberals. And its most progressive elements have made the French Church, at least in the persons of its leaders, virtually the most dynamic and aggressive in the world. The worker-priests and the Brotherhoods of Father de Foucauld are seeking at last to substitute the concept of social justice for that of charity, to speak of the oppressed and not just the poor. The Church in France is no longer a prop of bourgeois society; it sometimes even questions the virtues of that society. To be sure, all this arouses opposition. Rome hesitates, agrees, then counterattacks, condemns and maneuvers cagily. Some bishops accelerate the forward movement; others hamper it. Certain cities and suburbs acclaim it; certain provinces damn it.

The struggle between conservatives and progressives is sometimes ferocious. But more and more often, the Church hierarchy leans toward renewal and common sense. In France *real* Catholics are no longer very numerous, but at least they live their faith; they seem to live it fifty years ahead of Rome and two centuries ahead of Toledo.

SOCIAL STRUCTURES have altered and become more flexible, often in interrelated ways: farmers migrate to the cities, industries to the country; city dwellers now have country houses; dying businesses are replaced by new ones. These changes are still limited, but they have shattered the old equilibrium. Certain privileges are doomed, but, in turn, certain problems no longer seem hopeless.

Our agriculture is being modernized; migrant farm workers are being relocated in other jobs. Dying villages (sadly poetic imagery) will no longer bespeak the distress of one fifth of the nation, but will have found new reason for being. Television and the press will bring news, fashions, advice on beauty care, and all the latest gimmicks to the farmer and his family. New professional knowledge and competence will go hand in hand with a growing conformity in tastes and habits. Young farmers of Beauce already visit Spain and go skiing in the winter. Yet elsewhere, in Brittany and in central France, farmhouse floors are still beaten earth and the houses do not always have electricity. From now on, the pace of progress will quicken; it will abolish the old order and, with it, old injustices. It will prune what is weak and reinforce what is strong, it will build rational new structures where worm-riddled and dilapidated social scaffoldings have survived too long. If one must evaluate this evolution one has to judge it favorably. Who would dare condemn it?

The Real Frenchman

Only yesterday, French society was still haunted by the specter of revolution. Between the blue-collar worker in his cap and the white-collar worker in his hat, vast Marxist and romantic chasms yawned, foretelling the class struggle. Today, no man's hat symbolizes a class distinction. In less than twenty years Marx has gone out of style. It has been said that the proletariat turned middle-class when the traditional middle-class values were discredited. The bourgeoisie stood for thrift, family stability, discretion, and security. The grandchildren of the bourgeois heroes of yesterday squander, sell, spend, divorce, travel, flaunt their wealth. In other words, they are no longer a bourgeoisie. Their frenzy has infected everyone. Employers, employees, workers—all borrow, spend, drive a car, live beyond their means. The savings, woollen stockings, money tucked away in drawers, the old family farms—all the treasures accumulated son by son have been put into circulation to finance the new style of living, which gives the impression of affluence. Is it real affluence? I will try to answer this later. For the moment, let us simply note that spending old capital which has depreciated in value does not connote prosperity. At the most, it means having the common sense to realize that an era has ended, that its values have been superseded. It is far better to invest in the comforts and pleasures of life than to be the guardians of mildewed treasure.

Together with the depletion of peasant manpower and the new, realistic ambitions of the proletariat, the most important social phenomenon in France is undoubtedly the proliferation of skilled personnel. Managers, supervisors, technicians, engineers—all the middlemen of economic power—see their professional and social importance increase daily. Because they are well paid they accept the employee status; they try to better it and to buy as much comfort and pleasure

165

as possible. Unlike their forebears, they are no longer obsessed by the hope of being their own bosses, of becoming independent. All around them they see little private enterprises going on the rocks and they have no desire whatever to join those ranks. To hold a respectable job with a big company or the State suits them. Yesterday, all Frenchmen were more or less irascible Cyranos saying: " 'Tis a small glass I drink from—but the glass is my own!" Today, in place of this individualistic credo they prefer the free-flowing faucets of the electronics and chemical industries, and of government ministries.

The emergence of this new social category ("class" would be an improper and old-fashioned word) entails significant consequences. It is for these new ranks of employees that real-estate speculators build semiluxury dwellings, engineers create economy cars, and hotel owners attempt to modernize. Vacation clubs offer them a taste of the (well-explored) exotic at moderate prices. Newspaper publishers depoliticize the press to make it optimistic and appetizing; publishers step up their paperback lines, and so on. Homes, fashion, leisure pursuits, and culture have been geared to the pace of these newcomers. The problem is to win, flatter, and reassure them. Unfortunately, there is a tendency to offer them false luxury and showy junk, jerry-built houses decorated with marble, so-called sports cars, papers with scant or stereotyped news but rich in fashionable gossip and precooked, predigested features. The suppliers of cultural commodities are doing better. However much they may actually listen or read, never have people bought so much serious music and so many literary classics. Never have so many film societies and ambitious theater groups managed to operate in the black. Two parallel currents must be pointed out: the desire for a ready-made veneer of phony culture in some, and the desire for real information and learning in others. Some dream of joining the middle class and "getting with it," others of becoming civilized people.

The chaff is mixed with the wheat, the fake with the genuine. Some people buy art books to confer distinction on their libraries; others queue up in long lines to see fine exhibits. Some are ecstatic patrons of the predigested, vulgarized tourism of the vacation clubs; others venture forth in their little cars to travel far and wide through Europe. Who are the "real" Frenchmen? The young people one runs into in some godforsaken corner of Yugoslavia or Turkey, practically penniless but rolling merrily along in their little Citroëns? Or the bored, flabby ladies of the Club Méditerranée? And even within this club (one of the spectacular financial successes of the last ten years), who is the more real? The young doctor or engineer who takes advantage of a highly efficient organization to visit Morocco, Greece, Sicily, Tunisia, or even Tahiti intelligently and at a moderate price? Or the small-time Casanova who goes chasing after one-night stands in every village in the circuit? (I said that this chapter would try to make up for the presumptuousness of the rest of the book.)

If it is true that we can learn a great deal about a country simply by reading its newspapers, then we had best glance at the French press for a moment. The experience will be equally revealing and embarrassing.

Statistically, the French press is weak. *Le Parisien libéré*, which is the most widely read morning paper, has a circulation of 850,000. *France-Soir*, the most popular of the evening papers, publishes an edition of 1,300,000. In relative terms, the more serious press (*Le Monde*, 340,000) and the provincial press (*Ouest France*, 610,000; *Le Progrès*, 400,000) are more flourishing. The magazines, even the big ones, have quite modest circulations, compared to their Anglo-Saxon equivalents (*L'Echo de la Mode,* 1,000,000; *Paris-Match,* 1,500,000). The politically oriented papers barely scrape along. The Communist party's *L'Humanité* puts out an edition of under 200,000. All together, the three or four papers of the extreme Right do not have a total circulation of more than 100,000. Even that pillar of middle-class opinion, the venerable and cautious *Figaro,* which is rich in advertising, publishes an edition of only 500,000 copies.

But figures do not tell the whole story. Can one draw any general conclusions about this chronically jittery press, which is always on the brink of some crisis or other and is always casting about for ways to rejuvenate itself?

Let us say, broadly, that stability (*Figaro* and the provincial papers) and seriousness (*Le Monde, Le Nouvel Observateur*) pay off. A certain youthful dash (*Elle, L'Express*) has proved profitable between 1950 and the present, but it seems time now to replace polemics with objectivity and jokes and striking pictures with a more reassuring and classical tone.

Magazines such as *Elle* and *L'Express* exercised tremendous influence on women and on the opinions of the new bourgeoisie of technicians, especially from 1953 to about 1962. *Elle* taught Frenchwomen how to dress better, improve their personal hygiene, and examine their prejudices. *L'Express* was the bible of young people between eighteen and thirty-five who put a premium on style and taste and sound political feeling. But in 1966, sixteen-year-old girls were reading new publications that glorify jazz, popular singers, and adolescence. Forty-year-old women now prefer the conventional evening gowns and the gilded living rooms of *Jours de France* to *Elle*'s novelties. The ex-young men, now turned forty and dreaming of someday becoming general manager of their corporation, are dismayed by the pastiche of *Time* and *Der Spiegel* that *L'Express* of their youth has become.

Here again, to our consternation, all variations coexist: the popular successes (*Jours de France, Minute*), the juvenile successes (*Salut les copains*), the stability of old papers (*Figaro*), the steady growth of the serious (*Le Monde*), the prosperity of the noisily nonsensical (*France-Dimanche*). It is impossible to draw any clear conclusions from this tour of our press, and at most I may venture a few observations. In France, it is hard to keep alive intelligent and polished magazines, such as *The New Yorker* and *Esquire*. It is hard to keep big newspapers going that are at once serious and independent, critical and worthy of respect. In France, criticism is rather a matter of opinion; it quickly becomes polemical and therefore lacks authority. And finally, with perhaps two or three exceptions, the recent journalistic trend has been to cater to public taste rather than to offer it something better than what it apparently wants.

For a long time, and especially from 1952 to 1960, the French press has been bedeviled by censorship, confiscation, and politically inspired lawsuits brought against it by successive governments, and indirectly somewhat paralyzed by the state's monopolistic control of television. As a result, since about 1944 it has not managed to make itself felt as a powerful political or moral force. It has talented and courageous people at its disposal (Hubert Beuve-Méry, Hélène Lazareff, Raymond Cartier, Raymond Aron, Jean Daniel, Pierre Lazareff, Françoise Giroud), but it has been unable

169

to establish among itself, the government, and the public that constant interchange of news (and news officially withheld), evaluation, and comment which could constitute real progress in democracy and in public attitudes.

Because the French read very little and waver between credulity and distrust when confronted by the printed word, the press lacks readers, vigor, and, at times, ambition. Its international horizon is still narrow, and it is too much taken up with polemics and local affairs. If indeed the press is a mirror faithfully reflecting the French, then one still detects too much puttering, provincialism, and imitativeness. On the other hand (and this is no small compliment), ravages of conformity are infinitely less noticeable than are the benefits of freedom. You can write whatever you wish in France (since the end of the Algerian war, in 1962, government pressure on the press has been rare), though not always exactly where you might wish. Those who are dismayed by the inadequacies noted here can always join the 340,000 daily purchasers of *Le Monde,* which is still one of the good newspapers in the West.

ELSEWHERE I HAVE SPOKEN of the cultural inflation (at least in words, if not in taste and competence) that afflicts the idea the French entertain of France. It was long held to be self-evident that geniuses teemed among us and that Paris offered unrivaled hospitality to artists. In short, the French had some innate, unchallengeable predisposition that validated the equation Talent+Beauty+Aesthetic Sensitivity=France.

Let us skip the question of talent, which varies from decade to decade. Beauty I discuss elsewhere. So there remains the matter of sensitivity, aesthetic taste, and the regard the

French have for the creative people among them. How do we really stand on these points?

Probably the mistakes perpetrated between 1850 and 1914 by middle-class taste, the philistine irony with which Impressionist painting, in particular, was received, the astounding position won in the space of fifty years by work that had been derided earlier, and the tardy official recognition accorded gifted men (for example, the Nobel Prize to André Gide) —probably all these things have given Frenchmen today a bad conscience, with complications. The complications stem from the fact that the hope of speculating on the art market simmers side by side with the wish to be up-to-date, and a shameful confession that one is bored dares not compromise one's conformity in admiring whatever is in vogue. This is why some people rally round the talents that are currently "in." They are afraid that otherwise they will seem stupid.

"The "real" Frenchman—is he the big middle-class collector? The rich dentist who loves Bernard Buffet and reads Françoise Sagan? The grumbling Leftist teacher who swears by sociology and the New Novel? The student who devours paperbacks? The student who never opens a book? The elderly lady music lover of the Sunday-afternoon concerts? The man who buys LP's and never listens to them? Is he one of the ten thousand lovers of good literature? One of the three hundred thousand purchasers of the annual Goncourt Prize novel? The haunter of antique shops and the Flea Market? The subscriber to *L'Oeil*? Is he the museum champion who knows the Uffizi and the Prado the way others know the Metropolitan? The Parisian who dines out and is up on the week's literary gossip? The wife of the small-town lawyer who has read forty good books in a year but forgets to brag about it? The man who "has heard it said" or the man with an opinion? Is he the avant-garde fanatic or the man who longs for the bygone days when "at least they knew how to paint" —or write or compose or sculpt?

Having said that the average Frenchman cares little for music, is indifferent to sculpture, reactionary in his taste in painting, and only a small consumer of contemporary books, will we have moved ahead with our inquiry?

Is it true that our schools tend to freeze artistic creativity in boredom and academism? That our everyday life leaves little room for inventiveness? That our parents and teachers are so overwhelmed with respect for museums that they cannot guide ther children intelligently? Is our mistrust of "what is being done today" stronger, at all levels, than our snobbish infatuation with it? This snobbishness is less dynamic than would be a spontaneous, confident joy in the artistic creations of our time. A Chagall ceiling at the Opéra or the Maillol statues in the Tuileries provoke heated arguments because public opinion is not at all prepared to go along with Chagall and Maillol, reassuring as they should be. An avant-garde writer (even a writer of yesterday's avant-garde) becomes a celebrity (photographs, anecdotes, eccentricities in dress, gossip, etc.) more easily than a writer who is read by twenty thousand people. Without having listened to ten minutes of Pierre Boulez's music, the public becomes passionately excited over his wrangles with the authorities. And so it goes.

Respect, even superstitious regard, for artists is the rule in France, but unfortunately their works do not receive commensurate attention. The artist is permitted almost anything —unorthodox morals, eccentricities, provocative behavior of all kinds. He is protected by a nimbus of prestige and innocence. Even misdemeanors that would land anyone else before a judge are tolerated in his case. However, this generosity does not presuppose any aesthetic communion or even any intellectual solidarity with him. The artist is a great sorcerer. Great-granddaddy laughed at the sorcerers of his day; for this imprudence he was called a boor and deprived his heirs of several million francs. We aren't going to get caught like that. Who would dare say the Picasso canvas that people were still laughing at in 1945 is not *beautiful?* Picasso is sacred. In fact, for many he is the symbol of the sanctification of works of art for which those same people couldn't care less. The real Frenchman lacks any intuitive sense of what is ugly or beautiful, banal or noble, daring or flat. The real Frenchman grants the artists of his day a passport to the world of the sublime and the extraordinary on condition that he not be forced to go along.

IT IS IMPOSSIBLE, of course, to weave a harmonious conclusion to a chapter that is meant to illustrate the absurdity of its subject. Since these comments on the "real" Frenchman have been a series of sketches chosen to provoke reflection, let us now broaden the field and end with a small fresco. But where will we find a gathering of Frenchmen sufficiently dissimilar to comprise an illuminating sample and all typical enough to lend weight to the over-all impression they give?

Among a dozen other possible examples, I will imagine an informal evening gathering in the drawing room of a prefect in the *province.* As I see his residence, it is decorated in Napoleon III style. (Finer examples of this style are known to exist!) The prefect is about forty-five. His stiffness will vary according to his background; it will be attenuated if he comes from a "good family," accentuated if his present position represents for him the top of the social ladder. His manner is easy, though dignified. A touch of outspokenness or of caution reminds us of the ups and downs of an administrative career full of pitfalls. His wife is a bit younger. Undoubtedly, twenty years ago she married a man of "brilliant promise" for whom she was a "good match." She is, therefore, polished somewhat beyond the level of her present station. Practice in presiding over dull luncheons and official dinner parties has given her an assured ease. The house is decorated on the grand scale, a certain banality having been corrected by the hostess's taste, loans from the Mobilier National (a state depository of fine furniture available to high officials), the hand of a local interior decorator, and the addition of a few personal pieces. The ensemble may seem a bit ornate. The executive branch of our government likes its domestic "embassies" in the *départements* to be imposing.

The guests represent assorted varieties of social flora. The highest-ranking officials of the *département* may be present; a military man, if he is a "gentleman"; the prefect's *chef de cabinet* (young, with a keen eye and an ambitious jaw); a lawyer; a prominent doctor; perhaps even a teacher (provided he's not antigovernment)—all are at their ease here. The local business executives, who in the course of this or that scheme will eventually need the prefect's help, restrain the condescension that they, as the party of risk capital and private wealth, would otherwise freely express toward their host who, as the party of public service, is too much under the government's thumb and for too little pay. A few chatelains from the vicinity (yes indeed, they still exist, and their ancestral parks begin to be brightened by swimming pools) are trusted to add tone to the reception. In return, they will invite the prefect and his wife to dinner in their very historical dining rooms, a pleasure that somewhat relieves his administrative routine. If there is an artist or an intellectual around, and provided he is not a bearded, uncouth, or anti-social type, he will be invited. Millionaires, dukes, and artists are still the finest ornaments of a republican drawing room. We must not forget the children and the dogs. The former are almost grown up, and the latter shaggy and well-behaved. They will make a simultaneous appearance for about fifteen minutes at the end of the reception and confer on it the "happy family" note that cannot fail to please.

What is there in this imaginary scene that is worth noting?

Its naturalness first of all, its sober ease, and its devotion to the simple virtues of life. I purposely chose for my example (1) a provincial setting; (2) a gathering of prominent people; (3) a group that is involved in the basic administration of France. The *province* guarantees an easy-going, naïve tone. The middle-class element evokes the national dream of stability and security. And to choose as the central figure in the tableau a high-ranking civil servant is to salute one of our national myths. It may shock some to see wealth, tradition, and even talent mobilized around a representative of the state. Personally, in such a scene I would be more aware of the relative freedom and tolerance in human relations which it assumes. Notice that in this temple of authority which I have invented, no one is interested in the habits or secrets of the others, provided they are not thieves. A very considerable liberty obtains among the personages here. Although French society is burdened with age and custom, it is very fluid. Although it does not suffer from excessive imagination, it is not conformist. One senses in middle-class and provincial French life both solidity and flexibility, a tranquility, albeit within limited horizons, a rather quizzical awareness of being set apart and privileged. But before we cast our stone, we should weigh what measure of pleasure, boredom, generosity, and elegance could be found in a similar scene taking place in Valencia, Bologna, Stuttgart, Ghent, Leeds, Malmö, Lausanne, or in the country club of a Midwestern American city. It is not by chance that (in one of the rare compliments to be found in this book) I have stressed two qualities of French society which I believe have existed a long time and have remained virtually intact—freedom and tolerance. Above all, tolerance. If the obvious attachment so many foreigners feel for our country strikes us as a great mystery, there is no doubt that the quality of tolerance throws light on it. The spirit and the manners stemming from it would be equally characteristic of other social scenes that I could as well have invented.

What others? I could mention several that would supply images of the "real" Frenchmen no less real than those at the prefect's informal reception. However, other characteristics would then strike us. A dinner party in Paris: frivolity. A campsite near Saint-Tropez in August: vulgarity. A political meeting in the Salle de la Mutualité: fervor. A Boy Scout troop on a hike: foolishness. A factory gate at closing time: fatigue. A farmers' demonstration blocking the road with tractors: anger. On the rue des Saints-Pères, the students of the École Nationale d'Administration pouring out of an entrance flanked by two antique shops: ambition.

Frivolity, vulgarity, fervor, foolishness, fatigue, anger, ambition—are these feelings and qualities real? By shading them a bit, one could formulate them differently as brilliance simplicity, enthusiasm, good nature, resignation, incomprehension, cynicism. These are all ingredients that go into the French cocktail. My objective in listing them is to discourage too easy generalizations. What I have written here will not be pointless if it leaves with the reader a few useful notions. Which ones? My choices would be these: tolerance, frivolity, vulgarity, fatigue, and enthusiasm. Elsewhere I will speak of chauvinism, contentiousness, and that laziness we expediently term "philosophical."

CHAPTER XI:

Portrait Gallery

I F THE SCHOOLBAG of a French student were to lack a
history book, the bag would be empty. Our great passion
for factual history, for the dates of battles and treaties,
has been recently challenged, yet a French history text
would be held of small account if it failed to illustrate developments with documents and especially with portraits.
Ten centuries of our past are peopled with distinguished
personalities. They may be caricatured or idealized, lauded for
their lofty brows or held suspect because of their thick lips,
but the men whose likenesses embellish the ends of chapters
(between *Contents* and *Synoptic Table*) represent an inheritance of examples and anecdotes, a quarry where Frenchmen can dig for shared points of reference. Pupils from the
communal schools, sent forth into the wide world at fifteen
with a very small supply of ideas, and *lycée* students, for
decades nourished on the identical history text (written by
MM. Malet and Isaac and periodically updated for a quarter
of a century; now, alas, discarded)—all Frenchmen possess
this common capital which they make fun of, this language

which is at once secret and collective, these ghosts full of pride, torment, and daring ideas, who eternally inhabit the oversimple, idealized homeland about which our children are taught. These ghosts are the muses of the French elegy, the symbolic ancestors, the models, the foils, the depositories of several great—or supposedly great—traits of the national character.

I have chosen a few. Why these rather than others? Why not Bayard, Saint-Louis, Louis XI, whom Michelet so loved, Henri IV, Mazarin, Molière, Gambetta? Why not, halfway between the real and the imagined, and thereby all the more revealing, Cyrano de Bergerac or the heroes of *The Three Musketeers*? What meaning can an album of this kind have if it contains less than a thousand pages and a hundred portraits?

The few appearing here fulfill three conditions. First, it goes without saying that there are some who must be included; to omit them would be absurd. Second (with no duplications), each plays an indispensable role in the structure of our history. Finally, they all interest me. One can debate or enrich any such list, but one cannot deny that those who are included deserve to appear. The only complication that might arise would come from these demigods of French culture having been made what they are for fallacious reasons, or out of partisan passions. One ought simultaneously to ratify the choices, expose the illusions, and bring out the just claims to glory, these jobs being all remarkably intertwined.

HOW FAR BACK MUST ONE GO? To Gallic folklore and the Roman occupation? They are rather silted up in the sands of time. Like statues only half hewn from the marble, persons from that far back fail to emerge from the legends; they are swallowed up in the night of prehistory. On the other hand, with the dawning of the great medieval adventure, unique personalities and well-defined events loom large: religious faith; pilgrimages; the bright-burning flame of monasticism; the Crusades; that miracle of spiritual colonialism, the Frankish kingdom of Jerusalem; Provençal poetry and the birth of chivalric love; the first romances; the cathedrals. All our cities with their seven-hundred-year-old churches rising in their main squares! Narrow little streets twist around them still, as they did under Philip the Fair. Here is the heart of our cities, the hard core of our shared memories. The Middle Ages are the dike that buttresses our explorations and explanations of French history. Every schoolchild stumbles through a recitation of the *Chanson de Roland* and the list of the Crusades, sketches the rose window of Chartres and the plans of walled castles. Every pupil could be (or thinks he could be) the biographer of Joan of Arc.

How strange, amid the indisputable chronology of great deeds and battles, is the presence of this girl, burned alive at nineteen and whose destiny, unfolded in a mere three years, remains so stubbornly mysterious! For Joan belongs both to the school and to the Church, to the heroic chronicles of patriots and to the calendar of Catholic saints; her personality—so familiar, so exhaustively researched, so popularized in a thousand and one ways—becomes misleadingly simple. Amid the confusions of the early fifteenth century, her story defies explanation. Chosen of God, national heroine—the two roles smack of legend and compound our amazement. We have grown too accustomed to Joan; no one ever thinks about the short-lived wonder—really human and historic— she was.

Born in 1412; accepted, armed, and thrown into battle

in 1429; tried and burned in 1431; rehabilitated in 1455 but then rather forgotten; rediscovered around 1840 by Michelet in his *Histoire de France*; praised to the skies in the late nineteenth century by patriots who used her to whip up nationalistic feeling and prepared to avenge 1871; acceptable nonetheless to the republicans, who saw her as the victim of clerical obscurantism—she does not emerge from all this in a completely reassuring light.

In what survives of the transcript of her trial she seems to be transparent, a creature full of the grace of simplicity and fervor. At the same time the presence of a Jehanne des Armoises, resembling Joan like an identical twin, raises the ugly temptation to suspect some imposture. One is also tempted to explain the inexplicable, to imagine what "secret" Joan whispered in the ear of Charles VII at Chinon, which justified the King's confidence in her: bastard? daughter of the Blood Royal? The hypothesis is unsupported, but it is not absurd, and so the mystery thickens.

We do not have in France what could properly be called a religious cult of Joan of Arc. Yet it would be false to say that nationalism alone has placed the saint so high among our tutelary heroes. So? To Friedrich Sieburg's question— "Is God French?"—we love to answer in the affirmative. Between the darkness ahead and the lights from the past that guide us still, Joan, involved in both mystical and dynastic secrets, both saint and film heroine, flashing across that period of our past that is the best known and the most fully analyzed —Joan is a link between the kind of history we dream about and the kind we feed into a computer. Saint-Louis is an unknown quantity, a product of attitudes too remote from us; Louis XIV and Napoleon are almost close enough to be in our family circle. Midway between, Joan offers an illusion of innocence and of equivocal proximity. Like a little Christian Antigone, a serene, agonizing sister of all the great fighters and shrewd politicians who have built our patrimony, Joan looms on the horizon of our history like an enigma containing some mighty answer. An enigma too big for us ever to encompass.

THE FRENCH BELIEVE in all-powerful ministers, inflexible wills, hard workers, opposition smashers. From the long list of those who did great things, whether under a sovereign or at the orders of democracy, I propose two who seem to me strikingly akin: Richelieu and Clémenceau. Can we really bracket these two? There is no need for dismay. "I make war," Clémenceau said harshly. Richelieu might well have said, "I make the monarchy; I make France." Both men had to fight on several fronts. When the head and body of the state are soft, only a strong will can save the whole. Despite a weak and vacillating monarch, the cardinal conducted a state policy worthy of a king. The Tiger used all the remaining strength that an old man could muster in squeezing one last effort out of a nation already exhausted by three years of war. Each man had only contempt for other men, and each was surrounded by enemies. Richlieu faced conspiracies; Clémenceau, slander and ridicule.

The parallel should not be pushed to the point of absurdity. The lesson that the cardinal-duke and the old Jacobin *poilu* teaches us is the respect the French feel for strong and wily men when such men owe their power solely to personal character. We forgive them their intolerance, which is not a national shortcoming. We do not detest their brutality, provided it seems to be politically motivated.

The Frenchman, who is a mocker of authority and adept at avoiding constraint, always has a soft spot in his heart

for anyone who makes him toe the line because the job requires
it, but he is always ready to rebel against anyone who would
force his compliance merely by virtue of an official position.
A great upsetter and consumer of tyrants, the Frenchman likes
tyranny when it is exercised by an intermediary.

An evaluation of the two men's policies is not in order
here. Richelieu carried out two great designs—bringing the
nobles to heel and building up France, but he was guilty of
at least one mistake (attacking the Protestants) and of some
unfortunate excesses (too many executions hidden behind his
red robe). Clémenceau was always a fascinating personality,
but was he right in shifting from the radicalism of his youth
to the disdainful authoritarianism of 1918? Was he right in
raising the torch of his fight-to-the-bitter-end policy, seeing
that in the end we were undone by the too costly victory? No
matter. The cardinal striding up and down the sea wall
during the siege of La Rochelle, and the old premier slogging
through the mud of the World War I trenches are pictures
that we all carry in our hearts. We French are lovers of fine
poses, we are anarchists—but we quiver at the sound of the
drum, and in the case of such great lieutenants of the national
honor, we forgive them everything.

Clémenceau toppled ministries the way Richelieu lopped
off heads. The nobleman decapitating his peers for their
duelling, the parliamentarian unseating governments—this
pleases our simultaneously egalitarian and antidemocratic
tastes.

Their last moments were also alike: the exhaustion of the
ailing cardinal as they bore him back, dying, to Paris in the
scarlet litter for which walls had to be knocked down and the
gates of cities widened; the morose solitude of the Tiger
forgotten on the cliffs of the Vendée. These men of iron owe

themselves and us harsh deaths; the cable must stay taut to the end.

Mazarin, the skillful foreigner; Colbert, the rabid bourgeois; Carnot, the architect of victory; Jules Ferry, school and empire builder; Herriot, republican and man of letters—these are ministers who deserve our esteem and gratitude more, perhaps, than do the two I have discussed. But they have not passed into legend, perhaps because they did not sufficiently play upon the masochism of the French people—a national trait that must never be forgotten if we wish to understand who is ruling us, and why.

I AM NOT SURE that the French like Louis XIV. But we have been told so often that he was the monarch personified, that he himself comprised the drama of our greatest century and was the greatest actor in it, that he was the French contribution to monarchic theory; we have heard so much praise of Versailles and its Royal Sun, we have been so intoxicated with Louis XIV that to deny him a place of honor at our family party would be, in the true sense of the word, *lèse-majesté*.

As a myth, Louis XIV is overdecorated. He is a carriage overcrowded with passengers by the name of Racine, Molière, Pascal, Bossuet, Mansart, Colbert, Vauban, Louvois, Le Brun, Bruant, Boileau, La Fontaine, Mme. de Sévigné, Fénelon, Coysevox, Perrault, Le Vau, Le Nôtre, and even the acid Duc de Saint-Simon. Who could refuse passage to such a wagonload of celebrities, or anchorage to such an ark?

As the young king had wished, it was the façade that caught and ever since has held all eyes. Forgotten are the famines, the filthy hospitals, the persecutions and massacres of Huguenots, the youthful lawbreakers packed off to the galleys, the wars, the hundred thousand tax collectors. Versailles is the most beautiful palace in the Western world, but when it was built no one remembered to include toilets. What is this hygienic trifle in comparison to *Bérénice* and the great fountains?

Perhaps the French do not like the Louis XIV style, which runs counter to their feeling for restraint. But obsessed as they are with respect, are they free enough to realize this? Maybe when the *grand siècle* is compared to the effervescent Middle Ages and Renaissance, it is more sterile than it appears. It was a century of reaction and rigidity, of spontaneity frustrated. French society took on a Spanish formalism and was smothered in protocol; the letter triumphed over the spirit; absolutism was canonized. It was a period of war, boredom, vanity, grief, and, at the reign's end, sham piety. Between the days when the young king was in love with Marie Mancini and when the old king secretly married Mme. de Maintenon and aped her frenzied devotion, the mood of the century slipped into hypocrisy and gloom. Our most glorious sovereign left the country bled white; he died praying to be forgiven, praying that no one follow his example. In 1715 Louis XIV was harder on himself than legend and posterity have been.

He is the most celebrated of our kings because he has been the most "toured." In undertaking the thirty-one-year-long construction of Versailles, he was right to say that time judges monarchs by the buildings they put up. Compare Louis XIV and Napoleon Bonaparte: the emperor has the overwhelming advantage. He tried to put his brand on Europe; he so shook the continent that the repercussions were felt even in the waves of nationalist feeling at the end of the nineteenth century. He worked not to exclude but to reconcile. He left his mark on our laws, he projected his ideas far into the future. Compared to the conservative Louis le Grand, Napoleon seems extraordinarily modern. Louis XIV almost fossilized France. Luckily, the great stewards whom he had the intelligence to make his ministers, Colbert especially, spared him this historical bankruptcy.

By all the rules of logic, you would expect the French to detest the whole monarchic rigmarole: the court, the ritual surrounding the king's life, the royal household with its fourteen thousand military and civil retainers, the five hundred persons in the royal housekeeping corps alone (called *la bouche du roi*), and the huge, motley Versailles comedy that society was obliged to play. But when all humiliations and revolutions have been forgotten, the French still display a kind of ignorant deference for the least attractive of their kings; they are still tormented by nostalgia for absolutism and obsequiousness. There are recent examples at hand.

LOUIS XV, ON THE OTHER HAND, has had a bad press. He was a scamp and a rake, a lover of midnight suppers and loose women, a liquidator of colonies, an idler who deserved neither his pretty face nor the affection it at first inspired. All France could readily share the sentiments of Damiens, who, in 1757, struck him with a penknife. (Damiens was born in 1715, the year of Louis XIV's death, and thus almost ideally symbolizes how the disaffection of a whole people for their king could develop within a thirty-year period.)

But if his personality is not pleasing, his reign has many attractions. Why overstate the case against it? We always stress the high living, the girls the king lodged in the Hôtel Parc-aux-Cerfs, the collapse of John Law's credit system, the Treaty of 1763 (relinquishing Canada, part of Louisiana, and

India), but we pass over in silence the peace and prosperity at home, the flowering of talent, the urban beautification, the radiation of French culture.

In short, we may say that the Louis XV style was loved, the king himself unloved. And it is perhaps to the freedom of the period, although it was relative, that we owe indirectly the matchless ferment (Montesquieu, D'Alembert, Diderot, Rousseau, Voltaire) that quickened the French mind. For those who prefer prosperity to conquest, heckling to conformism, elegance to majesty, Louis XV remains the king of French vivacity and vitality. Versailles was intimidating, overwhelming; the Paris of 1750–70 was inviting and winning. Conversation became an art that swelled like a wave and overflowed salons and cafés; without that great spontaneous verbal effervescence, the creativity of the philosophers and writers of the period would not have been the same. Louis XV is the king of French chatter, repartee, the swift *mot juste*. He was suspicious of Voltaire, but it was during his reign that Voltaire composed the ten thousand most beautiful letters ever written in our language. The King was lazy, but his agents and provincial administrators put the nation on a prosperous footing and transformed cities such as Bordeaux, Nancy, Montepellier, and Nantes. He was a libertine, but Watteau, Fragonard, and Boucher gracefully ennobled what, without them, would have been mere wantonness. Throughout his fifty-nine-year reign, beauty triumphed daily in the architecture of Héré de Corny and Gabriel, and in the accomplishment of the finest cabinetmakers and ornamental ironworkers we have ever had. The style and décor of French life achieved a refinement that would have been unimaginable a century earlier. Ostentation was corrected, great open spaces were subdivided, dialogue and intimacy became possible. We may not love Louis XV—

but how can we not love the Louis XV style? The man, the monarch, is no longer in question, but the joyous, high-keyed, exhilarating fever that seized his subjects and made of them both the crowning generation of the *ancien régime* and the first generation to glimpse the new days ahead. Today we see things from the perspective of what followed; the early stirrings of catastrophe strike us more forcibly than the fruition of the old order's potentialities. This is doubly unjust— unjust to both the past and the future. For what was flowering was brilliant, and what was germinating would not be mediocre. Louis XV did not do things: he let things be done. Yet this liberalism brought us both a great, vital era and a great gestation period. We do not see clearly that what we love in Louis XV is that he was the pivotal king, a royal attestation to the days when our history was swinging from its old certainties to doubts, from proud lassitude to fresh certainties.

In that whirlwind of intellectual awakening and systematizing, of curiosity, rivalries, great accomplishments, and raillery, I believe it is in order to crown the prince of the scoffers "King Voltaire"—that tremendous worker who did not, as he believed, leave us tragedies, odes, and panoramic histories, but rather epigrams, lampoons, letters, a few stories, and the memory of his own stubborn courage.

We love Voltaire for a high-backed armchair that bears his name, a "hideous smile," a bad reputation, and the refrain of a song. We love in Voltaire the Bastille prisoner, the bastinado victim, the exile, the fierce defender of two unjustly sentenced Huguenots, Calas and Sirven. We love him despite his bad poetry and his business acumen. We love him because he was a great mocker, a great "destroyer" (his own boast), and an indefatigable skeptic—all reflecting precisely those virtues which the French mind needed at that time to loosen the hold of the preceding century.

There is a whole Voltairian iconography, which one must be wary of. When, around 1905, the wives of our subprefects were embellishing their drawing-room ottomans with church vestments to express their anticlericalism, they supposed they were being "Voltairian." They were being no such thing; they were being merely tiresome. One must take the man at his best; he was heavy as lead when he was being solemn, quicksilver when most himself. His quintessential attribute was irreverence. Even when he had become old and prosperous, his irreverence was wholesome and sound. After two centuries it has still not really aged.

IT IS GOOD that the severe face of Robespierre should briefly show itself here. I will simply point out that France loves now and then to indulge in a debauch of righteousness. The "pure, austere" republic like the republics of antiquity, an incorruptible passion for the public weal—we find such visions hard to resist. But alas, whether in 1793 or 1944, these lofty impulses take their toll of blood.

The Terror, whose soul and arm and supplier Robespierre was, seems for all its fury relatively innocent in retrospect. Compared with other civil atrocities (dragonnades, suppression of the Camisard revolt, recent colonial recrudescences), the Terror strikes one as remarkable for the clarity of its motives and the frenetic tension (dangerous even for its masters) of its rhetoric. It is, perhaps, a stain of blood on our history, but not of mud. More than anyone else, Robespierre was the impresario of the frenzy, blood-letting, idealism, and delusive visions of that period. He paid for this with a pistol shot, the guillotine, and the subsequent solicitude of radical historians, as was only fitting. Justice and injustice having thus been done, there is no reason here to smuggle this lawyer-deputy turned revolutionary archangel off our stage. His fanaticism counterbalances Richelieu's quite well.

PEOPLE VISIT THE TOMB of Napoleon in the Invalides a little less often than the Eiffel Tower but as much as Versailles. Publishers and souvenir manufacturers know that everything having to do with the emperor, from historical study to equestrian statuette, sells. A century and a half after his death, Napoleon is still the hottest item in our mythology. We really love him.

With him there is no fear of misunderstanding; we love him for the best of reasons: he is close to us. Close in temperament, for even his faults—grossness, impatience—are very French. Close in time, for of all our historic personages, including several still living, he is the most contemporary. Last and not least, he is close to us in his deepest impulses. Soldier, legislator, good writer, ideologist, snob, and a man of quick intelligence: Napoleon resembled the image that every Frenchman has of himself. Shall one be a great lawyer? Soldier? Republican? Monarchist? We keep hesitating. Napoleon rolled them all into one. The lawyer donned high boots, the soldier of the Revolution set up thrones and princes. A novelist at twenty, at forty he assisted in formulating the code of laws that govern us still, and he took time out to write some very beautiful love letters to the woman he did not take time to love. Briefly, and in perspective, Napoleon may fascinate M. Dupont, the average Frenchman, but he was no M. Dupont. He was very nearly a pure genius, the inventor and organizer of his own destiny, one of those men who owe virtually nothing to circumstance and almost everything to themselves. All our great public figures are either perpetuators or rebels—in other words, men who use existing materials, masons building or demolishing walls. Napoleon created out of nothing. He imitated no one, and he has had no successor.

The history of France is like a turbulent continent; Napoleon's resembles an island. A very large island, a little way off our coast. We have seen him being ridiculous—bedizening his courtesans, feathering his marshals, crowning his brothers—and we have forgiven him; the acid of ridicule will not eat into him. The Napoleonic epic left its survivors and its slightly dazed, eternally nostalgic witnesses. But the ship, unique in design and size, has foundered. After Napoleon, France was to grow rich, fat, staid, and sleepy. Never again would she resemble that entrenched position, that luxurious general staff tent. Never again would she march to the rapid, lean-rationed step of conquest. France has dreamed, and dreams still, of finding a master who dares all, loses all but the faith of his people. Among all the portraits, that of the little Corsican is supreme.

VICTOR HUGO'S was a noble life, a succession of apotheoses. Usually men dream of an ascending lifeline, of a final flowering. Hugo's eighty-three years amassed summit after summit. He was not a mountain, he was a mountain range.

He was born in the tumult of the Napoleonic wars, his father being a captain at the time. He was twenty when his first *Odes* were published, twenty-five when he wrote the preface to his *Cromwell*, twenty-eight at the "battle" over *Hernani*, thirty-nine when he was elected to the Academy, forty-three when made a peer of France. Whereupon he chose to become a republican. The success and the glory were followed by the bitter experiences of being a proscribed writer and an eighteen-year exile, by pamphlets, sublime poetry, and the pride of being alone and of being right. Napoleon III abdicated, France fell, Victor Hugo returned. Fourteen years remained to him, to be divided between political and poetic missions, the poems of a grandfather and those of a metaphysician, humanitarian oratory and love affairs. He was thus also the living symbol of the double life, the public and the private. And, at last, in 1885, came the state funeral, in which the pageantry was deployed around a pauper's hearse: a final gesture of perfect ostentation.

"Hugo? Our greatest poet, alas . . ." This dreadful joke did great harm to him. Some people are now ashamed to admire him. This wise man, this great bourgeois, this inexhaustible writer on all subjects—might not all this be a little inelegant? He knew how to do everything, and to do it well, too well. Isn't this a little fishy? But popular sentiment has not been wrong to endorse, as it steadily has endorsed, the resounding grandeur of Victor Hugo, a word king whose tradition has extended down to Paul Claudel and Aragon today. Democratic France—the France of public-school teachers and class dictations—has ranked Hugo among its great champions. Delicate spirits have poked fun at him in vain and to the speedy detriment of their own reputations.

They forgot the gold washed up by the torrent, the exquisite and masterful poems, the ringing prose, the heady shafts of sunlight at the end. They forgot the drawings; as a painter, Hugo might have surpassed Turner; as a visionary, he might have eclipsed Blake.

It is true that this thundering personality, all black and white and red and gold, appeals to simple people and jars on the refined. However, it is not in the name of the unsophisticated and over the protests of the cultivated that Victor Hugo is appropriately included in this little Pantheon: it is in the name of all, and to remind ourselves that the sophisticated are mistaken. It rarely happens that a creative man reaches the heart of the public at large, that he knows the secret of work at its highest level, and that level is also the level of the most humble and spontaneous among us. I have included no painter or musician here (the omission reflects our lack of creative sensibility in these fields, let it be said at the risk of offending), but it seems appropriate to close this review of our French traveling companions with a poet. Hugo, who so naturally offered himself as the beacon, the high priest, conscience, and guide for the French of another century, well deserves in our own day to be set up on the height surrounded by mists and lightning bolts that will remain this solid old Rhenish burgrave's impregnable position forever.

CHAPTER XII:

The Great Roles of la Comédie Française

I N THE REAL-LIFE COMEDY that all Frenchman play from one generation to the next, the repertory is aging perceptibly —as is the case with our symbolically named Théâtre Français. Some fine old roles have sunk into decay; ridicule and indifference will presently engulf others. Characters that only thirty years ago the average Frenchman wanted to resemble suddenly look like quaint, elderly mannequins. It makes one wonder about our children, who, in keeping with traditions as solid as the Christmas tree and going to the seashore, thrill every Thursday afternoon to *Le Cid* or nap through *Bajazet* at the Théâtre Français (the real red-and-gold one, with its grouchy ushers and its actors as truculent and snobbish as Breton squires). I often think how disturbingly unreal the "outside" world must seem to these youngsters when, as dusk falls and lamps are lit, they emerge to face the noise, the buses, and their nervous mothers.

The same sense of unreality closes in on us when we consider how radically French ambitions and roles have changed since our own childhood. It is a cherished commonplace that

Neapolitans are "born" actors; that from Bayreuth to Nuremberg, Germans have always excelled in staging grandiose Wagnerian spectacles; that the British play and listen to Shakespeare as naturally as in the days of the first Elizabeth. The arsenal of stereotypes is rich in theatrical metaphors. In the same vein, we say that only yesterday the French, standing between a casement window looking out on a garden and some gray chairs in what approximates a Louis XVI salon, were fated to perform in the melodramas of the middle-class repertoire. (They may find themselves cast in these roles longer than they suppose.)

The whole myth of a charming, antiquated, self-satisfied (perhaps also slightly inhuman) France could be accommodated in that Louis XVI drawing room. There I see the Graying Industrialist striding up and down, mustache drooping, goblet of champagne in hand. (Doesn't he appear still in the novels and plays of our utterly contemporary Sagan?) Enlarge the casement window, convert garden into park, diffuse into the air a hint of leather and stables, and onstage walks the Chatelain with his brusque language, imperious profile, and ruddy cheeks, unbeatable in hunting stories, irrepressible on the subject of family alliances, inimitable when chatting with the ladies. Reduce the salon to more modest proportions, and you will have the Prominent Provincial. He is a connoisseur of food, comfortably well off, a patriot, mayor of the town, general councilor, and maybe someday, come sixty, even a senator. Now add a touch of deliberate austerity and unintentional disorder, some Moroccan wall hangings, a tea table purchased in the casbah, some imitation Chinese knickknacks and paintings on silk; by thus evoking foreign tours of duty from the days of the Second Empire you will have created the lodgings of the Army Officer's Family. This one is not so remote! We might have thought that time had swept away such an antediluvian caste, compromised in the Dreyfus affair, decimated in 1914, impoverished by inflation, and disoriented by assorted military mishaps between 1940 and 1960. Nothing of the sort. Men we had imagined as merely shambling around the deserted streets of Versailles, lonesome old martinets with long names and small pensions, turned out to have had sons, brothers, imitators, as the fire-eaters in Indochina and especially Algeria proved to us—all with the same crewcuts and virile faces, who flung into the parachutist mystique and the spirit of the Western Christian Crusade the lonely aggressiveness they had inherited from their forebears. The tragic outcome of the Algerian war, with its intrigues and dissensions, in which honesty was often abused and courage often vain, belongs to these actors from another era. We saw the descendants of honorable old army families trailed by the police as clandestine members of the O.A.S., saw them hurled by the upheavals of our age from the respectable status of legends into passionate delinquency and notoriety.

Now arrange onstage a multitude of gilt chairs such as one rents for catered dinners, and you have the salon of a Great Designer, the mythical monster who guards the sacred pleats and hems, demigod of a race that will probably become extinct once Chanel and Balenciaga have disappeared, for who could imagine what beardless stripling or thirty-year-old female would dare follow in their footsteps? From the heights of Olympus and the social register the craft will descend into the street and into the hands of advertising men and youth. Now suspend a very official chandelier from the ceiling, and you may introduce the Young Embassy Attaché, destined to be an export item, and only yesterday highly valued as a romantic and conjugal commodity. Air travel, peaceful coexistence, and the telephone have relegated the elderly diplomat to editing his memoirs and led the young breed to dream of dabbling in steel or phosphates. The repertory is the poorer for the loss of these intelligent supernumeraries. In 1938, a fifteen-year-old boy could still dream of ambassadorships; today he would not even give them a thought, for he is obsessed with the need to play a *useful* role. One final scene shift: let the drawing-room windows open onto a broad lawn with a grove of trees beyond, and beyond that the misty emptiness of the sea. We are in a Breton gentleman's country house; this pale-eyed man of few words is the classic seducer of the years 1880–1920—the Navy Officer. After some farewell appearances in André Maurois's novels, in which he played the Lover, he too has vanished from our thoughts. Aircraft carriers and submarines do not require any Pierre Lotis who keep exotic journals and have a talent for drawing, but rather engineers whose cheeks are less and less likely to be etched by the salt spray.

Is anyone surprised that this gallery is composed exclusively of portraits of "gentlemen"? Châteaux, uniforms, old fortunes, and elegance—were these the only springs at which the collective imagination came to drink? No doubt the ordinary people dreamed of playing the roles of prominent people more than they yearned for the duties and triumphs of revolutionaries or trade unionists. But it is worthwhile to introduce some other roles and show how they also shared in the multifaceted middle-class ideal. The Farmer, the Gamekeeper, the Laborer, the Postman may be allowed a brief appearance at the drawing-room door. A few pleasant words are tossed their way, and of course the traditional glass of red wine is offered them in the kitchen. But they are obviously mere walk-ons in our drama. Other more complex characters, self-made yet resembling archetypes comparable to the Industrialist or Diplomat, occupied the thoughts of our fathers and grandfathers. The School Teacher, for example, that repository of primary and universal knowledge, of republican virtue and secular vigilance. His son would obtain two privileges: he would live in the city, and he would alarm the landed gentry. The seed of revolt could also grow in great houses protected by their parks. The thin, hot-headed, gifted young man who tutored the children and was in love with their mother comprised a classic but explosive mixture. A whole tradition and literature of the Tutor exists in France—the serpent that society unwittingly sheltered in its bosom. Julien Sorel could serve as the Byronic model for them all.

I would be inaccurate to devote too much space to these envious, angry, and threatening characters. What one dreamed of was a berth in society, an honorable position, and the possession, at last, of those external signs of wealth which denoted security to the keen-eyed revenue bureau and to youth's legitimate ambitions.

All these characters—the hunting squire, the retired colonel, the local politician, potbellied and demagogic, the café revolutionist, the militant school teacher, and the bitter socialist—all have gone out of style. The last specimens are aging and their last photographs are yellowing. With them is dying (has already died) that chimerical and slightly sour France of which the poets, the embittered and the naïfs, sang, from Balzac to Giraudoux, from Georges Ohnet to Jean Anouilh. Still, a few witnesses of this older era survive. Some portrayals are still extraordinarily close to us.

For example, one survival from bygone days—from the courts of Louis XIV or the two Napoleons or the social effer-

vescence of the nineteenth century—is the fascinating idea
of a Parisian Society. Despite all the social leveling, revolutions, scandals, and disillusionments that have intervened, it
still beguiles us. The gossip columnists believe in a *Tout-
Paris* (even if they are mistaken about its membership); the
mothers of young girls believe in car-racing competitions and
formal dances; theater managers believe in opening-night
audiences; public-relations men believe in cocktail parties.
Everybody has his "list," and the wonder of it is that the lists
partly overlap. The denizens of this common terrain, the geo-
metric locus of all snobberies, where all success, elegance, and
talent coalesce—these legendary people continue to cast their
spell over the French imagination (see the chapter on Paris).
The ambition to belong among these people busies French
heads by the tens of millions. The effort to make a place for
oneself in relation to them (and not only to make a place for
oneself but to dress, reside, and tailor one's manners according to their example and devisings) mobilizes immense
amounts of energy. So, although one cannot, without listing
the members of this club, describe them in detail, one must in
all justice discuss them *en bloc* as they stand midway between
the fallen and the living idols, between the old and the new
roles of our repertoire. Then, closer to real life and to familiar
longings (legendary but within reach, traditional yet attuned
to the times), we will be in a better position to review the
ten key characters in the contemporary *Comédie Française*—
being already clear that this is primarily a middle-class comedy.

No. 1 is the *Polytechnicien*. Notwithstanding his cocked
hat and sword, he is not so much dated as he is perennial.
He is not a relic of provincial conservatism, for he is too deeply

rooted in the nation; though the object of ridicule and flattery, he is nonetheless the man to whom each renders honor after his fashion. The modern *Polytechnicien* is no longer a student who attends a scientific school, Napoleonic in origin and military in nature, which was founded to supply the artillery with its officer corps. Neither is he the myopic, stringbean grind with egg-shaped head and flapping ears who appeared in caricatures some thirty years ago. For every ordinary Frenchman who has a son, the *Polytechnicien* is the image of Absolute Success. Just as, in theory, the ultimate weapon should make war impossible, so admission to the École Polytechnique with a high rating puts any young man in an unchallengeable position. A father whose son has been safely admitted can die in peace; he has propelled his offspring into orbit. Certain legends have become realities and will now *automatically* assure the newly admitted *Polytechnicien* a custom-made future. He knows that in his favor there will always be the famous mutual aid that the X's (in student slang a *Polytechnicien* is either a *pipo* or an X) extend to each other, the secret society of the math wizards, the Mafia of the equation jugglers. He knows, too, that the most powerful and munificent corporations will invite him to feather his nest with them, raising his salary tenfold. And that, as the facts demonstrate, the theoretical instruction of the École will be a prodigious preparation for him later to show initiative and assume command in the outside world. Even the irony that is heaped on the X's is useful; in a country that in certain periods of its history has known freedom of thought only via caricature, irony *consecrates.* One would suppose that terms like "key post" and "strong man" and "daring technician" had been invented to identify conveniently these protean managerial types who, from the heights of their success, from banking to the petroleum industry, from the steel industry to the Monnet Plan, cast their stimulating organizational eye over hypnotized France. But the *Polytechnicien* is not just an engineer called upon to shoulder managerial duties; he is the symbol of middle-class energy put at the service of technocracy and capital. There is as much magic as science in him, as much arrogance as competence. It cannot be doubted: the status of *Polytechnicien* clothes a man with the closest thing there is to supernatural power.

ACCORDING TO THE MYTH, the *Normalien* is a student at the École Normale Supérieure de Paris, humanities department. The title is enhanced by a proud diploma (*agrégation*) in philosophy, literature, or history. Originally destined to teach, as the *Polytechnicien* was destined for the army, the *Normalien* becomes a professor less infrequently today than the X becomes an officer. If he does condescend to teach, he is promptly offered the most desirable classes in the best *lycées*, before he is hastily given a university professorship. (One consequence of this snobbery is that the quality of secondary instruction is weakening while that at the university level is maintained.)

The *Normalien* is versatile and protean in the domain of ideas and speculation, as the *Polytechnicien* is in the area of technique and action. At this level, moreover, the two disciplines meet. Large private and State enterprises are permeated by superstitious respect for the diploma, and they tend increasingly to offer posts and power equally to the wizards with figures and the refiners of abstractions. What counts is intellectual caliber: mental agility, the ability to synthesize and to generalize, to which these prestigious titles attest. No one is going to waste these supermen by letting the one dabble in integrals and the other in Latin odes or the Treaty of West-phalia when fabulous futures await them in heavy industry, basic research, and politics. Georges Pompidou, a *Normalien* with a degree in literature, was successively a *lycée* professor (in Marseille, then in Paris), a Gaullist politician, a high-ranking government official (Council of State), director-general of a bank, president of General de Gaulle's Cabinet, and finally his prime minister. He is the most recent outstanding example of the *Normalien's* versatility and of the political opportunities offered in France to men with degrees in literature. His career may seem haphazard and erratic, but it is really a model of *Normalien* logic. While one finds *Normaliens* teaching in universities, of course, and in diplomacy, publishing, journalism, banking, and business, one may be sure that the twenty-year-old who has been "accepted at rue d'Ulm" dreams of a royal road that will lead him via the temptations of literature toward the certitudes of power. The three-generation social ladder I spoke of earlier still fires the imagination: the grandfather a teacher; the father a professor; the son a *Normalien,* then deputy, minister . . . It is too good to be true, and it is too true to be forgotten. From Herriot to Cardinal Beaudrillart, from Jean Giraudoux to the Nazi journalist Brasillach (executed in 1945), from Henri Bergson to the Gaullist banker Pompidou—the spectrum of destinies is too broad and too brilliant not to beguile ambitious men. And all the more so because here caste does not prevail. Elsewhere in France it is so important to "belong," to have been brought up in a certain milieu; there is an osmotic handing down of privilege from father to son, from family to children. But in the case of the École Normale it is not necessary to belong to anything, either to get in or to prosper there. There may be dynasties of diplomats, famous medical men, Inspectors of

Finance, and so on, but not of *Normaliens*. Appearances notwithstanding, the French social and university system is undemocratic and subtly closed to the nonbourgeois, but here it opens its doors wide—to workers, grinds, scholarship holders, all deserving young men—and owes perhaps a little of its popularity to a liberalism tempered only by the redoubted requirements of its diploma.

IN RECENT YEARS, a few words have come to sound like synonyms to the public ear: a high government official, an upper-echelon civil servant, a technocrat. The ordinary Frenchman confusedly senses here the real competence and authority, the rather mysterious ideas that affect his own future, sweeping plans, broad intelligence, a concept of the state and of the economy forged in the recesses of quiet offices by men both hungry for power and devoted to the public weal, calculating and disinterested. Among fathers who have "made it," the most intelligent dream of such a future for their sons. Why? Because it carries on a venerable fact of life in France and because it is well in accord with things as they are now and will be.

It is a truism that it was the great public servants of the kings who saved and prolonged the monarchy. Also, in Napoleon's immense effort to invent a modern state he took care to preserve and adapt the functions of the administrative cadres of the *ancien régime*. Finally, it is obvious that the chief civil servants of the Third and Fourth Republics, who were the direct heirs of those earlier men, worked in obscurity and behind the harrowingly disjointed façade of governmental instability to insure the continuity of government business. "Ministers come and go, the state services remain," was for seventy-five years the somewhat bitter reassurance. While

France's governments scarcely governed, her ranking officials, members of the civil services and executives in her ministries, administered the nation and guaranteed its survival. A probity and responsibility developed then which remain to our credit. It did happen, of course, that when confronted by political chaos, demagoguery, and folly, these men were tempted to tighten their hold on the country more firmly. Between 1940 and 1943, Marshal Pétain was surrounded by technocrats—big businessmen, actually, rather than senior civil servants, who thought that through a combination of public lassitude and their own hunger for hidden power they could exploit the national defeat and control the nation. History was not on their side. The so-called synarchists (because of their shared point of view, christened "synarchism," a half-real, half-occult theory by which an inner ring of men would rule the country) were unable to compromise the civil-service caste for any length of time. Once the revolutionary illusions of the Liberation were over, the members of the great public services quickly regained their positions in the state apparatus and their niche in the national saga. Inspectors of Finance, councilors of state, councilors to the auditor's office, senior officials in the ministries: they were sometimes harnessed to their usual tasks, sometimes "detached" and sent on special missions, parachuted into this ministerial cabinet or that nationalized industry, into a newly created state agency or an international organization. Expert advisers, anonymous and ubiquitous, adaptable, imperious, all speaking the same language, all coming from the same middle-class background, ambitious yet disinterested, fervent intellectuals but pragmatic men, their hold over France became stronger than ever.

Gaullism, suspicious of political parties, scornful of politicians (if they were not on its side), and indifferent to ide-

ologies has offered the technocrats their biggest chance since
Louis XIV. (There were, of course, technocrats before there
was the word "technocracy.") Inspectors of Finance have become ministers of finance or of foreign affairs; top civil servants have replaced politicians right and left. Whereas the
elected official perpetually blackmails the executive, the civil
servant is icily submissive to the best interests of the state,
having been trained to that end. Ministers no longer pirouetted
and promised, trembled and temporized; they ran their ministries. It bespoke discernment (probably derived from his
military experience) on the part of the president of the Republic that he did recognize the efficiency and the social reality of
this element in French life and that he placed the tools (if
not the strategy) of government in the hands of men who
were capable of using them.

Since all these important bourgeois careers are nurtured
in the schools, it is appropriate to speak here of the École
Nationale d'Administration. The E.N.A. was born in 1945, in
response to a wish to democratize public service and to prevent
the formation of *de facto* dynasties within the public services.
Has the E.N.A. fulfilled its mission? The problem was to put an
end to the snobbery and favoritism of the old École des Sciences
Politiques and to revise the qualifying procedure for admission to the civil services, which had been virtually colonized
(from father to son, uncle to nephew) by men whose style of
life, dress, speech, private fortunes, and family alliances guaranteed both status and distinction. The men who will form
our future administrative cadres have been burdened by a few
supplementary competitive requirements and examinations, but
they now benefit from the *esprit de corps* of their school and
have, on the whole, gained rather than not from the 1945 reform. The door has remained wide open for the traditional

recruits, and is more open than before to a few newcomers (officials with good performance ratings are admitted, after ten years of service, to try their chances in a less "elegant" entrance competition). The spirit has somewhat altered: there is less emphasis on chic and more on technical competence; less social life (a very little less) and a great deal of serious, voracious ambition.

To some the technocrat, whether from the Polytechnique, the Normale, some other university, or the E.N.A., is a chilly monster who lives on files and abstractions, and who is determined, no matter what the cost, to bend reality, despite its "human factors," to his conception of what France should be. To others he is the symbol of an effective nation, a nation that is preserving its customs and modernizing them at the same time; he is the competent, realistic, flexible man whom we need if we are to escape once and for all from the mists of our abstract principles and our demagoguery.

Whether the glacial manager of the "best of all worlds" or the instrument of a republic that is adult and creative at last, this upper-echelon civil servant more than ever haunts the dreams of the better neighborhoods. He is feared, respected; one tries to speak his language and copy his style. He holds the key to real power, one feels, and he will wring the necks of the various specters of Balzacian romanticism. Actually, he may be in the process of inventing a new romanticism, in modern dress. And why not?

NOW FOR THE PRIMA DONNAS. From our rather large collection, I will choose two: first, the famous writer; second, the medical demigod, surrounded by students and immersed in scientific academies and conventions, whom we call a *grand patron,* or "big wheel." (In passing, I may say that France has made much fun of yesterday's American passion for "the biggest [whatever] in the world," but in France the adjective "big" is very important. We say the *"grande bourgeoisie,"* and we speak of a *"grand genre"* and *"grand dîner"*; our nation is small, but its elegancies always seem tainted with "bigness.")

The big writer to whom everything is allowed is one of our familiar folkloric figures. In a nation where immorality (a predilection for boys or for little girls) torpedoes a politician, where stealing ruins any reputation, where extravagance is viewed with disfavor, and extreme opinions are increasingly unacceptable, the literary man can, on the contrary, permit himself anything. He can be a homosexual or erotomaniac (and boast of it); he can have done a stint in prison (and wax poetic over it); he can threaten society with destruction and damnation (and dine out regularly); he can be dirty, insolent, badly dressed, foul-mouthed—talent confers on him a permanent guarantee of impunity. The more he shout and shoves, the better people like it. For him it is almost impossible to create a scandal; amused indulgence smothers every attempt he makes and a delighted murmur drowns out all his vociferations. Decorated, received by the best families, welcomed into the Academy, the famous writer is one up on almost any other prominent figure. The vague distrust or disdain that surrounds him in Anglo-Saxon nations, the social and political isolation to which he is confined by elegant society in Italy and Spain—the writer in France knows nothing of this. Even if he is poor (or ostentatiously out at elbow), he is accepted and feted. He is a star. A leading character in the play. In the eyes of some young people with a smattering of talent, he is *the* important person, the man who plays the role (in the most diverse styles) that one hopes to play oneself. He can be an anarchistic, yapping fellow who hurls defiance and insults at the world, or he can be well-mannered, discreet, and influential; both kinds get an equally good press.

The *grand patron* is a doctor in the Paris hospitals who reigns like a tyrant over his practice, his assistants, and his patients; to his juniors he dispenses honors and positions on a competitive basis; he accumulates prestige as a scientist, influence as an expert, social renown, and opportunities for making lots of money. This "big wheel" does not merely hypnotize medical students and provincial M.D.'s: he is a real power. He can obtain membership in the academies and in administrative councils and influential political circles. He can afford to indulge in hobbies, in marginal activities that may soon occupy most of his time. He is a mixture of competence, cynicism, authority, and success. Any Frenchman equipped with a good memory, steady nerves, and patience in jockeying for position can dream of becoming him. For it goes without saying that the real medical aristocracy at the very top of the profession is a closed circle. Here one is recruited as to a board of trustees, by selection from within as much as on the merits of a diploma. This topmost plane is a kind of jungle whose resident wild beasts, by the way, do excellent work.

ONE FORMERLY MODEST and respected personage won a few stripes of added prestige in the postwar years. This was the teacher (*lycée* level). Or, more accurately, the teacher who rose above teaching.

Alain, master thinker of radical France, Sartre, Simone de Beauvoir—a number of people who took their degrees in literature were teachers and, theoretically speaking, still are. They filtered into politics (on the Left), journalism (like-

wise), and other fields such as the social sciences or the *cinéma-
vérité,* which are more chic and amusing than teaching. From
1944 to about 1955, these people reigned over the field of
ideas—which was quite normal—and also over talent and a
segment of the press, and they set the style and tone of what
was "being worn," intellectually, in those years. The middle
ranks of literature, criticism, and style were invaded by Sorbonne people. This status was accessible to many, was virtually
free of social restrictions, and readily attracted good graduates industrious enough to succeed, shrewd enough to see
which way the wind was blowing, and too faint of heart to
venture a career that demands true creativity or authority. The
times are changing, however. The rout of progressive ideas
and the proof of their inefficiency, the rising tide of the power
of money, plus the natural swing of the pendulum, have
tarnished the teacher's luster. The older men, who have won
their glory or security, ruminate over their well-founded rebellions. Younger men make themselves scarce or look enviously
at other and more desirable sinecures they may some day
capture.

Which brings me to try to pinpoint the ambitions of the
average Frenchman in the sixties. It is not true that everyone
aspires to play a leading role. Many people are sensible enough
instinctively to prefer reasonable goals rather than will-o'-the-
wisps. The limited dreams of a society tell us as much about
it as do the trumpetings of its heroes. True, there are great
and dazzling visions, but there is also an archetypal average
hope, a standard for the ordinary man. It would appear that
the ordinary Frenchman, in this sixth decade of the twentieth
century, has a new and rather flattering self-portrait. He aims
neither very high nor very far, but at least within his limits he
wants to succeed. "Success" means being well off, comfortable,

indistinguishable from his more glamorous neighbors, and free of basic worries.

The average masculine ambition is exemplified by a man in his forties, energetic, mindful of his weight, serious but skeptical. Fairly rich, of course—or if not rich, well paid. He wants to own things. He could easily become the servant of those symbolic things—their master and their slave. He has recently reached the point where he is able to acquire the appurtenances of the great Western ritual of comfort and status display—but he does not yet have a relaxed feeling of security. For him the pleasure of possession is still inseparable from its anxiety—which is the fear of losing what he possesses. All in all, his ambitions are those of a *nouveau riche*. He wants to live in a good neighborhood in a house that will awe his guests, to drive a big car (ten years ago his dream car was small, backfiring, unpredictable), and to exhibit a wife innocent of wrinkles and children who are, as he says, "well adjusted." He wants to travel, to acquire a sun tan, not to grow fat, not to think about dying, and to put off until some improbable, wintry future the cancer or heart attack that will one day strike him down.

The average Frenchwoman's ambition revolves more than ever around the magazines. Eternal youth and elegance—that goes without saying. A practical, secularized code of morality. Emotional attachments, but nothing too "serious." A husband, yes, but first some good job in publishing, interior decorating, the antique business, or fashion. For a girl of twenty from a good background, the dream revolves around symbolic visions of herself: me as a stylist; me in jeans and stockinged feet, dressing a shop window in a mildly surrealist style; me selling alabaster eggs in Jansen's; me unearthing rustic chests in the provinces for an antiquarian in the rue Jacob; me supervising an art gallery; me hostess in a club, or selling dresses in the rue de Sèvres; me secretary to a publisher, reporter on *Elle* . . .

All of this is, of course, only for the moment. "Until I'm twenty-seven." Then, a husband, "well-adjusted" children, a big car, Spain, a modernized farm forty miles outside Paris, to the west, always the west.

Obviously, average ambitions are not exactly inspired.

A FEW TURBULENT OBSESSIONS explode against this background of gilt and gray. The poor do not have a dozen ways of escaping. Only two, since we are not dealing in fairy stories here—sports and entertainment. Boxing, soccer, cycling, popular music, the movies—these are the blue skies that arch above their prison. Such and such a famous actor was a butcher's errand boy; such and such a singer sold vegetables in the market place. Middle-class youth dreams of ski championships, which from the point of view of making money is a modest enough ambition; young workers see themselves winning the Tour de France. The luxurious extravagances of the stars of sports and entertainment have never seemed more fascinating or more accessible. Fifty suits, six cars, a plane—they may be earned in three years with an electric guitar or in ten years on a bicycle. (Only popular singers, champion cyclists, industrial magnates, and Cabinet ministers travel by private plane, and in the case of the ministers it is an emolument attached to their office.) Never had fifteen-year-old boys been able *reasonably* to hope they would be millionaires before they were old enough to vote. Now this is a fact. Do they win competitions? Does victory go to the best man? Not at all. It is like a lottery. The winner can be, by pure coincidence, the most agile, or cynical, or clever, or handsome. Never have adolescents been offered so many chances. Never has the fact and prestige of an award been so utterly divested of any moral idea. Not that the fairy tales on which the more limited young minds feed are immoral. No. They flourish side by side with values that were only recently respected or ridiculed (which is to say, in one or another way recognized). The great adolescent dream of speed, ease, success, and money is secular, earthly, aseptic. If Satan reigns, he has chosen to assert himself in a baffling, neutral way. Rarely or never has a generation of young Frenchmen pitched its tents so far from the traditional territory of the tribe. "God is dead" is already a hackneyed expression. The mere *mention* of God is in poor taste. Perhaps what we are witnessing is the first wave of uprooted Frenchmen, living in a land and a historical context that for them is inappropriate. Noisy and insolently exclusive, our young people have their own heroes and their own fashions, and they are moving far away from the old family and social mores. The sons of miners will brandish no revolutionary clubs; in the depths of the champion's pink Cadillac or the singer's white Ferrari, they will loll in the proud confusion of having more of the things they thought they wanted than they know how to handle.

One senses a pervasive mediocrity in such images. All this is not good, not very promising, in the old-fashioned sense that there are people who are worthwhile and others who are not—although what does "worthwhile" mean today? Far removed from dreams of chivalry, of war and glory, of colonization by sword and cross, and apparently indifferent to the temptations of "wine, women, and song," the French, young and not so young alike, believe hardly at all in gastronomy or gallantry, and not at all in transcendent values. Some tens of thousands are striving to win, and especially to administer, power. They are preparing the elixirs and creature comforts that will guarantee euphoria to the nation. And the nation, meanwhile, dreams its dream of "air-cushioned ease." She shall have it. The rulers are eager to give their subjects what their subjects are eager to possess. Have the preconditions of peace and harmony every been so ideally conjoined? If I have chosen to round out my portrait gallery with pictures of sports champions and saccharine four-color blow-ups of entertainment idols, this is not merely a personal opinion. I am weighing my words when I say that never have the French so reduced life to its material and physical components. Is it because they are so free of anxiety? Or because anxiety is so profound that it cannot be acknowledged? How is one to say, without becoming either overlyrical or overindignant? It always used to seem that an ideal concept of life called for some metaphysical basis, some suprapersonal principle. As of now, however, and speaking for the majority, it seems that the French have almost managed to purge their covetousness of fear and to expunge from life any fear of death. Walk about, look, listen, read. This is the incredible evidence thrust upon you.

CHAPTER XIII:

The French and All Those Others

F OR THE FRENCHMAN, the realm of "other people" begins
very close to home—at his neighbor's doorstep, to be exact.
I do not know that any nation or language aside from our
own has invented a tautology to designate a stranger. "A
stranger who is not from these parts" is how people in our
villages used to refer (and not very long ago) to the resident
of an adjacent *département.*

In France, it was, and still is, usual to hear a city or a
region characterized by the circumspection of its inhabitants.
"Bordeaux people are proud," or "People in Lyon are distant," or "Lille is a very strict city," or "Bretons are always
suspicious." Every Frenchman feels, it seems, that the rest of
France is reticent and cold. And if to such local reputations
you add the great North-South division—the patronizing smile
with which every Northerner looks on the man from the
Midi, the slightly irritated and ironic astonishment that the
Southerner exhibits toward anyone from "north of the Loire"—
then you have some idea of the crosshatching of prudence and touchiness which has long governed the relation-

ships of the French among themselves. Differences have been attenuated by travel, the speed of communications, and the scope of the rural exodus to Paris and other cities. But the spirit remains; each family tends to be autarchic, each village has its little local patriotism—which amounts to denigrating other villages.

Cities are not free of this vice, but there it becomes aloofness. In Paris you can live for twenty years in an apartment house in a good residential area and never become acquainted with, and even scarcely speak to, a neighbor you meet regularly in the elevator or on the stairs. In poorer sections of the city, people will meet every day for years on end and chat, yet will never stop addressing each other ceremoniously as "Monsieur" and "Madame". One must turn to fashionable society or to the generation that is twenty today to hear the first names and familiar forms of address that elsewhere—in America and Italy, for instance—crop up in the first few minutes after meeting. Even the fashionable use of *"tu"*—our familiar form of "you"—and addressing others by their first name only, or by their last name only, which is now the rage in Paris among a couple of thousand people, expresses snobbery rather than intimacy. This ostentatious familiarity is pleasurable proof to the speaker and those whom he addresses that they all "belong," that they are all embarked on the same luxury cruise together; the names that they drop are really passwords. One could easily dissect this practice and expose the actual coldness, social scheming, and fear of being "dropped" that underly it.

THE MIDDLE-CLASS FAMILY—that fortress of tradition, that archetype in the dreams of some six generations of Frenchmen—was and to a lesser degree still is very much an enclave, a place in which to cultivate mistrust and let the seeds of misanthropy take root. Vanity, fear of other people, a readiness to despise or envy others from afar: even today these create the rarefied atmosphere which is French wariness. Fifty years ago French parents readily addressed their children with the formal *"vous."* It is still used in some families when children address their parents, or the parents each other. Traditionally, the home has been closed to the outside world and often still is. It is hard to disentangle in this what is arrogance and what is timidity, whether it is a sense of superiority or fear of a strange eye. One must never forget that even quite well-to-do French people have lived for a long time in surroundings that were ugly and uncomfortable almost to the point of squalor. (It is a revelation to visit apartments in Paris with an eye to buying one. You discover crumbling walls and a simplicity bordering on poverty, which are acceptable to people who in other respects live well.)

French squeamishness did not go so far as to correct the discomfort or to clean up ugly homes and make them attractive, but it was disturbing to have to display the truth for all to see. There is always a touch of shame in the haste with which a Frenchman shuts his door. The house and its furnishings—the background of daily life—are a kind of vague, unavowable family secret. The Frenchman who has been entertained abroad by people of his own social circumstances, who have opened their homes to him without the slightest embarrassment, appreciates and marvels at such hospitality. But he will hesitate to return it in kind when the opportunity presents itself. He would be humiliated to have to expose a style of life unworthy of his guests, his own means, and his self-esteem. Foreigners who find us so little hospitable and who complain about how difficult it is to get to know French families should never forget that this shame is real and, in most cases, justified. These observations of course do not apply to that small slice of the worldly and sophisticated middle class which has always bestowed great care on its surroundings and taken pleasure in living in style. Nor does it apply to the newly arrived generation—the technicians of our expanding industries, new bourgeois in the full flood of social change—to whom the habits of a consumer society and the need to display their recent elevation have given the desire and the means to make attractive homes and to throw open their doors. Nonetheless, it remains generally true that away from home the Frenchman lives above his means, and below them at home. Vacations, weekends, restaurants, a car—for the Frenchman these are the contemporary signs of luxury. But the home, the daily habitat, reveals his embarrassment and his acceptance of neglect and *laisser-aller*.

The Frenchman has never made a choice between the way of life at his northern frontiers, which tempts him, and that to the south, which makes him nostalgic. The former, with its religion of the hearth, its high rents, the smell of wax and burnished copper, counters the long winters of fog and rain with a passionate concern for the home. The latter, with its brick paving, scant furniture, and peeling walls, has conditioned people to urban habits, conversations on the terrace, and the evening stroll. The Frenchman does not display the passion of the Dutchman, Belgian, German, or Swiss for his home, but neither has he organized a social life in the open air, in the Italian or Spanish way, the agora taking precedence over the hearth. He hesitates between the two divisive influences, between Lille and Marseille, Alsace and Catalonia.

Sitting thus between two stools, the Frenchman has often botched his house; hence his reluctance to have people enter it. This reluctance is construed as hostility, and indeed to some extent has become hostility, although originally it was simply embarrassment.

TO THE CONTEMPORARY FRENCHMAN, determined to complete his conquest of stability and wealth, "the others" denote all those fellow Frenchmen who do not resemble his ideal self-portrait. Fringe people. People whom it is not flattering or agreeable to glimpse in the corner of the mirror when, with some satisfaction, one studies the reflection of what one is by way of becoming. The castoffs of affluence, the failures, or the obscure auxiliaries of expansion. They range from the Breton peasant to the bankrupt small tradesman, from the Spanish maid to the Portuguese laborer, from the ever-present Algerians of the road gangs and construction crews to the muffled-up, cough-wracked African sweepers of the Paris streets.

For our recent French affluence, solid or not, real or not, immediately created its disadvantaged groups. Having gorged for some fifteen years (from about 1940 to 1954) on their own misery, the French have now shifted the burden to other shoulders with an understandable but rather terrifying sense of relief. They would like to shut their eyes, not to see, not to know about it. This mixture of hardheartedness, haste to forget, and lack of imagination is of course complicated by a vague xenophobia and discreet racism. I will return to these, but they are not the principal elements. The principal element is the unspectacular, passive convenience of simply being oblivious.

What is the use of climbing to the top floor of houses

where the maids' rooms (now delicately called "servant quarters") were planned before 1914 without heat or running water and are left today in the same state? What is the use of verifying the sordid promiscuity in which Spanish hired help and girls fresh from the provinces live? What is the use, while driving on a Saturday along a country road, of making a detour to discover the immense shantytowns that reach to the gates of Paris and are inhabited generally by Arabs and the poorest of the newly arrived immigrants? (Eighty-nine shantytowns, comprising forty-two thousand people, was the official figure, according to a survey by Maurice Josco published in *France-Soir* in October 1965.) What point in making the rounds of the north and east sectors of Paris, to see with one's own eyes that the papers are not wrong when they intermittently denounce the scandal of bedrooms, cellars, and cubbyholes where four or more workers from Africa are crowded in together, there to wait, without jobs and almost unable to make themselves understood, for a good case of pleurisy to free them from the worry of how to earn a livelihood in this cold and noisy hell.

If the average Frenchman were confronted with the reality of this suffering and forced to look squarely at it, he would be troubled, filled with pity, and made to feel uneasy in the midst of his own comforts. But urban topography, official silence, and his own reassuring sense that he belongs to a decolonizing nation free of racial prejudice suffice to keep him in good conscience. Why be curious? New Yorkers living in the East Seventies do not care to walk along the Bowery; no more does the Parisian of Passy or Monceau want to venture into the Goutte d'Or or Ménilmontant neighborhoods. A few years ago, in November 1961, during the final and most confused, brutal months of the Algerian war, Algerians living on the outer boulevards descended one evening on the rich and commercial sectors of Paris—not to pillage or intimidate, but simply to testify to the fact of their existence. This created genuine surprise, even panic. And in the days that followed people preferred to turn a deaf ear to the outcries of the Leftist press, which criticized the violent, unnecessary measures taken by the police against nothing more than the silent, oppressive presence of these thousands of repugnant phantoms to whom France, in 1947, had rashly offered passports and the freedom to board a boat and disembark in metropolitan France to look for work.

The attitude of the French population toward its minorities is always equivocal. Peevish apprehension, mild repugnance—one must reach for words that express reticence or fear or a rather irascible impulse to turn away.

One minority group alone enjoys a privileged, flattering status—the Protestants. They number about eight hundred thousand. Once you have survived the period of persecutions, the fact of belonging to a religious, linguistic, or cultural minority—*provided the color of your skin is the same*—proves to be a stimulus. This is what happened with French Protestants. The state and public opinion left off maltreating them in the late seventeenth century. The Huguenots who had not chosen exile in Germany, the Low Countries, or Switzerland were proud, withdrawn, and very aware that the eyes of the country were upon them; they lived with a magnified sense of their own virtue and a nervous resolve to resist outside pressures. Congregating often in regions of great natural beauty and austere landscapes—Alsace, the spurs of the Rhône valley, the Cévennes—they gradually won the confused admiration of their erstwhile adversaries. Their industrial advance was aided by a profit motive less guilt-ridden than that of the Catholics (it was Protestant economists who evolved the theory and vouched for the morality of a rapidly expanding capitalism), and they achieved strong positions in commerce and finance. They established their reputation for probity and austerity at a time when, and with a class for whom, those qualities counted. Bourgeois among bourgeois, they have perennially fascinated and mildly intimidated other Frenchmen. The initials H.S.P. (High Protestant Society) are pronounced with whispered respect by people who scarcely know what the letters stand for. Some big industrial firms profit from the myth of Huguenot virtue; who can say what part it plays in the favor that the conservative Peugeots enjoy among well-bred Frenchmen? The "Protestant car" is what, with scarcely a glimmer of humor, forty-year-old French gentlemen call the Peugeot; it appeals to them for its lack of chrome and flashiness, its sensible lines, and the proverbial solidity that confirms them in their idea of what success is like. The idea that there might be vulgar or loud-mouthed Protestants does not enter the mind of the average Frenchman. In a word, within the national community, the Protestant benefits from all the prestige of "otherness" without falling victim to the mistrust that is instantly unleashed by ethnic differences. This is what I meant by the reference to color. What happens when we are dealing with a black man, a yellow man, or an Arab—that is, when racist reflexes come into play?

In 1959, when the Algerians had launched a campaign of terrorism in metropolitan France, two Portuguese workmen who happened to be chatting one evening under the Pont d'Auteuil were shot and killed. "What happened?" the police were asked. "We saw some swarthy-looking people in the dark, and we fired."

From 1954 to 1962 racial fear and brutality in France

reached their greatest intensity. Without question, almost the entire population reacted to the Algerians with anger and fear. It was the feeling of a well-to-do white majority toward a poor, dark-skinned minority, a subproletariat numbering some seven hundred thousand around 1950, willing to work cheap and, for the most part, drifting between strikes and common-law offenses in what amounted to total social and physical misery.

When the comforting statement is made that there is virtually no racial prejudice in the heart of the French community, we must not forget that the one time when that community found itself confronted with a truly heterogeneous population and a problem of major proportions, the response was one of fear and aggressiveness. Young French recruits could not have been permitted over a period of years to mop up, "pacify," occupy, and crush Algeria, if Frenchmen in general had not felt a deep and increasingly widespread and explicit racial contempt. If mobilized young French workers agreed (nine times out of ten without protest) to "beat the hell out of the gooks," it was because, in their factories and in the poor sections of Paris and the industrial cities, they had learned to look on North African workers with scorn or fear. If, between 1954 and 1962, the Communist party did not mount an effective campaign against the fighting in Algeria, it was not only that the anti-Stalin revelations of the Twentieth Congress of the Soviet Communist party had unsettled the whole ideology of the French Communists; it was not only the confusion that followed the crushing of the Budapest revolt; it was not only fear of putting the government in a position to outlaw the party; it was also that, once in uniform, militant workers more or less passively accepted "the long vacations in the sun"—operations in the Algerian hinterland that were spiced with a dash of violence and the agreeable sense of belonging to the master race.

So again we observe a typically French attitude: no great zest for aggressiveness toward others, but a mistrustful passivity that condones almost all violent measures and if there is a choice between protest and indifference, opts most often for indifference.

Let me note that for the Algerians our recourse to force paid off. It unleashed a repressive war that massacred some eight hundred thousand Algerians, but it won the country's independence. Also, it restored to the Algerian his dignity in the eyes of the French. In their hearts, all Frenchmen today recognize the heroism of the Algerian fighters. One stops despising people the moment one fears them.

THE SITUATION WITH REGARD to the Indochinese was different. The French did not have to wait for May 1954 and the battle of Dien Bien Phu to shift from a feeling of "white superiority" to one of admiring distrust toward all those whom they lumped together as "Indochinese."

Why? One need not refer to "ancient Chinese culture" or the "yellow peril," or recall Japanese victories in the Second World War. Well-to-do young Frenchmen had already assessed the Vietnamese in the persons of the brilliant and highly cultivated students who attended French universities in considerable numbers. Whether he was a restaurant owner in the Latin Quarter (and a revolutionary) or a mandarin's son studying at the Polytechnique (and a conservative), the Indochinese—ageless, courteous, elegant, slightly distant—conveyed to his French friends an uncomfortable sense of their own ungainliness and "barbarism." When extortion and violence were practiced from Hanoi to Saigon on the pretext of annihilating the Vietminh, there was not only a "this is war" feeling in France but also the fact that it was mercenaries and professionals who were doing the fighting on the French side, which allowed the prevailing French attitude to be one of vaguely disgusted indifference.

Considered as a whole, France was not guilty of anti-yellow racism. The one colonial nostalgia that afflicted the French—and it was a rather commendable nostalgia—was felt by the former plantation owners, civil servants, and even the military. They had fallen under the spell of Indochina. They had loved its natural beauty, its women, the finesse of its civilization quite as much as their quickly made money and their well-trained servants. For them, the "dirty war" was a frightful lovers' quarrel. Some have never recovered from their regret. Among the best-sellers of the last ten years, "Indochinese novels" stand high on the list. They express not so much a colonialist vanity as the confused fascination, compounded of sensuality, happiness, and peace, which was exercised over France by her most refined possession, the only colony (if one admits the century-old attachment of the *pieds-noirs* for Algeria to be somewhat different) we truly loved.

One unchallengeable sign of its privileged position is that virtually no sexual taboo ever prevailed between the Indochinese and the French. A young middle-class French girl who presented a Vietnamese to her parents as her future husband would certainly have met objections, but no absolute prohibition, because there would have been no reason to fear any profound group reaction, familial or social, against such a marriage. One would have anticipated, at the most, a mildly nervous surprise. (Obviously, this example refers only to a borderline case, and also an individual case. Single examples must not be taken as gospel truths.)

JUST AS A HANKERING for fascism constitutes a kind of tradition in French political life, anti-Semitism occupies a place in our collective unconscious that has not changed much in seventy-five years. Since the beginning of the Third Republic, in 1876, French opinion has always found room for extreme-Right ideology and agitation; good society has now and then fancied the extreme Right and its intoxicants: nationalism, the "strong man," "France for the French," and so on. This is more or less the situation of anti-Semitism; it is professed by a few overwrought individuals and the tiny factions that follow in their wake, and it is accepted in certain social circles with sometimes discreet, sometimes eager sympathy.

In the last years of the nineteenth century, the Dreyfus affair truly divided France into two camps. Basically it was a question of whether the quasi-religious respect for the army should force the state to cover up a judicial error on the pretext that the victim was merely a Jewish officer. The affair acted on the nation like a chemical reagent. It revealed the existence of two Frances. One belonged to the monarchical tradition and brought together army, aristocracy, a part—alas —of the Catholic clergy, people of influential standing, and all the partisans of nationalism and a policy of revenge toward Germany. The other camp, in the revolutionary and Jacobin tradition, attracted the intellectuals, socialists, liberals, and pacifists. A conflict that centered on the innocence of Captain Dreyfus pitted the future against the past, progressives against ultraconservatives, Zola against Barrès, the professors against the military, the more febrile attitudes of the cities against the ossified, nostalgic mood of the country, the schoolteacher against the chatelain and priest.

This schism, this chasm yawning between the two segments of society, is important. It constitutes the profound law and the inner dynamism of France; it lies at the root of many of her ills and quarrels. With every convulsion in French life one sees this division repeated. The two camps in the Dreyfus affair one finds again between 1940 and 1944, when the country was torn between Vichy and the Resistance, Pétain and de Gaulle; and again between 1945 and 1954, over the war in Indochina; and yet again, even more uncompromising and violent, between 1954 and 1962, over the Algerian war. You understand nothing about France if you do not see that while it is a great and apparently homogeneous social body, it is always capable of splitting into two opposing factions. Among the outstanding problems that testify to this, racism and xenophobia are probably the most revealing. The way a Frenchman looks at "other people"—whether Jews, Arabs, Negroes, or merely foreigners—is an entirely reliable clue as to what side he will line up on during the next crisis. All French anti-Semites, with the exception of some violently anti-German nationalists, stood behind Pétain and the French Nazis. And if the racial laws (decreed by Germany but carried out by French officials) and anti-Jewish persecutions were possible, if they did not arouse an indignant reaction throughout the country, that was because of the passivity, the toleration of crime, that corrodes the conscience of the middle classes in France. The yellow stars of David caused no feeling of shame. It would be going too far to say that France is anti-Semitic. It would be false to say that she is not. Anti-Semitism in France is endemic, prone to sudden outbursts of hate and violence. French society

—the middle class especially, for workers and peasants are scarcely concerned—is a soil where the seeds of anti-Jewish hostility can smugly develop. The French are not fanatics; they are content to listen to and, given the opportunity, to circulate "funny" stories or nasty gossip. You would astound a provincial doctor if you were to call him a racist because of his sarcastic remarks about "yids" or his comment about Mendès-France: "For the life of me, I just can't trust the fellow." Were you to accuse them *a posteriori* of complicity with Nazi crimes, you would astound the one hundred and fifty thousand people who, in a single month in the spring of 1965, fell on Roger Peyrefitte's novel *The Jews* and, with little shivers of appreciation, bruited about the pseudo-objectivity of what was really an insidious tract.

FRENCH ADULTS TODAY all remember an advertisement that delighted them in their childhood. There you saw (and still do, stylized), celebrating the merits of a chocolate and banana drink, a beaming Negro smacking his lips as he said: "Banania is sho nuff a heap o' goodness!"

The image of the childish black man, the brawny innocent, the goodnatured giant sharing in the general cheer for the greater glory of France and Empire pretty well expresses the superior yet warm French liking for the African. Relations with Senegal and French influence in Martinique and Guadeloupe, in the West Indies, date back three hundred years. Between 1900 and 1940, French imperialism (its apotheosis was the Colonial Exposition of 1931, in Paris) was peevish toward the Arabs, clumsy toward the Asians, but cordial toward black Africans. Basically, the French *love* the Negro, with a friendliness as little condescending as they can manage. They feel only a minimum of the sexual jealousy of the blacks and the fascinated revulsion for their alleged "bestiality" that have poisoned the relationships of other Westerners with the black man. The Senegalese infantryman, a soldier whom France used in ample numbers on the battlefields of 1914–18, was always popular. People in France laughed over the fear that legend claims German soldiers felt when they faced "our brave Senegalese." On quite another level, students from metropolitan France cannot very well fail to observe that their fellow-students from the Antilles speak a purer language than they, and display the kind of good manners that have fallen into disuse in France. When a Senegalese intellectual of the highest caliber, President Senghor, who is married to a Frenchwoman, says that he feels as if he were "at home" in the corner of Normandy where his wife was born and where he goes to spend his vacations, no one smiles. Regularly re-elected over a long period of years, the president of the French Senate (hence theoretically the second highest official of the state) is a Negro originally from the Antilles, Gaston Monnerville, who is also mayor of a town and senator from a *département* in the Massif Central. A few years ago, one of the stars in the riding competitions at the Étrier, in Paris—that is to say, a summit of snobbery and tradition—was a young African, the adopted son of a Paris banker, who was applauded when he appeared in the traditional white breeches and red jacket.

CONTRASTING with this idyllic picture, one could obviously cite a number of less reassuring episodes. Although the cities have become accustomed to people of color (Paris, the large ports like Marseille and Bordeaux, the university cities blessed with a warm climate, like Aix-en-Provence and Montpellier, to which students from abroad flock), the country at large is far from having achieved this liberal attitude. One could point out that "domino" couples, particularly in their more provocative form, black man and white woman, who are hardly if at all noticed in the Latin Quarter and along Saint-Germain-des-Prés, are sometimes followed by glowering looks in other parts of Paris. One could recall the difficulties students of color encounter when they try to rent rooms in private homes, or remember several incidents that exploded on the boulevard Saint-Michel during the feverish years 1958–62.

While all this is true, it nonetheless gives a false picture of the whole truth. The Frenchman, easily a racist where his Arab and Jewish "cousins" are concerned (we are all sons of Abraham), who are too close to him not to prove disturbing, has not had time to feel, organize, consolidate, and justify anti-black racism. One can account for this virtue. The closer the "other people" are the more quickly is racist feeling exacerbated. For Frenchmen and all other Christians the Jew plays a role in a very old antagonism. To tolerate him, persecute him, exploit him, and be exploited by him—all this is part of an old story, which is known before it is explicitly learned, which is absorbed from childhhod via books and the conversation of one's elders.

Black Africa was never a colony of settlers, like Algeria. It was the incompetent or daredevil sons that families dispatched to the colonies. When within the space of two or three years the Gaullist regime decreed independence for all black African territories controlled by France, no one made a fuss about France's multilated patrimony. Paradoxically, we felt no displeasure over seeing the "good black man" separate from France, whereas we pretended we could not tolerate that the "dirty Arab" should stop being "French." Probably relations between ethnic groups are really love affairs, and hence unleash many strong feelings. But between Negro and Frenchman, things never reached such extremes of passion.

WHEN THEY SEE FOREIGN TRAVELERS—especially Americans—flock happily together, go about in groups, and strike up friendships the moment they are far from home, Frenchmen are surprised or they wax ironic. They accuse non-French of lacking imagination and a sense of adventure or of being satisfied with a conformism that they, the French, allegedly escape by virtue of their well-known individualistic qualities. What about this?

Vain as the French are, they always forget how ashamed they are of each other. The Frenchman abroad is so pitiful in his confusion, aggressive in his behavior, uncouth in his comments, untidy in his appearance, dull in his responses, that to encounter the fellow is, for another Frenchman, like coming face to face with an unendurable mirror image. Thus, if he possesses ever so little sensitivity or national pride, a cultivated Frenchman abroad will avoid his fellow citizens. On a restaurant terrace, a beach, or in a hotel lobby, when he hears French being spoken he will take care to be stubbornly silent for as long as the risk of a meeting lasts. If he is not so fine-grained and feels the discomfort less acutely, he will—but with no particular warmth—surrender to the convenience of real French conversation devoted essentially to dazzling his interlocutor with the spectacle of his own efficient and blasé know-how. He will prove that he has visited more churches, traveled more kilometers, dined less badly but more cheaply—in a word, that he has been smarter than the other. The passing cronies of course will agree in deploring the absence in local eateries of the French national dish of steak and French fried potatoes, and in affirming dreamily that "their wines can't match a good Beaujolais . . ." (Let it be understood, once and for all that, except in the most expensive restaurants, the French are completely ignorant of the art of grilling a piece of beef, and that under the label "Beaujolais" twenty million Frenchmen are served daily a harsh bluish liquid guaranteed to induce stomach ulcers, heavy heads, and mottled cheeks, which came perhaps from Algeria, perhaps from Languedoc, which has nothing of Beaujolais about it but the name, nothing in common with wine except its appearance, and which contributes powerfully to a weakening of the national vim and vigor. Enough said.)

When our chance acquaintances on vacation have exhausted topics relating to food and money—the point being to prove that one has spent little (know-how), although one has the wherewithal (affluence)—they will respectfully broach the positive aspect of their travels. In a rapid, telegraphic code they will agree that Rome (or Toledo or the Parthenon or the Bavarian castles of Ludwig the Second) "is really something, after all." Then they will plunge into a brief denigration of France, as serenely uninformed on this score as they were ten minutes before when denigrating the country they are visiting. Most often they will admire trivial comforts—doors that close, clean public conveniences, efficient road signs, lawns around apartment houses—things to which French *laisser-aller* has evidently not accustomed them.

Finally, on a higher level of culture and patriotic responsibility, one last run-through will allow them to repossess their aplomb as Frenchmen, consumers of *"châteaubriands"* and connoisseurs of wine. They will hurtle up to the summits of architecture and refinement. They will conclude their dialogue, as the case may be, with either an "All in all, it's not worth

Versailles" or "Even so, I prefer Paris" or yet again—as crushing as the Battle of Austerlitz, less debatable than an article of faith, and permeated with the very essence of French civilization—some statement to the effect that "the *haute couture* of Paris will never be equaled" and that, furthermore, it "brings us in a tidy bit of foreign currency."

Of course, I should not want this mildly mocking thumbnail sketch to be taken for a thorough survey or these little anecdotes to be construed as a sociological treatise. I know that one would have to sharpen and classify and differentiate. In particular, one would have to draw distinctions within social classes and age groups.

There do exist Frenchmen, few in number, well-to-do and highly educated, experienced, widely traveled, who may be said to comprise one of the few truly civilized human groups the West can claim. But these people—businessmen who hop over to New York as casually as they shuttle between Paris and Lyon, rich amateurs of safaris and the Mexican sun, medical and university men who lecture and teach abroad and attend international conventions, artists who are more excited by an exhibit in New York than by an opening in the rue de Seine or the rue de Faubourg Saint-Honoré—these people are a thin gilt crust on the surface of French society as a whole; they are active, in step with the times, and have nothing in common with the "average" Frenchman except a passport and a language (if that). Certainly, if France remains an interesting and habitable country today, it is they who are responsible, but they are not the people whom foreigners meet on their travels, and they are not the people who go to make up the "average" person or the "average" quality to which all the bantering or distressed questions about France refer.

If it is true to say that an elite makes a country, it is equally fair and pertinent to say that, to the degree that members of the French elite are not involved in their country's derelictions, they live in it literally as exiles. At times a minority can function as the vital essence of a larger group; it also happens, alas, that an elite, with its will to go forward, may turn its back on the nation it cannot persuade or carry along with it.

The traditional "average" Frenchman with his little beard, his belly, and his decorations has disappeared from the gallery of international caricature. His metamorphosed successor is a kind of nervous Passepartout complete with his imposing D.S. —the most luxurious of the Citroën cars, today's symbol of the well-off middle-class man—his well-groomed wife, his nationalistic touchiness, his pragmatic approach tinged with militaristic nostalgia; for better or worse, this is the figure by which one should judge France and the French. He is the real Frenchman—not the aristocrat, not the writer, not the *grand-bourgeois* or the peasant. (As for the working man, he is striving with all his might, on the job and in his dreams, to become the man with the well-groomed wife. If one is to set up some French figure as a symbol, as a scapegoat, or as a witness—this is he.)

Candor compels another correction, which has to do with the difference between generations. The population growth that is taking place means that the increasing youthfulness of the population will entail a real change in the nature of Frenchmen and a new attitude toward their common heritage; so it is probable that the image of the typical Frenchman will undergo further metamorphoses. It is already impossible to mistake the fanatic vacation-club member, who is widely traveled and flexible in his morals, for good old "M. Prudhomme," who is a trifle ridiculous as he sets out on his once-a-year outing, his majesty weighed down by fat offspring and small valises. It is equally impossible to mistake the new-style junior executive—an aggressive, sinewy, athletic young man who talks straight to the point—for the provincial boss who is already on the way out, bundled up in his dark wool suits and his Principles, forever one revolution and one republic behind the times. The transformation is taking place right under our noses. The human material has already changed. How far and in what direction will the change go? It's anyone's guess. In any case, the young people who are now approaching maturity, who are naïvely fascinated by the gadgets the economy sells them and by a, to them, still rather legendary America, will unquestionably react differently to the examples, styles, and opinions coming to them from abroad. Chauvinism and xenophobia will not survive the experience of traveling and the chance to make comparisons. It remains to be seen whether that mysterious quality, overestimated yet vague, indefinable yet tenacious, by which the French used to recognize each other as compatriots and in terms of which they valued their national community will be able to adapt or will disappear completely, whether it can renew itself and survive all the varieties of ridicule that will be brought to bear against it and still not be pulverized and swept away in the immense mixing and leveling process which the modernization of Europe threatens to precipitate.

THE GENERAL OPINION people have of a country will be henceforth, for better or worse, a result of tourism. It is not businessmen or politicians but travelers who will voice the quick and rather random judgments handed down by the *vox populi*. Already, journalistic surveys and reports often merely formulate the questions raised by tourists or concoct simple answers to them.

France—romantic, picturesque, and cheap in the twenties;

chaotic but still picturesque in the thirties; impoverished but touching and picturesque still after World War II—the France of the tourists is now on trial. The rich and traveled West is now scathingly critical of what it once adored. French hotel accommodations and French prices work more to France's disadvantage than her supercilious, rigid diplomacy. Every year we receive not six million visitors but six million finicky inspectors and implacable judges. (In 1963, 1,100,000 Belgians spent 4,000,000 nights in France; 860,000 Americans spent 5,000,000 nights; 850,000 Germans, 5,000,000 nights; 860,000 British, 5,600,000 nights. The "nights" indicate the average length of stay.) How does the French population react to this immense, minute inspection?

First observation: around the first of August, when he sees the foreign cars trapped in the hellish road congestion of France at vacation time, or, better yet, when he watches the hordes of hapless, bewildered tourists carted by bus across a deserted Paris from the tomb of Napoleon to the prostitutes of the Place Pigalle, every thinking Frenchman murmurs to himself: "Those poor devils . . ."

Because of our pattern of vacationing *en masse* so as to enjoy the fine weather in August, the ordinary visitor is fated to discover French life at the wrong moment. He winds his way along the streets of a Paris of closed shops and suspended activities; his chances to judge us by hotel doormen and café waiters are far greater than his opportunities really to know France and perhaps to love her. If he risks traveling through the country, he will discover it in a feverish condition, overrun by belligerent road hogs and wailing children, the local people, meanwhile, armed from head to foot for their fierce war against the "vacationer," in which no quarter is given. He will join the largest contingent among the two million souls who scale the

Eiffel Tower annually, the million who visit the Louvre, the million who explore Versailles, or, in the more modest statistics from the provinces, the three hundred thousand more daring souls who will venture as far as Chenonceaux or Mont-Saint-Michel. Of us he will know only sleepy guides, the girls on the stages of burlesque shows, grasping short-order cooks, cynical headwaiters, a swarming countryside and deserted cities. After an average stay of 2.35 days—as the statistics (oh! so scientifically!) put it—he will return to Düsseldorf or Coventry or Houston or Ghent with a vaguely bitter feeling, happy and disappointed at the same time but above all confused; he will have seen nothing important, gained no insights, understood nothing.

Second observation: I have often found myself envying —yes, envying—the foreigners who have come to settle in France. I am thinking now not so much of businessmen who come to Europe for a tour of duty as of the painters, sculptors, writers, actors, students, or of the older people who have decided to live out the remainder of their lives in Provence or Touraine. Such persons, who come to France seeking a certain kind of simple peace or an opportunity to do creative work, really do find them here. Indeed, they are more successful in this search than the French themselves! There is a kind of special grace for these visitors; they expect something from France that the French like other people to expect from them. Accordingly, the French are cooperative and hospitable. Habitually distrustful, they open up to these foreigners who make an effort to speak the language and who, more French than the French themselves, sing the praises of crusty bread, red wine, Gitane and Gaulois cigarettes. If these foreigners go to live in a village, they are amazed to find how receptive the community is to them. If they live in Paris, they will find people grateful that they belie the stereotype of the tourist with his big movie camera and his small wit. These foreigners will be content to live in modest houses and in outlying areas. They will penetrate the real France rather than skim her misleading exterior. Rather than being the foreigners of the Place Vendôme and the Champs-Elysées they will become adopted Parisians of Auteuil and Mouffetard. They may perhaps have to be forgiven for fancying discomforts that do not redound to our glory, for playing too naïvely or indulgently at being French, for preferring the questionably picturesque to twentieth-century requirements. But it doesn't matter: these people will be happy here, and they will conceive—and later propagate—an idea of us that is vaguely archaic. Alluring, and too idyllic to be completely true.

Where is the truth, then, in this double-faced problem?

Bearing in mind that I have perhaps slightly overstated the optimistic point of view and painted a very rosy picture of the American artist come to work on the Left Bank or in Haute Provence, it would seem that the Frenchman accepts the foreigner willingly enough when he finds the latter's reasons for coming to live in France flattering and intelligent, but with all his greed and irony holds the tourist at arm's length. As a tour-taking robot, the foreigner is suspect; he is readily construed as a money-spouting robot.

However—and how curiously, typically "us" it is—although people will hope to fleece him, the tourist will not be treated obsequiously. On the contrary, he can hardly not notice how insolent, mocking, bad-tempered, and impatient are the very people who count on lining their pockets at his expense. What if he should happen to be received a little better, to be accepted? He will still have to detect the good will under a layer of surliness. An American journalist who lived

in France a long time, Mathilde Camacho, has put it well:
"But if what the tourist wants is an effusive embrace and servile
courtesy, he will be disappointed. This is not the French character. Independent, individualistic, and argumentative, the
Frenchman is not going to be any pleasanter to the tourist than
he is to his neighbor or his family. He will not be unpleasant.
He will be himself. He will start out by saying *non,* as a matter
of principle . . . By saying *non* first, he has shown his independence and the fact that he will do something only because
he wants to and not because he has to." Mrs. Camacho is here
calling attention to an essential trait. The Frenchman is a
grumbler by nature; he complains, he jeers, and he does not
confine the benefit of his bad disposition to foreigners; his wife,
children, colleagues, and neighbors are generously treated
to the same. It's nothing to boast about, but that's how it is.
Some of our newspapers carry special features saluting the
"Friendly Gesture." The garageman who does not turn away
the motorist with engine trouble and does not cheat him on
the repairs; the innkeeper who takes in late arrivals, feeds and
lodges them; these are cited as examples, congratulated, and
practically handed a medal. We organize "courtesy campaigns,"
"Operation Smile"—and it's a waste of time; the French go
on grumbling. Yet this intolerable habit of barking instead
of speaking can be matched by great dispatch and resourcefulness when the Frenchman finally opts to do you a favor.
But he will have started out with refusals and a sour face and
a reluctantly half-opened door; that way his honor is safe.

The tourist, then, faces the perils of a generalized aggressiveness. His appearance, his (supposed) wealth, his accent,
his hesitations, simply make him an easier prey to sarcasm,
ill will, and our I-don't-give-a-damn attitude. Actually, what
he is enduring is only an accelerated, aggravated form, prac-

ticed with impunity, of French boorishness—or is it only French exhaustion? For him the aftertaste may be more sour, but the rebuffs he encounters are one with those that the French exchange among themselves.

There remain all the things that do not have to do with temperament but rather with customs, conditions of life, and the national *laisser-aller*: the faulty plumbing, the dirty washrooms, the finger in the sauce, topics I will come back to. A good part of foreigners' complaints are addressed not so much to the French as to France. She is reproached for having grown old and, her official beauties aside, uglier. She is reproached for her decrepit buildings, lack of comfort, and, above all, for selling this discomfort and decrepitude ungraciously and at too high a price. All this is true; it is well known and endlessly harped on. The French themselves are quite aware of it. (Mrs. Camacho once more: "There was no time to lose. France must: build new hotels, smile, construct new roads, smile, establish *prix fixes* in restaurants with no unpleasant surprises, smile, put stronger bulbs in bedrooms so clients can read in bed, smile, install telephones, smile, put in plugs for electric razors, a carpet in the hall, smile, smile, smile.") Their erstwhile insouciant complacency has been replaced by scruples and masochistic anxiety. The nation shifts without transition from vanity—"our châteaux, our cuisine, our wonderful little roads"—to the depths of disenchantment—"we're the oldest, the least dynamic," and so on. The diagnosis has been made, the causes of the malady ascertained—but the cures are almost beyond reach. Our hotel system, for example. Its labor force is expensive—almost three times more so than in Spain; its welfare and social security costs are the heaviest in Europe—46.9 per cent of salaries as against 10 per cent in Switzerland, 15.5 per cent in England, 31 per cent in Germany, 35.8 per cent in Spain; and its tax burden is crushing—9.3 per cent of revenues as against 4 per cent in Germany and 1.3 per cent in Italy. Our excessive prices? It is true that Paris is one of the most expensive cities in the world. But, they will answer you, not more so than New York or London. A good hotel room in Strasbourg or Marseille costs a little less than the equivalent in San Francisco, and the same as in Brussels or Milan. Are such rebuttals convincing? Yes and no. No, because what France does offer for the same prices is offered less agreeably, and may not be as good. Yes, because often it is a lack of discernment on their own part that allows foreigners to be duped. They are wrong to confuse a glittering *brasserie* with a "great" restaurant, wrong to trust to high-sounding names of dishes that mask deplorable cooking, wrong not to verify the check, wrong not to explore side streets and places of more modest appearance. Not only do they spend too much; they spend it badly. The Ritz and the *bistro* frequented by people in the know (though the good guidebooks list it) represent two solutions, equally estimable but not equally ruinous. Between these extremes stretches the vast domain of phony ritziness, phony master chefs, questionable soufflés, and mislabeled wines. The domain of abused confidence and barefaced overcharging. France, very Latin in this respect and forever lying in wait for the "barbarians," demands a bit of flair and sense of adventure from her visitors. She fleeces the uninitiated but respects and showers her blessings on the connoisseur. To discover the France that is charming underneath an unprepossessing exterior, you must show that you too can be a little sharp. Comparable to Italy in this matter of restaurants and hotels, France is quite prepared to be—if not thievish—at least cynical and merciless in dealing with the simpleton. People will always be ready to speculate on the inexperience of the foreigner who, without so much as a frown, swallows a mediocre Bordeaux or warmed-over *filets de sole Mornay*. But what if he protests? If he sends the dish back to the kitchen? At once, as if by a miracle, he will be respected and better served. He will have entered into the great brotherhood of those who know their way around, those who don't get taken in. Is this attitude degrading? Obsolete? Exasperating? Yes, perhaps. Yes, of course. But my role here is to catch the candid camera shot, not to pass moral judgment. Take again the example of foreigners who have come to live in France, in villages or the quiet neighborhoods of Paris. They will not be cheated, because they will not have tried by pouring out their marks or their dollars without discernment or wit to buy a folklore or an exoticism that, rightly or wrongly, the French henceforth refuse to trade in honestly. As they rather confusedly see it, "France is something to be earned, to be savored, not something to be bought and sold on the spur of the moment."

It remains to be seen whether the world still wants to earn, to discover, and savor France. That is another story.

IN CONCLUSION, one should not underestimate the historical facts, the role played in all this by motions and memories of the collective unconscious.

Frenchmen born around 1890 (the generation that was decimated between 1914–18) had, until the mobilization in August 1914, lived with the certainty that they belonged to a great nation (the greatest, they thought privately), and had at the same time lived in a state of extraordinarily impassioned and vengeful chauvinism. On the pretext of keeping all eyes fixed on the "blue line of the Vosges" and preparing public

opinion for the reconquest of the lost provinces, a patriotic
fever and military excitement reigned in France for thirty
years.

Then came the much hoped for war. It was no high-
spirited charge, no rousing affair of cavalry and flags and heroism in fields of wheat and red poppies, but a nameless sinking
into quicksand, a bleak, revolting butchery of men bogged
down in mud. The dead numbered 1,350,000; the casualties
and war widows 2,500,000. It was a hemorrhage that bled
France white. The researchers and technicians we sorely lacked
between 1920 and 1940 had no doubt fallen somewhere between the Marne and the Chemin-des-Dames. Those who had
survived suffered from some malfunctioning inner mechanism,
some broken spring. They found satisfaction in a confused
war nostalgia; this was the "old soldier's mentality" that explains both the country's twenty-year-long sluggishness and
the support offered in 1940 to Pétain, the "victor of Verdun,"
and the last of the great legendary war leaders. These old
soldiers saw France harvest almost no fruit from her victory,
saw her, on the contrary, pay for her heroism with a declining
population and economic jitters. In contrast, Germany emerged
from chaos to embark on a strong-arm policy of belligerent expansion, Italy acquired a seemingly providential regime (and
both countries—monstrous status symbol!—were building
superhighways). England maintained her fine façade as an
imperial and maritime power; the United States paraded, at
least until the 1929 crisis, disgusting wealth. The former *poilu,*
the ex-soldier of Charleroi and the Somme, suffered from a
sense of scandalous injustice. He detested and despised the
innovations all around him, the dollar-rich travelers who
seemed to taunt him, the proud British commerce, the glittering uniforms in Rome and Nuremberg. He was torn between

nostalgia for a strong regime and xenophobia, between the temptation to give up a cult of the past, and fear.

The lightninglike, total defeat of 1940 humiliated France to the marrow. It completed in our national psyche that agonizing combination of emotions that one must never forget when one thinks of the spite the French exhibit toward others: a national pride justified by the victory of 1918; a sense of injustice caused by the country's decline between the two wars; the grinding ignominy of the 1940 collapse. Weighed down by this triple and contradictory burden, the Frenchmen felt himself the victim and the adversary of all those who had contributed to or witnessed his fall. (Add to this the exasperation of Dien Bien Phu and Algeria, when our own ineptitude turned a policy of decolonization into a succession of lost battles.) When General de Gaulle said to his foreign minister, "Monsieur le Ministre, a nation worthy of the name has no friends," he gave almost magical expression to the defiant rancor of the men of his generation. When, around 1950, the Communist party had its militants daub walls with the slogan "US go home," it was playing on a deeply rooted xenophobia. When official government progapanda or the big dailies play up some sports record, some economic achievement, the alleged timelessness of School of Paris painting, or the winning (finally!) of a Nobel Prize in science—a hundred examples would not suffice here—they are playing quite as much on the spirit of revenge as on national pride. Every French victory is won at the price of a struggle, a competition, a match *against* another nation. If France "is rising again," it is rising in relation to other countries, despite their countermaneuverings and their hostility. This must not be held too much against the French. Events between 1914 and 1945 inflicted severe wounds, and we are still traumatized by them. Our ex-serviceman spirit (in the 1966 budget, veterans' benefits are the third largest item, exceeded only by expenditures for defense and education) is complicated by a loser's mentality that does not help to right matters. We sense only ingratitude, selfishness, threats, military or financial pressures around us. England is having a crisis? Italy suffers from inflation? The dollar is weak? "Good—so much the better!" is more or less what the average Frenchman thinks. Every trial that befalls others in part re-establishes for him that mysterious balance which so long benefited him, as a Frenchman, until it plunged him into stagnation and defeat. Every Frenchman carries within him the whole of his national past—all the chapters in his history-of-France textbook. Every foreigner confronted by the overbearing mechanic, the insolent waiter, or the irascible president of the Republic, should be mindful that dreams and disappointments crowned French heads like a malignant tumor.

CHAPTER XIV:

Legends Dear to the French

IT HAS BEEN THIS BOOK'S LOT to be variously serious or grieving. Now, for the space of one chapter, let it be light-hearted. Some perspectives make us wince, others make us smile. We French have kept certain cherished legends alive among ourselves, we have managed to sell them to the travelers of yesteryear, and at least make them believable to those of yesterday; we are surprised to find the traveler of today challenging them, like a man who is indignant because his curiosity has been disappointed. The legends are touching, in part. Every family has its uncle who has his fund of anecdotes, its grandmother who rambles, and we listen to them, nodding patiently. We are indulgent toward the elderly beaux who believe in their unfading charm and the old ladies who, fifty years later, are still telling about their first ball, all the more so since their tales hold some truth, some traces of charm, flashes of color and music. We do not find it too hard, as we await more strident tomorrows, to love France's way of growing old, imperfect as it may be.

Tourism in Europe—even in the most ambitious sense—

is a lesson in the art of making fine distinctions and in disenchantment. I doubt if the hordes of Frenchmen and Germans who descend, in shorts and sun-visored hats, on summertime Venice are searching for the byways of bygone days. I doubt if the businessmen equipped with limousines, elegant wives, and blasé children, who whip like tornadoes through the Salzburg Festival, impatient to "make" Vicenza too, and Ludwig II's gingerbread chateaux, care overmuch for baroque marvels, Palladian symmetry, or a young king's folly, although these are among Europe's slumbering mysteries. Europeans themselves no longer know how to savor their continent. They prefer to stick to lofty commonplaces (which they never take the trouble to check) and, for the rest, to hasty but satisfying opinions.

So the old standbys still flourish: the Viennese are melancholy and breaded veal cutlets are heavy; Germans are industrious and their *Linzer Torte* are excellent; the Swiss have a sense of civic responsibility and clean hotels; Spanish pride is linked with the slightly ammoniac fragrance of *paella,* Italian seductiveness with the delicacy of Parma ham, London's gigantism with the low price of cashmere sweaters, the sublimity of ancient Greece with the acridness of *retsina.*

Depending on the locale in question, the continent may be melancholy, industrious, patriotic, proud, charming, populous, or sublime; this is what is called possessing culture. The rest is simply a matter of judging the food and hotel room. It is the European view in general and the French in particular that now one assesses other people solely by reference to these two criteria—the one abstract, the other tested, sometimes rather roughly, by the lining of the stomach and the bulge of the wallet.

Legends Dear to the French

By our "dear legends," I refer to French participation in this continental fresco painted in broad strokes by travel, the perusal of guidebooks, and cherished commonplaces. Trivialities and refinements, illusions and infelicities stand side by side. This France is not more false than any other. It is a France standing before her mirror, playing tricks with the lighting to look more beautiful, no longer knowing whether she is what she wishes to seem to be or whether she is what she appears to be in the eyes of foreigners. This France lulls herself with her old romantic notions, but is at the same time hesitant and fearful, asking herself whether she can hold out, whether her proud façades will not suddenly collapse under the joint blows of age and her own tough youngsters.

Holy Land of gastronomy, where one still eats so well and so badly; Olympus of viniculture, where the *grands crus* are matchless but the daily "Beaujolais" is murderous; sanctuary of historic monuments where beauty lives neglected; the tourist paradise that travelers avoid; citadel of elegance where women dress badly; conservatory of masculine gallantry where young men now care only for their hair styles, older men only for their cars; homeland of gracious living but always lagging behind the times by one *belle époque;* haven of good taste where taste has turned bad and so drives creative people into solitude; the nation of proportion, of Cartesianism, of gently sloping hills and formal gardens, which in two hundred years has produced manifold examples of frenzy and illogicality—who will tell us who we are and what our country is all about?

All our legends are false. All our legends are true. Depending on whether one is in good faith or not, aggressive or not, intuitive or not, one can, at will, turn all the familiar clichés into shining truths or into lies. Each fresh survey, analysis, or reportage stuns the Frenchman; to him it seems that those who made it were marvelous psychologists—but incurably blind.

Let us take, for example, among myths that are universal and current, *la belle époque.* It is universal because it is the latter-day French version of the Golden Age, current because references to it are frequent and we often still live in *fin-de-siècle* décors.

Actually, *la belle époque* is the period around 1900, but one could grow nostalgic about more remote periods. It was long agreed that anyone "who had not lived in France during the last years of the *ancien régime* had not known what gracious living means." Similarly, in the years 1815–40, people were feverishly nostalgic for the Napoleonic adventure, for the proud clash of victories and the soaring of our eagles over Europe. So, at the beginning of the nineteenth century the French already had two things to be nostalgic about. Around 1890, with *la belle époque* already in full flower, in the first glow of the Good Fairy Electricity, and amid the first traceries of the "vermicelli" style, elderly gentlemen were evoking the France of Offenbach and the fêtes at the Palais des Tuileries as if they represented paradise lost. Between 1950 and 1960, we witnessed the resurrection of the twenties, which were transformed from a fearfully harried period into one that elicited extravagant regret. From the Charleston to F. Scott Fitzgerald, from Poiret gowns to the Exposition des Arts Décoratifs, fashion's sleight-of-hand conferred dignity on what had been deemed negligible or, in any event, forgotten. We have here a constant in French psychology, which has to draw its images, inspiration, and regrets from years gone by. Probably the styles of 1935–39—great hooded capes, chairs shaped languidly like the chassis of slow-moving Renaults, the tandem bicycle, the early songs of Charles Trenet—will presently be rehabilitated and receive our doting smiles.

However, the 1900 era generated more literature, clichés, cults, and legends than the others. So it poses a double question: Was the *fin de siècle* the miracle that people claim it was, or not? Did it supply an ideal response to some national longing?

Actually, our opinions of the 1900 era have changed. Today we tend rather to denigrate it. If the myths are stripped away, it was a period in which wealth was shamelessly flaunted in the face of frightful poverty; scarcely any regulations protected working women and children; the right to strike was challenged; the poor lived in filthy slums while the bourgeoisie gorged themselves in their townhouses and in the red-velveted seclusion of private dining rooms. It was the era of the Panama scandal, the injustice visited on Dreyfus, the vulgarity of the cocottes and dandies, artistic affectations, the fashionable young "consumptives," the ravages of syphilis; if these are cherished today, it is only from a kind of snobbery. The 1900 era might be described briefly as a mixture of the worst and the best, but the best was not Maxim's restaurant and the worst was truly abominable.

If we look dispassionately at those years from 1875 to 1914—forty years of peace, affluence, and security hardly disturbed by colonial conquests—how do we see them?

Technically, France was moving ahead. M. Eiffel built his symbol of industrial dynamism. Steel bridges sprang up everywhere. Urbanization was ugly but vital and audacious. The Paris Métro was dug in record time. Economically, a colonial empire was established at no great expense. Politically, the Panama affair could be held to have demonstrated the health of parliamentary government and the Dreyfus affair did, in the end, see justice triumph. Religious stirrings were less im-

portant, historically, than advances in education. The ideological wounds of the Commune were healing. The country
recovered in five years from the 1870 defeat. Significant social
legislation was passed. The International was organized. On
the other hand, the bourgeoisie, ascendant since 1830, was
reaping the harvest of its labors and was at the peak of its
power, which was, in fact, the peak of French power. In 1900,
France was competing successfully with British mercantilism
and German imperialism. It was the last time that she was to
play this role—the role of a genuine star—on the world stage.

The middle-class style of living reached a kind of perfection. I am thinking less of elegant private suppers than of
family living patterns. The Impressionists have left us images
of that well-being—walks along the Seine, picnics on the grass,
summer Sundays in the pleasure gardens oustide the city,
Etretat or Trouville beaches, homage to the blond beauty of
women and the pleasures of the sun.

The extreme baroque of a Huysmans or a Montesquiou
or the smutty audacities of a Willy must not make us overlook
Gide, Claudel, Valéry, Barrès, Jammes. In 1900, Proust was
working on his *Remembrance of Things Past.* There were
Bizet, Debussy. The 1880–1910 period nourished the youth of
a generation of creative men such as France had not known
since the reign of Louis XIV or the ferment preceding the
Revolution.

It would be futile to try to imprison *la belle époque* in
any single one of its possible qualifications—Maxim's, syphilis,
the Eiffel Tower, the secular public school, the sensuality of
Renoir, the genius of Claudel—and just as futile to believe
that people have loved 1900 only for good reasons. Everything
was inextricably intertangled. Intertangled in a unique, glorious, earthy image of wealth and well-being. It was a period

that denied God, that looked only to itself and the future, and that grew drunk on its belief in the limitless progress of human capabilities. French hedonism and optimism, which in 1775 had been reserved for a minority, were suddenly democratized. Well-being could be enjoyed in Parisian luxury or provincial châteaux, but also of a Sunday along the banks of the Marne. If the big industrialists believed in the future, so did the little schoolteachers.

Paunchy, self-satisfied, mustachioed—fabulous—*la belle époque* nevertheless represents a kind of summit for France. The summit may have lacked elevation, but not power or vitality. Is the legend excessively silly? Nonetheless, it contains truths correctly sensed. It was, in fact, an asset on which the country lived until 1950. Of all our tiresome tales of the "good old days," this is perhaps the one that history and common sense will most willingly endorse.

A FAMILIAR LITTLE BOOK, the size of a missal but bound in red, travels in French automobiles—the *Guide Michelin*. Theoretically it tells everything there is to know about hotels and garages; it provides excellent maps of towns and cities; it mentions briefly the points of interest to tourists. It indicates distances, altitudes, population figures, mountain passes, customs regulations. But above and beyond all else, it assigns stars for gastronomic ratings.

Every year at Easter, when the new edition of the *Guide Michelin* is issued, gastronomy columnist and ordinary Sunday stroller alike hurl themselves on the little red book with the same hair-splitting and suspicious passion to find out which restaurant owner has won—or lost—his third star. Polemics rage, counterexpertise is advanced. The *Guide's* culinary consecrations are endlessly discussed in the bosom of the family and among friends; the press comments are furious or ironic. In place of the currently glorious chefs and fashionable hostelries, this or that allegedly unknown little bistro is proposed, past journeys toward the stars are evoked, which ended in disaster and setbacks, or turned into triumphs. Gastronomy really is a national topic. It knows almost no social distinctions. The man of limited resources who has not yet attained the serene self-possession that allows him to prefer grilled meat to game served with a rich sauce, or Vittel water to Gigondas, still sacrifices a sound liver and heart to the vanity of overheavy meals. At lunchtime, however, all Frenchmen are rich; the amounts of money consumed in mediocre restaurants would baffle all the economists. His car and his food are the two items in his budget for which the average Frenchman lives above his means.

The religion of the table (with its confessional annexes, superstitions about wine and the science of cheeses) is celebrated in many ways. The famous restaurant, the pretentious inn with its heavy beams and fireplace, and the overwhelmingly friendly little café must not make one forget the secrets of home cooking, the recipes handed down from mother to daughter, the husbands of whom we say that the way to their hearts is via their stomachs. The restaurant business, with its hierarchies, its chefs who are handled as gingerly as film stars, its legends, and its pitiless prices, is simply the external, publicity-minded, and gilded projection of a long family tradition. The passion for cooking has been so profound for so long that one still sees elderly concierges, widowed and fat, in the dark solitude of their little rooms (redolent of fried onions) hovering over the simmering stews with which they sweeten their last years. It is a point of honor with women of almost all classes, and with a goodly number of men (the upper classes foremost among them), to know how to cook. In France, one never loses caste for knowing how to prepare a mayonnaise or how to knead pastry dough, or for begging a friend to share the recipe for some dish one has just enjoyed at his table. The little housewife who will spend the whole day preparing a meal for a few guests and the mistress of a great house renowned for its table (and for its chef or caterer) share a common language, a happy complicity, a secret respect for good food and for those who appreciate it. If there is any place in the world where the quality of the *gourmandise* is a part of the civilization, that place is France. It may be a question of truly fine cuisine, discernment, and a worthy tradition, or only of the myth and the outer trimmings —the food itself having miserably deteriorated—for gastronomic pretensions and genuflections flourish side by side with genuine quality.

For there is, alas, a gastronomic farce. The self-styled great chef, the restarurant with its phony chic and phony sauces, and the incompetent, pretentious housewife make up the cast. The nuisance of it all is that the French are allowing themselves to be taken in more and more by the sets and staging of this comedy, and they play it far too often for foreigners. The "good" restaurant that is really very so-so and the wine bearing a label that strangely resembles that of a *grand cru* are swindles on a par with the business of face-lifting second-hand cars. Vulgarity reigns supreme. How many inns along our highways substitute for real quality the Gothic-lettered sign, the staggeringly polysyllabic names of dishes, the disdainful insolence of the maître d'hotel, and an astronomical check? Such dens of contempt, fraud, and theft resemble— I come back to my comparison—the shadowy garages around the Porte Champerret, where gentlemen straight out of a

Grade B movie, sporting lizard shoes and flashy rings, sell you a "dandy little '58 Chevvie, good as new" that will die on the first hill.

In all fairness, one must not forget the restaurants that still have an exquisite regard for culinary traditions, as nearly perfect as they are expensive, the truck drivers' stopovers where anyone who ventures into them will be served honest food and wine at popular prices, and the few celebrated three-starred restaurants belonging to chef-proprietors who are venerated like royal dukes and have not yet consented to mass-produce their art. All these blessings are within the reach of the exacting amateur; they deserve to be viewed as phenomena of civilization, for that is indeed what they are. To deny this you must never have been regaled by one of those sublime repasts where the cunning lightness of each dish, the choice of wines, the sense of balance and measure, the art of stopping in time, of savoring without ever entirely sating one's appetite, all contribute to creating—without drunkenness, flushed faces, or heaviness, without fatigue or surfeit—a euphoria conducive to good conversation.

Need I say that these masterpieces of science and prescience are now scarcely to be had anywhere, at any price, and that only a few patient, cultivated, and meticulous millionaires, hidden in the depths of their mysterious mansions, are in a position to offer them.

The pleasant talent of a provincial housewife and the good honest fare provided by an honorable restaurant owner are to *haute cuisine* what a pretty village square is to the Place de la Concorde, or the notary's house to the Château of Chenonceaux. It is a great pity that inflated dreams of restaurants like Baumanière or Le Grand Véflour ferment in the brain of every third-rate cook and that the lowliest Mme. Dupont

feels herself part of the ineffable destiny of French gastronomy
the moment she serves up a rabbit stew. We are perennially
relapsing into these soaring ambitions, these feverish dreams,
and while they are the funniest of all French afflictions, they
do no end of damage to our reputation. The inadequacies
themselves are less grave than our illusion of being inimitable.
It is common knowledge that three hundred years ago our
country received the doubtful honor of having the pox baptized "the French sickness." Well, things have changed.
Today the real French sickness is our gastronomic illusion,
with all its concomitant ills—fancy wines, commercial proliferation of types of cheese, misuse of "Provençal" herbs,
shameless prices, poor taste in dining-room décor. In the vast
gulf between a simple meal and luxury, between the family
soup tureen and the ovens of a millionaire, our gastronomic
hallucination rages more and more seriously, as merciless on
the pocketbook as on the digestion.

THE MANIA FOR ANYTHING HISTORICAL and the lazy
eagerness of tourists are, in French eyes, merely adjuncts to
eating well. The most insignificant machicolated turret, the
most modest Renaissance bell tower are pretexts to sit down
and consume a *civet de porcelet* or a *feuilleté de morilles*
in a so-called "rustic" dining room or a Rotisserie de Château
or, yet again, a Relais des Princes Noirs, where the wine card
is more impressive than the public conveniences. It is a recognized law of travel today in France that the only safe time
to drive is during lunch, when everyone else spends two hours
busily building up his cholesterol count. Thereafter, allowing
the necessary time for digestion, our roads become more
than usually fearsome, crowded as they are by drivers lost
in the fumes of the Bourgueil, Sancerre, Muscadet, Brouilly,

Fleurie, Juliénas, Arbois, Tavel, Côtes du Rhône, and the
petit vin de Cahors that they have just been relishing. The
after-dinner befuddlement in which the French murmur the
names of vintage wines, vineyards, hillsides, and villages, as
if they were telling their beads, is as sweet as a poem.

These marriages of a château with a wine, a *cassoulet*
with a Roman gate, a cognac with a feudal ruin are indisputable national inventions. The same verb—*goûter* ("to taste,
enjoy, or relish")—is used interchangeably for places, persons,
music, drinks, and dishes. "Gourmet"—a word as round,
smooth, and polished as a pebble in a stream—has always
been an appreciative compliment. With time it has acquired
connotations more and more ethereal. The gourmet is not
only the man who knows how to appreciate fine fare and the
correct wines to go with it, but also, this art being the symbol
of refinement, any man who knows how to combine his pleasures with the right places, people, and styles. At its best,
French civilization has been and is, metaphorically, a kind
of ideal meal in which everything conspires to make pleasure
perfect. The charm of the house and its furnishings, the
smoothness of the service, the excellence of the dishes, the
liveliness of the conversation, the intellectual agility—all
these contribute to a single triumph rather comparable to a
successful meal. For that matter, this unostentatious hedonism,
which you enjoy without letting it throw you, is called knowing how to *goûter la vie* ("enjoy life") and clearly the phrase
denotes an all-embracing program. This talent for enjoying
life has had its superlative moments—the reign of Louis XV,
the waltzes of the Second Empire, the charms of *la belle
époque*—and if we are to be indulgent toward our nostalgia,
these are the true voyages through time that we should take.

Through time—the eternal backward glance is perhaps

the whole secret. Whatever a Frenchman may be doing by way of enjoying life, whatever general opinion he may express about himself or his country, will, in one way or another, refer to the past. The past is a value in itself, and the shortest route back to it is via whatever is old or old-fashioned. As I have said so often, the equation: quality = age, is deeply rooted in us. The whole Tourism-Archaeology-Gastronomy complex, which so completely expresses what we are proud of and how we think of ourselves, is saturated with the past. When the antique dealers, those dignitaries of France for the last twenty years, say of an old piece of furniture that it is *dans son jus* ("in its juice") or that it is *bon,* they are using words which —by an apparent coincidence—are applicable to a *pot-au-feu* or a cheese, but which here, with the color and brevity of a secret language, convey a double and absolute value: distinction and authenticity. In France, a value is all the more unchallengeable if it emerges untouched and untouchable from the past. A *pâté* must be cooked as a *pâté* was cooked under Louis XIII; silk must be woven, wood must be dowelled, joists set up, wine bottled and decanted, chairs upholstered as they used to be. Whether in a meal, a piece of furniture, or a house, this is the magic formula that alone respects the delicate essence preserved by so many decades or centuries of care.

One must not make too much fun of the *Guides Bleus Hachette* or the *Guide Michelin.* Publishing corporation and tire manufacturer are of one accord—their business is not to invent France but to hold up mirrors to her. The blue book dwells on the views, hills, mountain peaks, geological marvels, chasms, grottoes, sinks, underground streams—everything that climbs or burrows, unveils a landscape or leads to a cathedral or museum. The red book is devoted to the table and the car, our double weakness. It appears to marvel every time it discovers a hotel (marked in the Guide by an "M" enclosed in a square) where faucets supply water, elevators go up and down, the electric current allows you to shave, and the morning coffee wakes you up. "M" stands for "modern"—with an accent of surprise. All the ideal aspects of France are contained within these fat, sober little books. The France of vistas and historic monuments and roads "bordered with green" (a symbol on the irreproachable Michelin maps, published by the same firm as the *Guide,* which indicates "particularly picturesque roads"), and of the *bistros* and the inns. By relishing all these virtues of France together, by contracting them within the hurried perfection of a Sunday outing or on a leisurely vacation, the Frenchman feels that he has reached the peak: his own complete and perfect fulfillment. He has the impression that he is what he was born to be, that the world he is in fits him like a glove.

The nationalistic spirit, which is discussed elsewhere in this book as one of the worst of our collective ailments, also has its light, almost innocent sides. I wonder whether Germans ever happen to say, with utter naturalness, as if it were self-evident, "We who are the most industrious people in the world . . ." or whether New Yorkers proclaim themselves citizens of the most beautiful city in the world, or Italians calmly declare themselves the cleverest men in the world . . .

It is not surprising that the Chinese speak of how numerous they are or that the Swiss refer proudly to their postal service; these are statements of fact. What is surprising is to see the French pass from fact to hypothesis, from statement to legend, and treat hypotheses and legends as unshakable dogmas. When phrases such as "most harmonious landscape" or "most elegant women" or "inimitable charm" are applied to France and its inhabitants, they do not even elicit a smile or a doubt. Our excellence and our pre-eminence in certain domains—sense of proportion, fashions, charm—go without saying. The disorders and fevers we have known in our past in no way challenge our innate, intuitive sense of balance and prudence. The daily spectacle of so many badly dressed women who are comically "stylish" and not very clean in no way compromises the sublime chapter in our history text entitled "Haute Couture." The Frenchman in his suspenders and slippers, with a sleezy tie and filthy socks, preserves intact his reputation as a seducer, won for him by—who knows?—François I, the Regent, or the heroes of Guy de Maupassant. As for Paris, it is like a huge abscess deliberately created to drain all the infection into one place; nothing is too lyrical, too grandiloquent, too vacuous, or too obvious to say about Paris. This haughty, familiar, querulous, exhausting capital will ultimately make itself detested by dint of believing its charm is self-evident. The fashions-perfume-Paris complex is as indestructable as the historic sites-starred inns complex. The strange thing is that both are justified but also exasperating. Everything truly good about France is in danger of going bad because of the abuses of our national self-complacency. One good quality attempts to cover up ten deficiencies; one lovely façade tries to excuse the ugliness of a whole neighborhood. We who claim to be champions of reason lack good sense and a sense of proportion. Cartesianism, which, together with quick and intelligent head, we all supposedly receive as our inheritance at birth, developed systematic doubt into a system of thought. But of all people, it is the Frenchman who, although once he could correctly believe himself irreverent, irreligious, and iconoclastic, has now become a paragon of credulity. He questions his legends no longer. He is the misty-eyed spectator of his own make-believe. Nothing if not generous, he believes in the elegance of his women; nothing if not optimistic, he believes in his own powers of seduction. I am not talking of the beautiful actresses and the playboy sons of rich magnates, which all Western countries have, or of the glamorous beings in the slick magazines, but of the Frenchman himself and the archetypal image that the French of both sexes all carry with them; a mop of chestnut hair, eyes more and more blue and less and less hazel (statistics tell us), an indestructible little Renault, and treasures as glorious and inalienable as Chartres and Versailles that, it seems, are found by the shovelful between the Place Vendôme and the Seine—all of which comprise the exquisite privilege of being born French. As latter-day compatriots of the heroes of Marivaux, Beaumarchais, Voltaire, and Musset, if we are to resist our own virtues we are now left with no choice other than to arm ourselves with irony, for irony is a fault that has outlived all the good qualities that should have purged us of it.

CHAPTER XV:

The French and Beauty

A PEOPLE AS OLD AS OURS has lived for a long time in close communion with beauty. I mean humanized beauty, beauty conceived and expressed in the measure of man, whether splendid or modest, beauty equally capable of celebrating a faith or adorning wealth, and in which nature collaborates in only a remote or secondary way. We do not possess the immensity of the steppes or deserts, the prodigious gash of the Colorado or the traces of those geological furies which are the Andes or the Himalayas. Our forests are sparse, our countryside having long since submitted to the peasant and his plow; our riverbanks are moderately scenic, our Alps discreetly dramatic. We are—and Heaven knows we have often enough been told so, often enough have been rocked to sleep with this refrain—we are born in the land of measure.

The atavistic, almost visceral sense of beauty which has little by little been deposited in the national unconscious owes very little to the natural theater of the French countryside aside from a taste for harmony and an intuitive appreciation of the golden mean. It owes almost everything to the way in

which, for almost ten centuries, the inhabitants of the country
have left their mark upon it and made it their own. Villages,
bridges, churches, châteaux, and cities are evidence of, and
lessons in, beauty. If ever there existed in the eye and taste of
a Frenchman a certain conception of balance, charm, nobility,
and intimacy, it has been his stones that have instructed him.
To a lesser degree, also the accomplishments of his craftsmen—furniture, woodwork and stucco of houses, stained-
glass windows of cathedrals, skillfully trimmed stone or sculp-
tured doors. If one wanted to put this more categorically, one
would say that before being an artist, the Frenchman was an
architect and artisan. All members of a community are exposed
to works of beauty, and the French learned the art of
seeing and sharpened their taste for the beautiful by looking
at churches, houses, and châteaux. The fine arts—literature and
easel painting—always more or less eluded the use and even
the attention of simple people. On the other hand, when the
moment came for putting up his own house, any villager of
the seventeenth century or bourgeois of the eighteenth had
only to lift his eyes to find his model in the arch of a church
or the wrought-iron work on some gentleman's mansion.
Whence the unity and almost miraculous soundness of taste
that pervades all our "great periods." From the oldest Roman-
esque churches of the Auvergne to the sober buildings of the
first half of the nineteenth century, passing en route through
what has survived, despite violence and fire, of medieval cities
and the luxuries of the Renaissance—Lyon, Troyes, Dijon,
Sarlat, Chinon—and through places in which we still live
today: the Place des Vosges, the townhouses of the Marais,
the great eighteenth-century Atlantic ports, Aix-en-Provence,
Montpellier, countless châteaux, palaces, and middle-class
mansions, the proud rue de Varenne and the dwellings built

near Paris by the bankers of the Restoration, the immense
adventure of church architecture from Le Puy to Chartres
to Saint Etienne-du-Mont, from Tournus to Strasbourg to
Val-de-Grâce . . . we pass through a thousand years of imagination, extravagance, austerity, levity, multiform inventiveness, a succession of regimes and wars, religious struggles and
revolutions, periods of power and periods of eclipse. A thousand years of true and unchallengeable beauty endlessly re-
newed . . . A thousand years that variously inflame, encumber,
or benumb the judgment of the Frenchman today . . .

Nothing is more odious or more futile than "beauty
contests," i.e., rivalries among countries, cities, and museums;
the comparison shopper's evaluation of ruins; touristic and
cultural terrorism. What country of Europe—Italy or Spain,
Germany East or West, Switzerland, Holland or England;
what region—the Tyrol or the Engadine, Tuscany or the Val
de Loire, the shores of Ireland or the banks of the Rhine; what
city—Prague or Vienna, Rome or Toledo, London or Paris,
Bruges or Heidelberg—has accumulated over the centuries
the most prodigious capital of beauty? The question is irrele-
vant.

On the other hand, we can try aesthetically to link as
intimately as possible men with monuments, landscape with
history. Anyone who loves Europe deeply has attempted this,
and when he has best perceived the hidden correspondences,
the somewhat mysterious triumphs of time, he finds that he
prefers this place to that, an English castle rather than one in
Touraine, a Bavarian rather than a Provençal village, or vice
versa. That is what it means to love Europe. It means discover-
ing where this reciprocal impregnation of time and place offers
us the truest joy. It does not mean vying for first prize or competing for vacation statistics. So let us overcome the French

weakness for cultural competitiveness, for the unstated but persistent implication of their supremacy in tourist attractions, Gothic hegemony, classical superiority, baroque primacy, and, in the matter of museums, battlements, and gardens—total victory.

Once stated, this reservation must be clearly understood. It is not intended to underestimate what our public officials call the nation's "artistic patrimony." Hopefully, it may simply deter competition with others, localize our capital more realistically, measure the precise place it occupies in our ideas and actions, determine with what comforting dreams it has clouded our reflections, and understand in what form it flowers in us today.

However, a search for common sense in this area explodes a mine at every step. Insofar as artistic patrimony is concerned, everything said about it in France, aside from the fact of its abundance, is pretty much false. First of all, the most astonishing beauty of France is not what the posters in our tourist offices glorify; it is difficult of approach and hidden from the curiosity of strangers. Then, the French, who talk about that beauty so readily, do not give a damn about it, really. In appearance, we are a nation of museum guards, but in fact we are a nation of vandals. Lastly—and strangest of all—collectively we may be considered to have lost, about a hundred years ago, the intimate physical contact with beauty which time and our forbears had established.

I doubt that the hurried traveler ever suspects what treasures the French countryside conceals. Who will point out to him the Norman manors, the country houses of Périgord or Provence or Touraine—those thousands of restored, furnished, occupied dwellings that are as closed to the curiosity of the tourist as they are to the acquisitiveness of the antique

dealer? Their unpretentious perfections, their luxurious or
accidental distinctions, their natural harmonies born of centuries of time compose chapters in a history it is almost impossible to tell in words. One should wander aimlessly, get lost
down small lanes, venture into courtyards—and, above all,
chat, strike up friendships, open doors part way but never force
them. It is possible never to have visited Mont-Saint-Michel
or Versailles or the Place Stanislas in Nancy, or the Louvre,
and yet to know, thanks to some Charente home or some
Montpellier townhouse, how the heart of this country beats.
This I believe very deeply: France is more beautiful than we
say she is, but her beauty is worn, fragile, and, to an extraordinary degree, hidden. The local amateur antiquarians—a
vanishing species—hardly manage to get to know their own
département within the space of a lifetime. What they do
acquire, on the other hand, is an acute, fervent intuition of
what their province once was, and the virtual certainty that,
in every essential respect, it is doomed to destruction.

It is hard to find anywhere else in Europe such disregard
for and neglect of the vestiges of the past, and such a daily
assault on taste, as is exhibited so widely and with such impunity in France. Left to his own devices—and there is no
government statute with the authority to protect him against
himself—the Frenchman sacks and botches ("modernizes" and
"embellishes"), remodels, fragments, and destroys what was
once the proud setting for French life. Our cities and villages,
no matter how historic the former or impoverished the latter,
are the victims of the suffocating lapses of taste epitomized in
the multicolored jerry-built villa. Whether the Frenchman is
setting up a café, modernizing a shop, renovating a house, or
building a shed, he perpetrates a kind of outrage. Ninety-
nine out of a hundred Frenchmen lack not only a sense of

beauty but also common sense. They even lack the commercial intuition that would tell them that beauty "sells," that harmoniously planned cities are "good business." For a century we have been bedeviled by a feeling that springs partly from individualism, do-it-yourselfism, and partly from a pure pleasure in destruction. The sudden wealth of the last few years and the availability of new materials (plastics and cheap, mass-produced items) have multiplied the manifestations of ugliness both in quantity and virulence. Villages in underdeveloped regions, long preserved from desecration because they were underpopulated and poor, have succumbed in the last decade to roughcasting their walls in ultramarine or canary yellow, to "bold new" town improvements, and flashing lights. Shops that had resisted a hundred years with their charm intact (and such charm had, in its way, become a work of art) are now, thanks to flourishing business, transformed in six months into juke-box joints or public lavatories of 1930. If to the crimes against the past you add the aberrations tolerated in the name of the present (service stations randomly placed, new buildings outdoing each other in inferior design, the tangle of miscellaneous overhead wires, perennially unfinished constructions, futuristic signs and novelties, plus the leprous infection of the automobile penetrating to the fragile core of our cities), you will understand that while French beauty has become increasingly anemic since about 1850, it may well have been mortally wounded in the last ten years. Rhapsodized in our schools, our textbooks, by our propagandists and by ourselves, this august entity has had it. Here and there it is already dead and everywhere else it is dying.

No sensational feats of artificial restoration will give back to the French the essential thing without which the outward appearance (which is to say also, the inner spirit) of their country can only degenerate—the innate taste for living in surroundings worthy of what men want to be.

When did this age-old stream of French aesthetic sensitivity run dry? When did our eye stop seeing clearly, our hand stop knowing how to design, our wealth stop creating worthy investments?

A rapid backward glance at houses, interiors, and furniture will promptly convince us: somewhere between 1840 and 1870—during the Second Empire, that is—the continuity in French taste was broken. I grant the attempt to rehabilitate, à la Visconti, the final splendors of the baroque (Traviata style) and, as at present, the ingenuities of 1900. These are merely small flurries, the nervous responses of a dilettantism afraid that it will not invent a contemporary beauty. Two or three lavishly overdone and affected Napoleon III décors (the Château de Ferrières, the only building in France designed by the architect of the Crystal Palace, Sir Joseph Paxton), the prettily lascivious small bronzes of the turn of the century, and the delicious Mucha, will not controvert the evidence, which shows that the great flow of creativity, of innate inventiveness and stylistic competence, was lost to us somewhere between 1840 (when the last beautiful houses were built in Paris) and 1870 (when the Empire collapsed, and the Offenbach style began to degenerate into the President Fallières style). A walk through our streets will confirm this abundantly. Up until about the 1848 Revolution, the middle class, particularly in the provinces, built itself solid, nononsense houses, vigorous and well set in attractive surroundings, with gardens, grille gates, and such. The change occurred within a few years. The reign of brick and iron brought with it the fad for metalwork, which was to leave virtually no trace worthy of mention; the cult of the copy

resulted in fake Louis XV, as in the Napoleon III palaces, and
the abandonment by the cabinetmakers (among the best craftsmen we have ever had) of all true originality in favor of
variations on the themes of earlier styles.

All this can perhaps be explained, with a generous assist
from the sociologists, but it is unmistakably evident that
French aesthetic decadence did set in at the beginning of the
Second Empire. Thenceforth, we were to have nothing but
1880 Gothic, 1890 Renaissance, and 1900 châteaux, complete
with towers and battlements; filthy-rich mansions in the
residential sections; Basque villas, Tudor replicas, and Swiss
chalets in the suburban nightmares; the disastrous reconstruc-
tion of areas that had been devastated during World War I,
the delirium of suburban mediocrity that raged from 1920 to
1931, and toward the end of the period between the two world
wars, the abandonment of any pretense of architectural
quality or originality.

Were we to examine the background of family living—the
furniture, the everyday functional tools or objects with some
claim to artistic content—we would find everything moving,
in the same downhill direction, faster and faster. Nothing—
no protest, no aesthetic hairsplitting—can belie the fact that
the France of Chartres became the France of the Sacré-
Coeur in Montmartre; that the Louvre was succeeded by the
two Trocadéros; that the France of Aix-en-Provence and
Nancy declined to the level of the ostentatious streets of the
16ème *Arrondisement* in Paris and petered out somewhere
among the shrubberies of Le Vésinet. From Coysevox to
Barbedienne, from Mansart and Gabriel to Viollet-le-Duc and
Garnier: everywhere the same metamorphosis took place.
There was only one—albeit tremendous—ray of light in all

that grayness, and it was provided by the painters who, to the accompaniment of jeers and catcalls, reinvented painting between 1860 and 1914, while daubers like Bouguereau and Boldini were riding high. But it is obvious that the Impressionists were not able, alas, to redeem French taste in that half-century of bad taste. And one remembers how they were either neglected or despised at the time. (Who, among *their* contemporaries, had mocked Fragonard in 1770, the two Le Nains in 1650, or Clouet in 1550?) What I call the "bystander arts," those points of contact between the people at large and those who are creating standards of taste, notably architects and artisans, had entered an empty twilight zone from which, by all indications, they have not yet emerged.

The same lack of drive that prevents our maintaining or restoring a certain level of taste also prevents us from being effective in searching for or inventing something new. Foreigners driving from Orly into Paris for the first time are stunned by the blocks of housing units which have been put up among the scattering of small detached homes in our suburbs—as ill-matched as tomatoes with chocolate sauce. This is ugliness on the colossal fake scale succeeding ugliness on the intimate fake scale. It is jerry-built collectivism crushing anarchic individualism. It is the regimented man living in the inhuman housing project, gregarious and conformist, longing to be in all things indistinguishable from his neighbor, who has received the torch from that earlier Frenchman whose belligerent individuality carried within it a mistrust of his fellow man, whose appreciation of privacy was more nearly a need for aggressive solitude, and whose closed, narrow life amounted to a kind of sociological sickness. But whatever the scale, both uglinesses live under the same sooty sky, outlined against a horizon stolen from beautiful landscapes. In much the same vein, it was startling to hear some eight years ago the spokesman for an auto manufacturer previously known for his good taste state that the firm had decided to cover the seats of its small cars with extremely ugly upholstery in the future because, he said: "From now on, we're aiming at a lower-class buying public." This blatant cynicism sums up all the disparate evidence that we have tried to gather together in a quick glance, and from which there is perhaps a single lesson to be drawn.

Am I wrong to invest such things as walls and interiors, streets and living rooms, gardens and armchairs, châteaux and low-income housing, cars and snack bars, with this exorbitant importance? Am I wrong to believe that in a materialistic and, in fact, a de-Christianized society, that kernel of tenderness in a human being (which, in other circumstances, we would call "soul") can be found in the attachment that binds him to wherever he lives and has his roots? I don't think so. There are few "profundities" to speak of in talking about a country. Ideologies, in particular, are passionate and ephemeral. On the other hand, certain themes are essential to whoever wants to sense what a nation is really like. The great muscles of the social corpus are bunched around the couple and the home, childhood and education, tolerance and racism. Man and his house, man and his village—man face to face with the equation of time and beauty, in which he himself is the unknown quantity—this is a key issue. One—perhaps the most spectacular—part of the French malaise is found in the litanies we chant over our historical monuments, and in the squares of our disfigured villages. It is an unhealthy and unproductive way of "living in the past." It is living in the past only in words, not in the very stones from which it has been made. The title of a well-known book by Henry Bordeaux, which was widely read in early twentieth-century bourgeois circles, expressed their respectable *idée fixe* in four words: *The Walls Are Sound.* I can sum up my present point simply by noting that they are so no longer.

CHAPTER XVI:

A Miscellany of Endemic Ailments

FOR A FRENCHMAN there is no more salubrious intellectual exercise than criticizing France. I do not mean systematically to discredit her or to cast aspersions on her honor or merits, but simply to challenge the national posture of self-satisfaction, vanity, and self-deception.

A critical attitude is actually more widespread than people believe or than the above would seem to suggest. The opposition denigrates the government; the reactionary attacks democracy; the republican sees reaction looming on all horizons; each man arraigns the entire nation through his neighbor. However, these criticisms are conceived in terms of a flattering, Platonic idea of the country; they refer to an ideal France that unquestionably exists but is being perverted or brought into disrepute by the government or democracy or reactionaries or fools or whatever. They are criticisms formulated from the perspective of our collective lack of realism. It is precisely this notion of an ideal France that we must get rid of, this national unreality that we must chasten once and for all. The French are intoxicated by their famous "sense of

A Miscellany of Endemic Ailments

proportion," but they have no sense of France's own true proportions. A study called *Mesure de la France,* by Pierre Drieu
la Rochelle, was published soon after World War I. Appearing
when our post-victory euphoria was in full flood (Treaty of
Versailles, League of Nations, "Germany will pay," etc.), it
was a cry of alarm and grief, an assessment of French decline.
The most admirable leaps forward, courageous actions, useful
sacrifices, and painful reforms are too often administered by
a self-satisfied determination to gain time or to prepare for
revenge.

In an atmosphere of inflated self-contentment, it is un-
popular to stand back, to try to assay the country's true weight.
Objectivity is all the less appreciated for seeming, at least
initially, to be negative criticism. But, in fact, how can one fail
to find that the aging coquette still convinced of her beauty is
a little faded? Criticizing France means, first of all, making use
of what I will call the principle of challenge, which has so
often stood her in good stead; second, it is doing her the
service of being in some small measure loyal.

The trouble is, we so easily get carried away. Surveys turn
into indictments; declarations of love become angry tirades.
"We are always accused of thinking *anti,* but that is because
there are not so many reasons for thinking *pro,*" Jean-François
Revel wrote in his angry but carefully reasoned pamphlet *En
France.* It is a fact that if you are traveling down the hill of
bitterness and disenchantment—in other words, of rational
patriotism—you quickly pick up speed. I had made up a list
of ninety-eight major flaws and outstanding oddities that, it
seemed to me, must be noted in order to be honest. However,
experience teaches that if readers sometimes do read a chapter
of a book in its entirety, they never retain more than one para-
graph or quote more than one sentence. This is why the mildest

criticisms take on an irritating tone of excess and violence. Therefore, my list of French ailments will include only a dozen and will, furthermore, treat them with a gentleness in which the reader will be entirely right to find love and caution conjoined.

I HAVE ALREADY DEALT at considerable length with the first of our complaints—the nationalistic dithyramb. It contains, controls, colors, and subsumes almost all the others. It is not only the first; it is also prime—fundamental. Together with love of the past, it is the mother-malady of French bad health. Its manifestations are numberless. It affects sports, diplomacy, science, communications, artistic and literary creativity, technology. We French have got into the habit of talking about a victory in a ski meet, an art competition, or an auto race as if it were a challenge that French ardor, astuteness, and genius defiantly hurled at the rest of the world. France is forever finding herself confronted by the brute strength of Soviet barbell stars, the massive power of Detroit's big cylinders, or the blind power of dollar millionaires. Pluckily, she fights back with a mixture of fury, flexibility, irony, resourcefulness, and wild audacity. We are unbeatable little Davids facing all those Goliaths which the twentieth century has manufactured expressly to ruffle French pride. So, when a young girl or a horse or a cyclist manages to hold his or her own, perilously and pathetically, against the horde of the rivals of France, our delirium knows no limits. At such times, the commentators on international sports matches or newsmen on TV (television is a marvelous medium for testing France because it uniquely and slavishly echoes her "master's voice") produce some memorable rhetoric. They oscillate between a godlike calm and the fervor with which one might report a miracle. Either French victories are the fruit of a basic, quasi-fabulous superiority and happen as a matter of course, or they are snatched from destiny, from one second to the next, only by the prodigious, desperate effort of some sublimely deserving youngster. It is never merely a matter of reporting a win in a rugby match, a race, or a sailing competition as a happy conjunction of muscle, endurance, and stop watches. That would be trampling underfoot the French idea; i.e., the legitimacy of French victory that, from Poitiers to the Innsbruck games, from Marignan and Austerlitz to the Five Nations Tournament and the Tour de France, has never been usurped or challenged.

In areas other than sports, the national panegyric becomes infinitely nuanced. In painting, the Catalan Picasso and the Swiss Giacometti, as in sports-car design the Italian Gordini, simply become naturalized Frenchmen; this then sanctions certain aberrations beyond the native French genius as embodied in, say, Poussin, Rodin, or Louis Blériot. When, on the occasion of a visit to the White House, our minister of culture wished to make a specifically French gesture in the area of his special interest, he arranged for the solemn loan of a Leonardo da Vinci canvas, annexing it as French for the occasion. Its "Frenchness" had been conferred on it, presumably, by the fact of the Louvre's having accepted it in the museum collection. France handed over political refugees to Hitler in 1940, but salvaged all the stateless talents in the name of the School of Paris. Similarly, the soccer player who scores goals ceases to be a Polish miner or a North African laborer and is admitted to the club of tricolor prowess; as a new arrival, he seems to exude more quickly than another the virtues he acquires by osmosis the moment he comes to live in France. For better or worse, all activity carried out inside the hexagon of metropolitan France contributes to the greater glory of the nation. It is a melting pot . . . of vanity.

One has scruples about peevishly cataloguing the weaknesses of one's own country. If only one could be sure that the reassuring old adage "Spare the rod and spoil the child" is true. But I feel I should go on. After all, scruples themselves are a part of this self-satisfaction I am tracking down, and especially of the French monolithic stance whereby to challenge a detail is equivalent to condemning the whole. Careful as one may be to guard against such excess, the habit is so ingrained that one is more or less contaminated by it. I am no exception. The need I feel to justify myself shows the extent to which I am troubled by the grievances I am articulating, how much they hurt me personally, and how difficult it is for a Frenchman to consider objectively the land in which chance decreed that he be born and the passport that the law places in his hands.

In putting my country under a miscroscope, I feel as if I were committing a sin against her every time I discover and name a microbe. This is an unpleasant feeling. Also, I would wish to know, sin for sin, which it is better to be guilty of: complacency or captiousness, apathy or acerbity.

Even when one believes—as I do—that objectivity and rigorous self-analysis are both healthy and loyal, they may foster troubling alliances. Large-scale evaluations, syntheses, and programs are always political maneuvers. The figures and judgments that I have put together here for whatever they may be worth, in order to draw some lesson from them, are the kind usually hurled back and forth between rival political camps in order to denigrate the opponent and bestow a certificate of merit on one's own side. It is just as uncomfortable to howl with the wolves as to parade with the peacocks.

A Miscellany of Endemic Ailments

But let me go ahead with a clear Puritan conscience, a Savonarola threading my way between Joan of Arc and President Poincaré, to enumerate our French maladies. I will pass quickly over the best known to expatiate, with all the pleasure of floundering among generalities, on those that are most commonly overlooked and also the most mysterious.

That France, in the second half of this century, possesses no more than 950 miles of superhighways, that her telephone system is the most decrepit of any in the Common Market—these, after all, are merely matters of asphalt, screwdrivers, and recalcitrant credit. They are technical shortcomings, *ergo* curable in a flourishing economy. There is no point in lingering here over the relevant statistics; as we all know, they are depressing.

It is more interesting to contrast the high points of achievement with the low, and ask why the national effort has been directed in this rather than in that direction, why certain advances seem to have been possible only at the price of enormous negligence in other areas.

In the ratio of cars to population, France ranks immediately after the United States and ahead of all other developed countries; her railroads, which were admirably restored after the Liberation, are excellent; until recently, her postal service functioned rather better than that of some of her neighbors; her secondary-road system, established early in the century and modernized up until 1939, is most adequate, efficient, and scenic; her cherished Caravelle (of which Frenchmen are as proud as they are of Versailles) not only provides first-rate plane service at home but also has become a successful export item; everything having to do with electrical power is administered by a very competent governmental agency.

This honors list is not intended to flatter our vanity but

to illustrate complex questions. Why do the technicians who build superb dams not build telephone exchanges? Why has the country that was able to develop or modernize some sectors of the economy (automobiles, aviation, railroads) remained impotent in coping with other and comparable problems (housing, highway construction)? Why such dynamism on the one hand and such inertia on the other? To contrast private initiative and state planning throws no light on the question, for it happens that some nationalized sectors of the economy are lively, some private sectors sluggish, and vice versa.

It is true that on several occasions there have been what one might call organized mistakes. That is, the choice of the easier of two policies: inflation rather than austerity in 1945; cars rather than housing, consumer soft goods rather than factory retooling. Why? For one thing, because after the French emerged from their 1940–5 tunnel, they hankered for a little butter on their bread. It was also simpler to disarm social unrest than to attack its causes. A succession of short-lived governments had need of a demobilized public opinion in order to impose on it their colonialist military adventures. Comfort, rather than tension and effort, emasculates a society. Fate was unquestionably on the side of the short-view strategists; hence, France kept her rendezvous with expansion in 1952–7, and the debtors were shielded from the painful moment when the note falls due. The country muddled along between successes and failures, living better and better, and agreeably surprised that the over-all picture was not so black.

Nonetheless, there is a bit of mystery here. Men of the same generation, who had been brought up in the same traditions and known the same difficulties, succeeded in certain areas and failed in others. It is like some incoherent kind of magic. Sclerosis and daring, technical apathy and technical resourcefulness have coexisted in France; one may state this as a fact, deplore it, but not explain it.

Do economic factors provide any light? In other words, is French affluence perhaps misleading? Perhaps we have not got enough money to do everything?

To put matters in this way is to take the short view. The programs of development and modernization which have been brought to fruition do not absorb but rather generate wealth; they create needs, jobs, vitality. When the rate of economic growth is steadily accelerated, all investments show more or less immediate profits. What then?

Then, no doubt, one must shift from "rigorous analysis" to interpretation and hypothesis. There is an element in French life that is not susceptible to logical explanation; there are areas of absurdity, blundering, a fuzziness that technocrats, Gaullists, Leftist sociologists, and highly placed, liberal government officials alike have not managed to dissipate.

Why are the French heavy drinkers, dirty, bad-tempered, and prone to cheating? Why are these stormers of bastilles and upsetters of thrones willing to lap up the pablum that their government disdainfully condescends to feed them in the guise of information? How is it that the heirs of such great builders of cities as Le Nôtre and Mansart, have let themselves be infected by the urban illness known as the "suburb" and love it? How has this skeptical, mocking old country been able to engender so quickly millions of short-tempered, murderous bullies who, once at the wheels of their cars, forget the basic tenets of the social contract? What is the virus—for it is a virus—that spreads feverishness and lethargy, passivity and vulgarity?

Someone will reply that by amalgamating quite different

issues, by deliberately mixing together kinds and degrees of problems, I am polemicizing and making my task too easy. It is too much to ask for permanent rebellion. It is useless to hope that France will demonstrate such a high level of culture and such a lively sense of civic responsibility that her people will pour out into the streets to demand, in one fell swoop, the razing of the monstrous little one-family houses of La Garenne-Bezons, installation of bathtubs, a fair and respect-worthy fiscal policy, courteous drivers, the restraint of bootleg distillers, radio and television newscasts that do better than reflect contempt for the public's intelligence. This is asking too much. The list is crushing. One can simply hope, if not to cure, then to understand.

Plumbing does not create public hygiene; the bootlegger does not create alcoholism; flaws in the tax laws do not automatically engender fraud. Behind these phenomena there are rules and customs. The rule and custom of questionable body linen and sour smells. The rule and custom of the nation-wide red wine, of Calvados in Normandy, *pastis* in the Midi, the cosmopolitan apéritif. Or the rule and custom of chiseling the boss, the organization, or the government. These are all open sores, all French, and they supply material for endless jokes and songs.

It is surprising that often one finds at the root of an aberrant state of affairs the organizing impulse of law. It is the law, acting through a system of bonuses and easy credit, which has allowed the lower middle class to surround cities, notably Paris, with a suburban leprosy. It is the law, first by demogogic reaction against an abuse of the *ancien régime* and later out of inertia, that for a century and a half has allowed contraband alcohol to rot the brain and harden the arteries of eight generations of Frenchmen. (Napoleon, in 1806, granted every owner of fruit trees the right to distill for his private use without being taxed. Obviously, this opened the door to extravagant abuses of the privilege and to an immense illegal traffic.) It is law that meticulously leveled a tax on salaries but tolerates great vagueness as far as taxation of other income is concerned, and thus encourages misrepresentation and fraud among the most favored professional and social groups. Lastly, it is the law that established a virtual state monopoly in radio and an absolute monopoly in television, thereby releasing the torrents of conformity and sweetness and light that are overwhelming the eyes and ears of all France.

It does not absolve the lawmaker to say that people have the laws they deserve. On the other hand, how can one avoid saying just that? The strange marriage linking a people and its laws is never a matter of chance.

Among the various phenomena I have mentioned, one, I think, deserves more attention: the suburb. Actually, that the French drink a lot, bathe little, drive fast, curse each other, and play hanky-panky with the tax collector—all this is dreary, commonplace folklore; one knows what to think of it. But the suburb—its appearance, sociology, scope, and recent changes—constitutes a typically French situation, worth looking at more closely because it teaches us something about ourselves.

Our decaying cities, stagnant construction industry, and the insensate individualism of the working-class Frenchman have created the suburbs.

The outskirts of the big English cities, the approaches to Genoa and Milan, and the unplanned, unsightly landscape that stretches for miles and miles along American highways can convey some physical impression of the Parisian suburb, some sense of its visual and psychological disarray, but will not evoke its essence. That essence partakes simultaneously of ugliness, smallness, hostility for men and things, misanthropy, and a petty sense of privacy and proprietorship. The suburb is the answer to the choice—the wish—to live this way. The suburb embodies the idea that millions of Frenchmen have fashioned for themselves of what makes for happiness here on earth.

The sociologists will do well, of course, to study what economic and other pressures have made the suburbanites accept their suburbanite fate. The sociologists will point to the lack of city planning, directives, and controls, but only later will they grapple with the essential cause—psychological aberration. If for fifty years millions of French people have been left completely free to choose, in an administrative vacuum, the place where they wanted to live, and there, in a veritable paroxysm of individuality, to build the homes they wanted, then one can deduce that the result—the suburb—is the spontaneous expression of the character and taste of the interested parties. No one helped or advised them; neither did anyone force them. Actually, things were facilitated for them since, in terms of aesthetics, their own wishes were respected and, in the sacred name of liberty, they were allowed to do as they pleased. The record is there for all to see. The lover of facts can stroll from Issy-les-Moulineaux to Drancy, from Levallois-Perret to Villemomble, from Kremlin-Bicêtre to Pantin. Let him open his eyes and look around him: he will see a genuine slice of France.

The legendary characteristics of the suburb are the fence, the iron gate (locked and embellished with a sign announcing "Beware Dog"), the little garden, the small detached house, and its larger, more expensive neighbor. The most jealous individualism governs all things. The idea that two adjacent houses might look alike gravely offends their owners' sensibilities. If, in some rare instance, it happens that two houses have been built like identical twins, a riot of superfluous ornamentation and aggressively contrasting colors will express the idiosyncrasy of each and symbolize the immense distance that separates the neighbors.

Each plot must be hermetically closed, girdled with walls, picket fences, trellises, and even barbed wire. In the case of new construction, the enclosure always comes before the building itself. The first concern of a man who has acquired a building site is to forbid the rest of the world access to it, even though he may not intend to lay the foundations of his house for several years. He will embellish his fencing with a porch, a gate, and a lock. Of a Sunday he will come, open his gate, drive his car into his domain, close the gate, and indulge in the pleasures of absolute possession by clearing away a bit of underbrush or perhaps laying out a picnic. If he lacks a house and, therefore, a "Beware Dog" sign, he will plant in the middle of his empty terrain a sign reading "Private Property. No Trespassing."

The simple and noble word "house" has been abandoned in favor of the two terms preferred by suburbia: *"pavillon,"* designating the more modest structure, and "villa," in which appear vaster social and architectural pretensions. The word "house" is no longer used except to admonish children guilty of playing in the streets: "Come into the house this minute!"

The essential quality common to both villa and *pavillon* is that both are single, detached houses. To live in them or, rather, to own them, represents a victory over the collective enslavement of the apartment building and urban uniformity. One feels very much "at home," as people put it with evident and endlessly repeated satisfaction. The implication is that

"One is better off in one's own house than in other people's." This conviction (which children do not necessarily share) lies at the root of the obscure rivalries and sly battles between inhabitants of the same street. As a general rule, the winner is held to be the person who manages to slam his door shut first. "Each to himself." Accordingly, suburban localities do not form communities in the image of our older villages, but are simply a juxtaposition of fiercely autonomous cells. Humanly and socially, the suburb represents a regression of several centuries. In another sense, it is the faithful mirror of twentieth-century France, a state of mutation between the earlier rural, stable, hierarchized order and the order of tomorrow, which is still to be invented. The intermediate stage —urbanization, that is—has been simply telescoped and spoiled.

The two do-it-yourself religions of the suburbanite are gardening and tinkering. Both allow him to work unremittingly to improve the appearance of his abode. The appearance is for him a source of pride, an invitation to dream—the one touching chapter of folly in a life that is otherwise nothing if not prudent.

The basis of everything is four walls roofed with bright-red machine-made tiles. With the passing of time, the building material has evolved from limestone (which gave a solidity that precluded any trouble with one's walls) to brick, to cinder block (a veritable find for the suburbanite, this porous, rough stone looks like a mustard-colored sponge and is guaranteed to skin any hand that ventures to rub against it), to, finally, the various industrial compositions that can be finished in poetic ultramarine or lemon-yellow roughcasting.

From the early years of the century until today, styles have defied counting. We have lived through turrets and towers;

A Miscellany of Endemic Ailments

Style Hôtel-de-Ville 1900; fake Tudor half-timbering; Anglo-Norman; Basque; Swiss chalet; Provençal. One homeowner's pride might be expressed in a minature château of the Loire; the modesty of another would take shape in a hybrid structure built by the family, without architect or plan, and enlarged as needed. Since the average plot is about a quarter of an acre, the result is a prodigious conglomeration, each house's originality being heightened by the mere proximity of all its incompatible neighbors.

Decoration has followed technological developments closely. Iron (grille gates, marquees, shutters) triumphed around 1900. Then came the era of ceramics (Walt Disney characters wandering over tiny lawns), fitted metal tubing, and the manifold possibilities of plastics. The poorest suburbs have at times resorted to piling old tires one on another, painting them red, and planting geraniums in them. Recently, the brightly colored, rough-surfaced boxlike houses have benefited from outdoor tokens of wealth garnered from the interior-decorating magazines or the family's jaunts to the south—hammocks, deck chairs, and so forth. Gardens where iron arches and bits and pieces of grillework reign (the eternal obsession to enclose everything, even if only a begonia bed) are, by a mystery both horticultural and psychological, stocked with botanical specimens unknown anywhere else. Surburban gardens were very likely created by God on the eighth day, with the connivance of local nurserymen. They are so ugly that one comes to consider positively majestic the cedars in the "parks" of the older and more beautiful villas (these villas are the property of doctors, occasionally of unambitious lawyers).

Were we to explore this sociological phenomenon in its fullest dimensions, we should have to speak of childhood, school, and adolescence in the suburbs, the first romantic flutterings, the morning and evening trains that transport daily a million white-collar workers to Paris and back, the love affairs, engagements, adulteries—and later, old age, retirement, cats, the traditional mania to enclose everything now pushed to the point of actual hatred between neighbors; death, and burial in cemeteries that are enlarged every twenty years, that are always sticky with clay and mud, and that present rows upon rows of gravestones as stupid, pretentious, and touching as the rows of *pavillons* that line the water-tower streets, the avenue de Paris and avenue Félix-Faure, the boulevards Jean-Jaurès and Général-de-Gaulle. O suburban cemetery! What would Mary McCarthy, who can make such clever fun of the august Père Lachaise cemetery, say of you? What would she say of your Breton granite, your truncated columns, the hackneyed sentiments chiseled in your slabs, your silver-plated vases and crowns of pearls and artificial flowers? The suburb of the dead matches the suburb of the living. The suburbanite enters into his eternal rest the way he lived—dedicated to a concern for, an affirmation of, proprietorship and precedence and mournful flowers, and tormented by the demon of embellishment. The suburban dead will rot according to the logic of the same system by which they lived, and in the funereal equivalents of their *pavillons,* for every self-respecting family has taken care to buy its burial vault—waterproof, divided into several levels, and referred to by a sublime expression which couples the eternity of death with the inalienable property rights of the municipality as "grants in perpetuity."

Maybe the suburb has lost some of its more ridiculous aspects in the last ten years, but it is acquiring others.

The urban population explosion, the construction of huge multiple dwellings, and the increasing number of cars are peopling the suburbs more and more densely. The remaining big park areas, the last shaded refuges, are no longer being automatically parceled out in small plots, but are sometimes excavated and studded with enormous apartment complexes. As a result, around the cities we now find coexisting the miniature world of the *pavillon* and the outsize world of the apartment bloc, the ugliness of the very little and of the too big, the solitude of retired people burrowing inside their tiny boxes and the new-style solitude of the apartment-barracks. Bare façades are profiled against the horizons of formless landscapes; muddy or desert-like streets are unfinished and unnamed; bands of children rove around, just as bored and abandoned as those of yesterday, who were kept safely in the nest and forbidden street and group play in the name of *petit-bourgeois* respectability. The suburb is changing without growing either worse or better. It has moved into the second half of the century with all the baggage of anarchy and ugliness which has always been its lot. In many places, it is devouring more space. The loveliest of the small French cities, fragile jewels that are already flawed but still beautiful, such as Senlis, Sarlat, Uzès (there are at least fifty of these cities in France, each of which merit a visit), see burgeoning around them these multicolored eruptions of villas and low-income apartment complexes. Today, increasing prosperity and economic vitality are creating suburbs, as formerly thrift and lethargy did. So the suburb is one of France's little mysteries, and even obeys the unknown laws of the Eternal Circle.

To THOSE WHO will be irritated by this chapter—and I am thinking especially of French readers—I offer, by way of conclusion, the following food for thought.

Do they ever stop to think about the men whose job it is

to address some public: the writer speaking to his readers; the deputy to his constituents; the civil servant devising some plan for the anonymous mass of eventual consumers; the statesman conjuring with that still more baffling and indistinguishable mass he calls "the French," believing that he knows them or despairing that he ever will know them? Does the irritated reader think of the effort these men must make to imagine, in the true sense of the word, this France—to conjure up the image of the people to whom they speak, for whom they work, on whom they count, whom they hope to lead or mislead or convince or electrify or lull to sleep? What images do such men see?

We write and speak about "the French"; we make plans, we compare, we dream of power and grandeur, of taste and generosity; but at that very moment millions of plays are being enacted that are France. One man is watching a black-skinned, exotic president ascend the Champs-Elysées to "rekindle the flame" of the Unknown Soldier. Another is signing a check to pay for a refrigerator, fudging his expense account to cheat his boss a little, playing soccer, risking his savings on the races at the Pari Mutuel Urbain, drinking his sixth apéritif, pushing a little car made to go 75 miles per hour up to 85, fornicating, praying, listening to M. Jean Nocher's drivel on the radio (without smashing his set!), queueing up in front of a movie house, sleeping. It is evening, and on village squares men are bowling, chatting, revving their motor-bikes, watching girls. It is evening, and in expensive neighborhoods people are drinking whisky, dressing, getting ready to dine in town. They are listening to the idols whose voices are reproduced on records by the millions. They are studying for exams; dying, well drugged, of cancer; looking up a Michelin-starred restaurant where they will enjoy a well-grilled chop; thinking of money, amusement, boredom, their children, their enemies. It is evening, and the TV is presenting a minister's fireside chat. He, too, talks as if he knew what is meant by "France" and "the French." But if only for a moment he thinks of the extravagant tangle of situations, of this swarming termites' nest or submarine floor, of the accents, voices, laughter, and sighs—if for one instant he thinks of the folly of his over-simplifications, how can he go on talking so urbanely?

One could say the same thing about all societies, I know. A nation is exactly that—the miracle of all these things more or less holding together. A nation exists because the factors making for cohesion outweigh by just a little the factors of self-destruction. Because the ants agree to say that they are all from the same anthill, to wear its colors, and, for better or worse, to act accordingly.

However, because my evocation of France has been brief and its conclusions can be even more briefly refuted, I will say only that the extravagance, fragility, and unreality of France's destiny seem to me to have become more pronounced. The French "miracle" seems to me a little more miraculous than one should reasonably wish; the abyss that yawns between the idea of France and the reality of France is dizzying.

The kinds of behavior that I have listed as national maladies are those which seem to me to be leading to the point where the tension between general ideas and individual destinies, between what one would wish France to be and what she is, will—quite simply—snap.

CHAPTER XVII:

Figaro; or, A Few Reasons for Loving Even the French

A ND NOW, allow me to drop the famous objective tone of the essayist for a moment to evoke an evening in Paris. An evening in the winter of 1965.

It was the week when everyone was coming back to town from a snowy holiday or from celebrating New Year's in the country. Death awaited us on our return. A highly regarded actress had killed herself. Perhaps her suicide implied, among other things, condemnation of a certain way we have in Paris of working, loving, judging, living at once too close together and too far apart. The editor of a big newspaper had also died, and behind the stiff official condolences we seemed to hear murmurs of intrigue, whispered speculation. Who was getting his spot? Who was taking over his influence and power? That evening (January 7, 1965, to be exact) at the Théâtre de France, the intermission chatter was all about these two disappearances and the questions they raised, all the "whys" a city feeds on—or, rather, that a certain circle feeds on, the people of whom other people say and who say of themselves that they *are* the city.

So coming back this time was like relapsing into illness or smothering. You returned to the familiar faces, the passwords, the touch of cynicism without which you would not survive, and the still more threadbare locutions of friendship. It was like an interminable "Monday morning feeling" in Paris that January, when you asked yourself why the dawn, the week, life itself, should begin again and what it all might mean.

Suddenly something happened. A whiff of oxygen, a breath of crisp, dry, bracing air passed over us. What was it? Simply this: they presented a performance of *Le Mariage de Figaro*. We do not ordinarily fire a twenty-one-gun salute for such evenings: old Uncle Beaumarchais is a member of the family. And yet, when the music of French speech at its audacious best began, when the quips and retorts rang out— terse, intact, as indestructible as when, in 1785, they had rocked all the old complacencies to the cheers of the guillotine's future victims—it did not take us five minutes to identify with French traits which are often caricatured, to sense an agreeable feeling of youthfulness rekindle, to feel we were once again at our best. Measuring my words, I would put it this way: we were rather proud to have been born French.

What a relief it was, all of a sudden! Suddenly we were escaping from our Paris doldrums in the only way that really counts—on wings. It had nothing to do with cultural piety, cult of the "classics," or any such drivel. No, it had to do with youth and delight. There are several reasons why.

First of all, the language. A society that speaks well

breathes free. Men think and fight the way they talk. As the professors of literature say, the Duc de Saint-Simon's style explains and contains the best of monarchical society. A century later, the intense eloquence of Saint-Just burned with true revolutionary fire. A nation that stammers is bogging down, is falling asleep on its feet. There is more reason to fear for France in the impoverished writing of her *lycée* students, the inflated nonsense of her newscasts, and the insipid whey of her popular music than in I don't know what technical difficulties she runs into in puttering with her rockets and superplanes. Our best statesmen would understand what I mean—Mendès-France, who speaks calmly, precisely, and without demagogic flourish; or the General, who annually presents his public with two or three wonderfully turned and unexpected phrases. But the speech of Mendès is that of an accomplished technician, and however astonishing the Gaullist register may be, it is even so only a compound of archaism, sarcasm, and military coarseness. The language of Beaumarchais, on the other hand, is the acme of freshness and genuine elegance. It is not true that "everybody spoke well in those days." The pastorales which so enchanted the Trianon were flat and affected, and the monarchy expired humming them.

Secondly, the gaiety. Figaro is joyously pitiless. Suzanne resists the count with peals of laughter. As we listen to this limpid, laughing speech, suddenly we discover how formal, bombastic, inflated, and carping we have become. When we are serious we are heavy but carry no weight. Beaumarchais did not turn his world upside down by lecturing it; he made it laugh. Better by far to laugh at ourselves, come what may, than to bore ourselves. Frenchmen today would do well to ponder this, faced as they are with a choice between *La Nation,*

Figaro: or, A Few Reasons for Loving Even the French

a little Gaullist sheet that no one reads, and *Le Canard enchaîné*.

The third reason for our enjoyment: the play's common sense. You could equally well say, its irreverence. There comes a time in the life of all societies when such confusion and disorder reign both in ideas and alliances that plain common sense proves more salubriously destructive than all the analysis in the world. It is not by chance that in *The Marriage* the home truths are dealt out to us by a scamp of sorts. Was not Beaumarchais the typical scamp of his day? Who, we may ask, is the scamp of modern France? Who, twenty or a hundred years from now, will make his readers—our sons—proud?

Which brings us to the heart—and the end—of the matter. We are sick and tired of being talked at. The martial tune of French *grandeur* has gone sour. But that evening, it was that good-for-nothing Figaro on the stage who, after a hundred and eighty years, was giving us our "French lesson." It was Beaumarchais—adventurer, clockmaker, ex-commoner, marrier of wealthy widows, overventuresome financier, ambassador of intrigues, leader of cabals, released prisoner, an inspired rascal thought up by an effete society for its own pleasure and unhappiness—it was Beaumarchais who made us long for the days when, in the face of vested power and injustice, courage spoke out so firmly—and with a smile.

Yes, there was, there still is, a French *grandeur*. But it displays itself better via challenge than affirmation. Its glory lies in preventing the people and their princes from falling asleep, not in lulling them to sleep. The role of French greatness today—if we absolutely must dream of it and seek it— would be to expose absurdities, hypocrisies, abuses of power and of language, and to laugh at them, not to disguise them with borrowed nobility. If he were alive today, Beaumarchais would prefer *Dr. Strangelove* to military parades on Bastille Day.

I do not mean by this to substitute one chauvinism for another, to replace bluff and military bluster with heroes by the name of Beaumarchais, Voltaire, Laclos, Diderot, Stendhal. I am simply thinking of the young and insolent nation France once was. Does anyone, anywhere, still expect anything from us? Influential voices soothe us by saying, Yes, indeed. If so, would it not be in order for us to analyze what our country was, and why, at several periods in its history? This function of free inquiry has traditionally been better filled by liberal thinkers than by zealous defenders of tradition, à la Maurras. But look at the men of the Left and of progressivism over the last twenty years. Their sort of realism and the trend of events have impelled them from alarm to anger, from bitterness to vilification, until they have come to be accused of constituting an "anti-France." This is not a charge to be lightly dismissed. The contrast between their vigorous criticism and their inaction is what has particularly struck their opponents. Because they are specialists in pessimistic diagnosis and quibbling, but are practically ineffective, they have come to appear like saboteurs. They were somehow fated to foresee the worst and to think the worst—and thus to be right!—but also to envisage heaven-sent solutions requiring no help from them. As a result, their position became more ambiguous and they themselves more disenchanted. All of which is to say that to me Figaro does not seem at all to be the great-grandfather of a Left-wing editorialist—he is too modern for that!

When one faces up to the sheer volume of work to be done, to the delays and failures and misrepresentations, the temptation to take refuge in sarcasm is strong. But to take refuge means to halt, and if there is one lost secret of French intelligence—or, if you prefer a more modest term, of a particularity compounded of perpetually shifting good and bad qualities—it is mobility. A systematic pessimism and demythologizing are no longer useful prescriptions for our troubles; today they are the mask of inaction. But when we see Figaro bound onstage, see him dance around an elegantly bewildered Almaviva, hear him pour out the truths of his day in the most beautiful French prose there ever was— then we are overcome with longing for such vivacity. This is how we want to be. Let us not be parrots, not even of the slogans of revolt. Let us inject some life into the persistent twaddle that our quarreling still feeds on. Let others tax us for our frivolity, denounce our mania for challenging everything. These shortcomings constitute at least half of what it means to be French. The other half—the Louis XIV and the Napoleonic, the authoritarian and centralizing, the Jacobin and universal, adept in the outline and the generalization, at ease in categories and systems—this part will always be strong enough.

Among the several exciting reasons for loving the French, I should like to underline these, conceding that they are equivocal: the French deserve esteem for having invented the monarchy and for having overthrown it; for having devised the Civil Code and for having then, without relinquishing their passion for the law, sustained a state of permanent anarchy. Between the two traditions, the hierarchic and the libertarian, the royal and the rebel, I confess that my heart leans toward the side of lucidity, restiveness, challenge. But if there is one reproach to be leveled against France as she has been for the last fifty years, it is that she has lacked both firmness in public policy and imagination in challenging that policy. In the past, we have been capable of building, capable of questioning, and twice we wrought something we believed to have universal validity. From the eleventh to the eighteenth century, we supplied the West with the model of that prodigious apparatus, absolute monarchy, which rose slowly and despite a thousand besetting perils out of feudal anarchy. Thereupon, everywhere in the world we shook to their foundations the dynastic edifices that had been built in the image of our own, we invented new concepts of human happiness and liberty, stimulated revolt, and quickened the sense of nationalism. After offering the idea of monarchy to Europe as the finest obtainable kit of building blocks, we offered it the idea of the Nation as the most sublime of dreams. The Europe of fatherlands, bickering, and beauty, the continental seedbed of ideas that between 1795 and 1871 (let us forget about 1920 and the Treaty of Versailles!) were to sprout all over the world—that Europe was formed in the light of French imagination. We taught kings how to be kings, then taught the people how to rid themselves of kings. In the process of hinging these two periods of history and articulating these two great systems, which are complementary and not contradictory, France perfected a certain kind of man—quick, insolent, fired by his conquests and the vision of his future. If we entertain aspirations toward pride and importance, they must be measured against him. While I have deplored the excessively long shadow the past often casts over us, it is nonetheless in the past that we find the star to hitch our wagon to. Is this paradoxical? It is always easy to draw up a list of programs that must be carried out and then to wax euphoric over the benefits that will be gained once those programs have been faithfully executed. It is more important to know to what kind of man one wishes to entrust the architecture of one's future. It is better to choose a model from the past than to copy the square-jawed, insipid virility of the recruiting poster. The engineer-with-a-mission and the architect-paterfamilias are less to my taste than Figaro. Is that a crime? In any event, it is proof that, more than some of my criticisms might suggest, I belong to the great French adventure.

OF COURSE, one can always go about this the other way round. I will now imagine that I am offering the French people my best wishes for the New Year or on the threshold of a new seven-year term, I will list the tasks that must be accomplished, carefully balancing the unwelcome chores and the exciting frontiers of the national destiny. But something in me—a smile, a suspicion, a quick, argumentative reflex—will always prefer the sharp question to the fruity answer, the perked ear to the hand on the heart. We confront the necessity of building homes, modernizing professions, salvaging cities, educating children, extending political stability—and something in us thinks of Figaro. Is this perhaps why it is so hard to be French?

CHAPTER XVIII:

The Difficulty of Being French

THE VIRTUES THAT I CLAIM as ours were precious to a strong and inventive nation; in a weary or too credulous society they are sterile, and can therefore quickly turn frivolous or sour. In that case, it may serve no great purpose to evoke a symbolic personality or a typical character that would be generally acceptable.

The difficulty of being French is a feeling of discomfort and perplexity, as if one did not belong in one's own skin. It is something one feels in the innermost self, and is as hard as it is distasteful to formulate. We can ask ourselves whether, among the various French categories, there is one that, for the moment, is more habitable than the others—or is the malaise general? We can list the crises and the tasks ahead and tell ourselves that small victories and sporadic displays of courage will accumulate until ultimately we will be more at ease with ourselves. But to grope toward the heart of the matter like that does not allow one to grasp the problem in all its elusive imprecision (any more than does the nostalgic portrait of a Beaumarchais hero). All the same, let us try.

First, the categories:

The Difficulty of Being French

Are you better off being a young or an old Frenchman? The young one feels important but neglected; the old one feels important but guilty of neglect. The glorification of youth is now fashionable; it seems silly and muddle-headed to older people, who for the moment still hold the reins of power. But for the moment only . . . To be twenty in France today is to feel like the unexpected guest at a stupid, anachronistic ceremony; the less that is expected from you, the more you are (clumsily!) fussed over. To be sixty is to face the choice between speeding up, which will crush you in the end, or applying the brakes, which would be bitter and futile. Which role is easier?

To be a city dweller is to live an absurd and exhausting tragicomedy (each season it gets harder to play), which you despair of seeing improved by remedies that, for that matter, you put off administering. To be a peasant is to belong to a community two thirds of which is doomed in the near future, and to suffer from the most spectacular collective confusion now raging in French society. To be a peasant is to realize that the next ten years condemn you either to winning wealth that lies beyond your reach or to becoming a second-class city dweller. To be a worker is to live through the transformation of a proletariat that so far has neither completely given up its revolutionary spirit nor yet achieved the standard of living, security, and dignity which would make the socialist dream definitively obsolete. To be a worker is to see capitalism and the State now reconciled in an effective partnership, following paths that parallel the very ones the workers would have liked to impose. To be a worker is to live better and better, but out of one's element, in a society that resembles neither what one once feared nor what one once hoped for. It is to dream of joining the middle class while making fun of the idea of be-

299

coming middle-class. It is to be no longer a slave—but it will never mean being free. It is to regret, at times, that the old class enemy is no longer so clearly marked out for vengeance because of his unjustices and stupidities. French workers of forty and fifty feel like the half-pay troops of the revolutionary dream.

To be an employer is to belong still to what M. Guy Mollet used to call "the dumbest Right in the world," that is to say, the most timorous, least aggressive employer group that ever was. However, it means also to face the first large-scale industrial and banking consolidations, an intensified competition, legislation that at last is abandoning a blindly protectionist policy, and finally, the upsurge of a rejuvenation as maddening to older people as it is exhilarating for youth. It is to know that in the years ahead you are condemned to expand, to enlarge. It is to feel the old home, although its doors are firmly closed, invaded by squalls. It is to have understood in less than ten years that after fifty somnolent years natural selection will be merciless this time. Exciting? Yes, but scarcely comforting.

The old distinctions of Right versus Left, conservatism versus change, which I have referred to so often, seem out of date to the rest of the world, yet in French thought they preserve their prestige and they paralyze our national debates by couching them in outworn terms. As we have seen, these distinctions bespeak a genuine division of French society into two forces that are always poised to split national unity. In this context, which is both archaic and true, in this jungle of slogans that are both anachronistic and exact, where does one take one's stand?

To align oneself with the Right is to shoulder the great guilt that, from the Dreyfus affair to the O.A.S. (by way of

Vichy and the various forms of French fascism and militarism),
has afflicted reactionary ideology.

To align oneself with the Left is to share in the burden of
having been visionary, ineffective, divided, unrealistic, and
virtually useless for the last twenty years.

To declare that the concepts of Right and Left are out of
date or to claim to be apolitical is to be automatically branded
a shameful reactionary.

To play the political empiricist or technician is to go
against the grain, because the French political temperament remains incurably ideological and partisan.

To be a nationalist is to make powerful nations snicker
and to distress the weak (who love only the powerful). It is to
pose for the banal caricature of the Frenchman which, for the
last fifteen years (or the last century and a half), has been
sketched in newspapers throughout the world.

To be a cosmopolite is, for a Frenchman, to think and
judge profoundly against his own nature. Universalist?—yes.
Cosmopolite?—no. The Frenchman's habit is to see the world
in his own image or not to see it at all.

To be a European is to feel as dull as a Christian Demo-
crat, a secretary to Chancellor Adenauer, or an old Boy Scout
stuffed with uplifting touristic illusions.

To be a Catholic is to have to choose—our eternal
dualism!—between integrationists and progressives, Roman
cardinals and worker-priests, confidants of the military and
fellow travelers of Communism, Vaticanist and Gallican.

To be a believer in this country (which theoretically is
Christianized to the marrow) is to feel oneself in the social
mainstream but in a spiritual minority. It is to take part in a
modern morality play, but to find at each step that Christ is
forgotten or flouted.

To say that one is an atheist is to slip inside the old skin of the early-twentieth-century anticlericals or else to feel excluded from a conformism that is very much alive, even if nine times out of ten devoid of faith.

BRIEFLY, FRENCH SOCIETY no longer fosters, at any of its various levels, those patterns of collective behavior to which once one needed only to subscribe in order to feel right in oneself and in one's milieu. Over a long period in Europe, solidly knit and seasoned groups offered the individual refuge and comfort; here and there, they still do. To be a Spanish aristocrat, a Roman churchman, a Swiss from the less advanced cantons, a Belgian cleric from around Louvain—these are social roles that can still offer to those who fit them a well-assorted choice of opinions and behavior norms. For a long time, the provincial French middle class was one such closed circle—content to live in intellectual autarchy, suspicious of the outside world. But three quarters of these fortresses have fallen. Groups which only yesterday were the most rigid and stable—Catholic Breton peasants, Protestants of the Cévennes, the landowning and Parisian aristocracies—are now subject to various pressures. The agricultural crisis and exodus are disorganizing the old rural societies; unsuccessful marriages and café society are smudging the social register. The reassuring, well-articulated structures of a social milieu, a faith, a repertory of opinions and how-to-live rules of thumb are today found nowhere.

The social mutation inseparable from population growth accentuates the disintegration of the old ways of thinking and living. As late as 1914 and even 1945, "being French" could be linked to several long-cherished popular assumptions. Everyone chose and knew his part in the play. (You even knew

302

from which and to which rung on the ladder the social climbers were struggling to ascend.) Now to be French is to be the actor or walk-on in a hastily produced film, without having had time to learn your lines or to find out how the story ends. It is now a matter of having to improvise and invent an ending. There no longer exists any formula for How to Be French.

This lack is aggravated because, when others judge us, they apply the old formulas to the new society. France (like Italy, which resembles her on this score) is no longer the inn of tradition where the foreigner used to find everything just as he had expected it would be. Perhaps the confusion and irritation of our visitors come from this disparity between our legend and our reality, as well as between their preconceived ideas and the verification they attempt on the spot. The French often feel attacked on a terrain they no longer particularly wish to occupy or defend. What does it matter to them, after all, whether they are or no longer are famous seducers, champion lovers, accomplished conversationalists, lords and masters of women of "inimitable elegance"? Some mythical redoubts are deserted even before they are attacked. One cannot hold against the French their having stripped off tattered finery that no longer became them.

On the other hand, we are tellingly attacked at many other points for actual defects in our society. Rather than plead guilty, we pretend not to understand. The reproaches are justified, but we do not want to hear them. This may be purely and simply turning a deaf ear, or it may have to do with traits so deeply rooted in our character, weaknesses so essential to us, that we refuse in advance to correct them. A man is the sum total of his faults and virtues, or so every Frenchman unconsciously thinks. As an individual, he lends scant credence to psychoanalysis because he cherishes the architecture of his own conflicts and believes that were this to collapse, he would too. Collectively, he resists all self-critcism, all analysis that would force him to face up to French inconsistencies. He hopes that circumstances will change and somehow make the nation and the State shed their old skins without requiring too much of an assist from mere citizens. A little anarchy, a little alcoholism, a little irresponsibility, a little *laisser-aller* have never kept a nation from getting along, have they? Or a hankering for fantasies and pleasures, either.

The self-indulgence practiced by the Frenchman is not the result only of being uninformed. Of course, he often does have to down poison and cure, harsh truth and soothing comment, with one and the same swallow. But anyone with an iota of curiosity has the option of sorting out the information officially fed him. The truth is not concealed from the French; it is sugar-coated for them, yes, gilded to suit the national palate for gilt; but scratch a little, and you will find it. Most of the foreigner's grievances against the French—whether they concern diplomacy or hostelry, aggressive attitudes or antiquated accommodations—are brought to public attention. It is simply that they are accompanied by commentaries that soften the blow. If it is the government talking, the speaker waxes ironic, tricolor style, about those barbarians and their complaints; if the opposition is speaking, it converts the same reproaches, a little basely, into criticisms of the administration. In both instances, the truth is blunted by the way it is either presented or exploited before it can have struck home. All foreign analysis of the facts of French life is subjected unfailingly to this dual treatment, and it is not easy for the ordinary citizen to find the honorable position he should take with regard to them. He is afraid to join either of the two equally exasperating camps, both of which solicit his adherence: the camp of self-complacency or the camp of self-denigration. He *would* like France to have more highways, schools, housing, research scientists, stadiums; he *would* prefer the French to be less heavy drinkers and better architects, given less to playing politics and more to being good citizens. But he would not like these hopes to turn him into a perennial grumbler or lone wolf or prophet of doom and disaster. It becomes difficult and almost illusory to be right in a period and in a country in which common sense is so unevenly shared.

A possible cure for the good conscience of the complacent ones and the bad conscience of the Cassandras might perhaps be to dedramatize the enumeration of the jobs we have to do. The plans, programs, and resolutions should no longer serve as campaign arguments and polemical weapons. After all, a president elected by a fifty-five-per-cent majority should, from the day of his election, be the president of the whole nation, just as, hopefully, the work to be done should be the task of all Frenchmen and not an arsenal of accusations or statistics to be hurled at the heads of one's opponents.

The list of our national aspirations might then read more or less as follows: (1) update the entire educational and vocational training system; (2) develop scientific and industrial research; (3) throttle real-estate and construction speculation; (4) plan both the exodus from rural areas and urban growth; (5) rehabilitate neglected areas of the country; (6) clean up certain wholesale and retail distribution channels; (7) update certain professions that are antiquated—for example, medicine and law; (8) modernize the highway system and devise an urban traffic plan; (9) organize the use of leisure time, shifting the emphasis from spectator to active sports, and from speculation to competition; (10) free the law from Catholic pressures; (11) free radio and television from government

monopoly and pressure; (12) help public opinion to con-
centrate on political techniques rather than ideologies; (13)
revitalize the press; (14) foster good taste and simultaneously
demolish the dusty myth of "French beauty."

This is an edifying, banal and tedious list. It outlines an
ideal program for any serious government in any country of
western Europe that is moving toward modernization. However, some items are typically French, such as the wish to be
free of the tyranny of the wholesaler, food-produce agent,
pharmacist, and notary. And the need for roads and for common sense in city planning. Other preoccupations concern
our Latin neighbors as well: the need to secularize legislation,
to do away with censorship once and for all, to dispel the confusion between information and propaganda. Italy has her
Mezzogiorno; we have our Brittany and our "deserts" south
of the Loire. In recent years, Spain has experienced a building
fever that rages without regard for the beauty of sites or the
laws of reason. Public desire for a press at once technically
advanced and civically responsible is evident in Italy, England,
Germany—indeed, wherever scandals, leaks, polemics, and the
outright fabrication of news are rampant.

I have not included these comparisons to minimize
the magnitude of French needs but rather to place them in their
proper context, which is Latin and Catholic rather than
Northern and Protestant. For example, Italian problems in
particular exhibit characteristics common to our own, whereas
Holland, the German part of Switzerland, and the Scandi-
navian countries have rapidly developed toward a socio-
economic situation very different from ours. France is divided
(the famous Le Havre-Geneva line) between the peoples, traditions, and ways of life of northern and of southern Europe.

Just as her dynamism relates her to Belgium and Germany, her archaisms link her to Iberian and Italian societies. This duality is found at all levels of life. General de Gaulle—Flemish, educated in Paris and in Belgium, and a resident of Champagne—is a man of the Northeast and he governs a France which he feels to be Northeast. Southern France—wine-growing, underdeveloped, and Leftist by inclination—voted against him in December 1965. From the Albigensian crusade led by Northern barons in the thirteenth century to the revolutionary anarchy in the South that followed on the Liberation, in August 1944, this has been the one division to threaten French unity seriously. Today it manifests itself in terms of economic disparity. The man from Lille and the Parisian, who hold the bulk of French capital and are the favored instruments of our national expansion, feel that they must "carry" the South of France, which is poor, sparsely populated, and stagnant. Because of this, it is more difficult to be a Frenchman of the Southwest than a Frenchman of the Northeast. Differences of speech, mentality, and temperament accentuate the dissimilarity.

LET US INJECT a small dose of melancholy and cynicism into this concluding panorama. One could truthfully say that until recently, when France began to turn the big corner, the last of her sons who found it easy to be French were the people who felt angry or threatened or nostalgic. The "little France" of the first half of the twentieth century was torn between universalist ideas and small-time politics, between pride in past battles and prestige and the timidities of an old woman; among her defenders, this France numbered the last Frenchmen to feel that they belonged where they were.

They were bitter, they were determined to throw a monkey wrench into the wheels of history and to try to block the crushing onslaught of progress, but in a way these were comfortable positions. These rear-guard fighters were the last among us to believe blindly and absurdly that their cause was just. Angry peasants who lined up their tractors to barricade the roads in 1961; small-business syndicates stirred up by a certain M. Gingembre; butchers exasperated to the point of violence and bomb-throwing by government intervention in their anarchic trade; Bretons in revolt dumping tons of unsold artichokes into the city streets; small tradesmen incited to a boycott of the income tax and to political violence by Pierre Poujade; officers in 1960–2 rebelling to "save" Asia and Christianity and *la Patrie*—such are the last of yesterday's Frenchmen to have fought the future without misgivings or reservation. Tomorrow, the recollection of their anger, confusion, and rebellion will be part of the legend of the great French mutation. While we wait for France to change from a bourgeois to a technocratic nation, a lesser shift is already underway—from a small-middle-class, small-owning, small-exploiting country to a society of the "tertiary" sector: the middle-class cadres. Between 1955 and, roughly, 1965, we witnessed one of the final rebellions of the small town against the administrative control of the top echelon of civil servants in Paris; of the small farmers against the inevitable urbanization and the land-reallocation program; of the small crafts, businesses, and industries against the ineluctable law of concentration. The old, miniaturized France of garden plot and province is dying painfully and nervously, without having yet devised ideas around which it can organize its future. Yesterday's residents are going to have to build tomorrow's houses. They still do not know how to; they still are not sure they want to. The various forms of revolt that some Frenchmen thought might be remedies have turned out to be illusory: Poujadist anarchy, socialist upheaval, and the dream of a Catholic-military crusade are equally out of date. The hour has passed for these three calls to arms, paradoxically associated in their common cult of the past. But let us be fair: their roots went deep into the national soil; their weaknesses and their strengths were consubstantial with old traditions. No one sees clearly what the forces to replace them will be like. Hence the disenchantment, the sense of having been swindled, that bests many Frenchmen. Swindled they are not. Fate has simply set them down at the point of greatest tension and most rapid change in the modern history of their country. Not all of them have yet understood that instead of being the last inhabitants of one era, they could be the first of another. Some do know this. They have purged their will of partisan passions and replaced them with empirical attitudes. They reject the division of ideas into two competing crusades and of the world into two blocs between which they have to choose. They have renounced romanticism and messianic missions. They have decided that they will be simply the managers of a thriving business. They are girding themselves to enroll twenty-five million new arrivals who will find the liquidation of sacred cows less of a problem than their fathers do. Thus resolved, will they save their own souls? Will they preserve the intuitive sense that belonging to an old nation, to *the* nation par excellence, is a more complex destiny than to be in the upper echelon of some supranational corporation, an interchangeable cog in the development of a century? This book will be published, read, and forgotten before the answer to this question is given. The French have lived only to cultivate the garden of their individualism to the point of intoxication.

They very nearly died of that intoxication. They now run the risk of committing suicide—tidily and efficiently—if they permit this individualism of theirs to be altered beyond what the excusable wish to survive requires. It is not going to be easy to continue being French.

A NOTE ABOUT THE AUTHOR

FRANÇOIS NOURISSIER was born in Paris on May 18, 1927, of mixed French, Flemish, and English ancestry. He was educated in Paris, eventually specializing in political science. Widely traveled—with visits to many parts of Europe, North Africa, the Near East, and America—he has been a literary adviser to the publisher Bernard Grasset and a member of the staff of *Vogue* (Paris). In addition to contributing to such periodicals as the *Nouvelle Revue Française, Réalités, Plaisir de France, Figaro Littéraire, Nouvelles Littéraires, Paris-Match,* and *Le Monde,* Nourissier has published a dozen books, beginning in 1950 with *L'Homme Humilié* and including the novel *Une Histoire Française,* which won the Prix Littéraire de la Guilde du Livre for 1965. He divides his time between France (Paris and a country home) and Switzerland. M. Nourissier is married and the father of three children.

A NOTE ON THE TYPE

THE TEXT of this book was set in *Garamond*, a modern rendering of the type first cut in the sixteenth century by CLAUDE GARAMOND (1510-1561). He was a pupil of Geoffroy Tory and is believed to have based his letters on the Venetian models, although he introduced a number of important differences, and it is to him we owe the letter which we know as Old Style. He gave to his letters a certain elegance and a feeling of movement which won for their creator an immediate reputation and the patronage of the French King, Francis I.

Composed, printed, and bound by The Haddon Craftsmen, Inc.,
Scranton, Pennsylvania. Typography and binding design by

WARREN  CHAPPELL